7 Figure Publications Presents . . .

Life after Life

by

Falicia Rose Blakely

7 Figure Publications
PO Box 9334
Augusta, GA 30916
http://7figurepublications.com

(Hardcover)

ISBN-13: 9781732914544

Library of Congress Cataloging-In-Publication Data:
LCCN 2019939585

Editor, Linda Wilson

Cover design by Lisa Sims of Passionate2Design

Published April 2019

Dedication

*Almighty God, full of mercy and compassion to Your people!
Thank You for seeing fit for this to become a reality for me. Your plans
for my life are beyond me. I didn't think I would even see twenty-one,
but You predestined something different. Thank you for not allowing
me to die in my sins and putting some of the most amazing people in
my life! I am in love with you, Lord. You're the greatest!*

To my son, because you give me reason to live.

Acknowledgments

I would like to give thanks to my Higher Power for giving me the patience, strength, and the ability to pen my second novel. I give great thanks for being blessed to have a beautiful family, who are indeed my motivation to overcome my struggles.

Introduction

Who am I . . .

I am the voice that cries out in the night. The soul that longs to be a mother to her son. I am the strong woman who refuses to give up . . . circumstances forced me to grow up. I am the one serving this Life sentence for a man who is free. I am the heart who chooses to forgive and vow to never intentionally hurt again.

I am the one that the system has raised, but I'll be damned if you think I'm just another phrase . . . 'a smarter convict,' 'manipulator of the system,' or 'an inmate.' I am the one who fights to uphold my morals and press to obtain my fullest potential. I am a lover of many, hated by few, chosen by God, yet discovering my purpose but recognize the power in my suffering! I am feared by those who are intimidated by change. I am brave, courageous, and a force to be reckoned with.

I am more than my comprehension, stronger than my abilities. Formed from an Infinite Image. Created to live forever . . . eternally. I am a mother, a daughter, best friend, a niece, the kind of wife you spend time praying to receive and to know me is to love me. One who is missed dearly . . . I'm just trying to help you see, Who I am.

One who is still standing. One whose story is still unfolding. One who is physically bound but have long ago been set free mentally and emotionally, by the grace of God! I am Falicia Rose Blakely, a thirty-five-year-old woman serving life without parole. One who desires the forgiveness of all. Beautiful and black, sincere and understanding. Weary and down at times, but *always* rising back up! This is a part of who I am.

CHAPTER 1

"Momma, don't cry." I thought about my mother's anguished face as I lay prostrate on the conference room floor. The judge had allowed us to visit there before they transported me back to jail. I wished I could have truly comforted her, reassured her somehow, even though her only child had just been sentenced to life without the possibility of parole. In the natural realm I may never see turf, sit down at the dining room table and eat a meal as a family, see my son start school, nor celebrate a birthday. I was still trusting that God had other plans for me. And I did believe, but my heart was aching.

"God, You got me. I'm not gon' worry. You got me," I encouraged myself in the Lord. "You were there. You know why I did what I did. Help me . . . I'm not getting up until you strengthen me. I need you!" I cried out. I didn't even hear the knock at the door, nor observe the deputy opening the door. By the time I looked up, my face was covered in snot and tears. The handsome, middle-age man stared at me with tears welling in his eyes.

"Miss Blakely, you about ready?" he said with his southern accent, looking so sympathetically toward me.

"Yes, sir." I slowly gathered myself to my feet as I adjusted the skirt of my baby blue suit.

"You need some tissue?" he asked.

"Please." I leaned my head back and looked toward the ceiling as if I could catch a glimpse of heaven. "Lord, guard my heart. I want to trust you," I continued to pray. I thought about the comment the last victim's mother made.

"God already dealt with the death sentence, so we're not concerned with that anymore." She was referring to my HIV status.

"Father, please don't let me die in these people's prison."

1

Moments later, I was in a holding cell removing my civilian clothes and putting back on my jail house smocks. I accepted that this was the life I had chosen for myself. How I wished I could turn back the hands of time. I would have never allowed an Ike Berry, or the likes of him a chance. Ken Driggs, my attorney, and Ann Crail, one of the many who were on my defense team came to collect my clothes and check on me.

"You all right, kid?" Ken asked. I gave him a weak smile, trying to be brave. "I'll be at the jail on Sunday to see you." He was faithful about visiting me.

"Come here." Ann pulled me into her embrace. "It's all right. You're gonna be fine. At least you can raise your son. He needs you." She did her best to comfort me. After they were gone, I just sat in that cell thinking about the day:

The only reason we requested the death penalty was because I wanted Falicia to sit in a room alone thinking about what she did to my son, every single day," the mother had said. She didn't know I didn't need a lonely cell to do that. I could be in a roomful of people, and my mind would drift to the day when everything changed.

Arriving back at DeKalb County jail seemed like another obstacle I had to face. I already knew the people I stayed with had lined up in front of the TV watching the news to find out as much as possible about my business. But could you blame them? So focused on what the next person has going on, they miss out on their opportunity to better themselves, especially when they aren't *as bad* as some of us.

It seemed like the longest walk as I made my way on and off the elevator, down the hallway, and into the multi-purpose room, where the officer removed my cuffs.

"I'll be praying for you," one officer told me. I walked up to the door that led to my pod.

"Keep your head up, Miss Blakely," the Correctional Officer (CO) Mrs. Dorsey said through the intercom. "I'll be in there to check on you before my shift ends, okay?" She smiled pleasantly as I smiled back. She had always been considerate and fair with all the inmates. She was one of the few whom I was transparent with. If she told me she was praying for me, I knew she meant it. I took a deep breath as the door popped open, and I walked back into pod 200, the place I had resided for the past nineteen months. As to be expected, all eyes were on me. Some sympathetic, some judgmental, and a few undecided.

"Hey, sis! We been praying for you." A couple of girls I often grouped up with to pray approached me.

"Thank you! It's been emotional. I'll see you later. I need to go pray." I hugged those who I truly believed cared about my mental state and proceeded to my cell.

"That bitch walking around like she holier than thou and done killed all them damn people!" a woman named Yvette popped off right as I stepped into my cell. I stopped dead in my tracks. She didn't understand today wouldn't be a good day for her to be running her mouth. According to the judge I had nothing to lose.

"You wrong for that, Yvette," one of the girls told her.

Lord, is she for real? I prayed as my heart began to race. I had made the decision to dedicate the rest of my life striving to live a life that was pleasing to God. But that wasn't as easy as it sounded, and right now was clearly one of those times. Several people were giving her the business about her remark, but I speak my mind. I turned on my heels and stepped out of my cell.

"Falicia, don't pay her no mind," one girl admonished. I knew to ignore her because not everything deserved a reply, but my adrenaline was pumping! It had been a long time since I slapped a broad.

"What you say?" I asked so calmly it scared me.

"Falicia, it ain't worth it! She ain't God, don't worry about it!" another girl said, standing in front of me.

She didn't even understand; Yvette was about to pay for everything! The agony my ignorant ass had caused my family and the victims, as well as for all the times that coward beat me—every lie he told me—everything the news reporters said I was—every accusation the victims' friends and family made against me—and the disappointment my son would soon feel because I couldn't come home. I was getting ready to unleash on this broad!

"Say it again." I walked around those who were in front of me. Her lips were moving, but the chaos turned up real thick. I couldn't see anybody but Yvette as I moved people out of my way. She stepped out of her flip-flops and threw her hands up like she was ready. So was I!

God, I'm telling you now. I'm getting ready to murk this 'ho! If I get to her . . . Tears welled up in my eyes. I was mad as hell, but not just with her—with myself for actually killing those men and not Ike's dumb ass!

"Falicia! Falicia!" Mrs. Dorsey suddenly appeared directly in front of me. Her presence threw me off. *When had she come in?* I looked around swiftly. Another CO was present and instructed the other inmates to go to their rooms. What else could I do but stop in my tracks?

But there was always tomorrow.

CHAPTER 2

My life doesn't seem that much different than after I first heard the judge declare, "Life without parole." However, I know it's official now! What I had been trying to prepare myself for mentally was my new reality. Those people (judge and prosecutor) had concluded that I am never again to walk a day in the park, stroll along the shore of the beach, celebrate another birthday with my son or nephews and so on . . . Well, at least that's what they hope! But for some reason I can't accept that. Not that I feel I should get away with murder because I shouldn't, but I can't set aside the fact God knows why I pulled that trigger, and I just don't believe He's going to let this be the final say! The conclusion of the matter . . .

My Bible rested in my lap as I sat on my bottom bunk. I did my best to relax, trying to hear if there was anything that God desired me to know this morning. Eventually, the door popped and I jumped to my feet, already prepared to walk out the door. I got up earlier this morning to spend a little extra time on my hair, and then I pulled my new uniform from beneath my mat. I wanted to be creased up today. Ken, in his compassion, had arranged for me to have a sit down with the District Attorneys. Considering the fact I was just sentenced, this meeting was blowing my mind because the case was "closed," as some would say. So what might we possibly have to talk about?

My stomach did a few flips as I walked into the multi-purpose room. The two familiar faces rose to their feet as Ken approached me when I opened the door. We embraced.

"Falicia." District Attorney Tom Clegg extended his hand. I thought twice about shaking it, being that this was the man who had portrayed me as one cold-hearted child, but now more than ever was an opportunity for me to allow my heavenly Father to be glorified! So I would conduct myself in such a way that all the evil things they said about me would be a reproach to them. This was my quest for life.

"Good morning, sir," I said, accepting Clegg's handshake with a firm shake of my own. The simple gesture spoke volumes about the individual.

"Mr. Morgan." I shook the other District Attorney's hand who had the same first name as Clegg. He didn't address the court, but was the enforcer behind my sentence and created the direction in which my case went. We all sat down. I took a deep breath and prepared myself for what was to come.

"Ms. Blakely, I want to get straight to the point," Mr. Clegg began. I tried not to shift in my chair, so I would avoid giving off the impression I was nervous. "We believe you." I blinked a few times to make sure I heard correctly! "We believe everything happened as you said it did. All of Ike Berry's involvements, but we don't have enough evidence to prosecute him. If your co-defendant isn't willing to testify against him, we can't convict him." Mr. Clegg looked me straight in the eyes as if he could feel my pain. I looked over at Ken. He already knew what I was thinking. Getting Pumpkin to talk would be like pulling teeth. From what I heard, she hadn't even been honest with her family about the depths of her dealings in the streets with me and the other girls. I just sat back in my chair; this would be a situation that God alone would handle.

At least the truth is out there . . . I suppose, I thought.

Fulton County didn't waste time coming to pick me up to sentence me on all my pending charges after Ken notified them of my sentencing in DeKalb County. He sympathized with my longing to just get it over with and head to prison. Between DeKalb and Fulton County, I had spent almost two years in those county jails. One evening I was picked up and shuttled to Fulton County along with three others. This would be the second time and my final trip going on a loan out, which is when you are arrested in one county but have pending charges in another. The arresting county will lend you out to the county where your pending charges exist, but they eventually send you back.

This time I would be facing the judge, and whoever the prick was that called himself representing me! I didn't expect him to be like Ken and come see me once a week, but knowing he never took a single day to at least introduce himself and get a feel of who I am is a great injustice in my eyes! How can an attorney fight for your life, and he or she doesn't have the slightest idea concerning you, your motives, or your mental state? So Ken took the initiative to contact him and give him a brief on what I was just sentenced to in DeKalb.

Afterward, I was placed in a holding cell with other women. Most of them were waiting for a signature bond. I sat trying to mind my own business as they talked about everything under the sun! Men, sex, drugs, partying, and shopping. My heart began to ache because as we all sat in the area together for over an hour, I never heard anyone say a word about God.

"What you in here for?" a dark-haired female asked. Based on me overhearing her previous conversation, she seemed a little dingy. The beautiful girl wore a pair of jeans that clung to her hips and butt and a cute T-shirt that she possibly got snatched out of the house lounging around in. I turned and looked at her for a long moment before responding. I was considering my words.

"If I tell you, will you answer something for me?" I finally asked. It was apparent I threw her off a little. She glanced around the room; we had everyone's undivided attention. With a little hesitation, she agreed.

"I'm here for armed robbery. Several," I admitted.

"You don't look like you would do something like that. What, were you with the wrong people at the wrong time?" she asked.

"I wish . . . What do I look like?" I replied.

"Like you could have possibly used somebody credit cards or wrote a bad check." She looked around to see if anyone agreed with her. "How much time you looking at? I should be out of here before the sun rise," she assumed.

"Me too!" another girl spoke up. My mind went to the time I got arrested, and Ike bonded me straight out.

"It really doesn't matter, because I just got sentenced to life in DeKalb," I spoke nonchalantly. The whole room went silent.

"What the hell! Are you serious?" someone asked.

"Yeah. Dead serious. So let me ask y'all something. Do you think it's possible that God tries to intervene in your life by allowing lil' road blocks like this to happen?" Everyone just looked at me. "Like, consider the times you almost got raped or shot . . . the times you almost got hit by a car or hit someone else. Think about how you got caught for one thing, but knowing you really could have gotten cased up for more. Maybe even those times you prayed and asked God to deliver you from something and promised if He did, you wouldn't do this or that anymore. How many of your friends will have to overdose before you realize you need to get some help? You sit wondering what you could have done to receive the kind of sentence you have, but did anyone consider maybe, just maybe, God was sparing your life! How many times he tried to intervene on the path you were on, but you didn't have an eye to see or an ear to hear the warnings that He was placing right before your eyes. Don't be another Falicia Blakely, who had to hit rock bottom in order for God to get my attention. Wake up now, before it's too late. Your rock bottom may not be mine, but it could very well feel like it is. Understand, life is more than just what you want to do. It's about a purpose that God sent you into the earth for. Just think about what I'm saying, that's all I'm asking." I sat back in silence, feeling as if God was using me to give these young women another perspective to consider, and I wanted to make sure I said everything that was necessary. Nervous, I glanced down at my shaking hands and wanted to flap my arms because of my sweaty armpits. The nagging feeling in my gut let me know what God wanted me to do, but despite how openly I spoke, I felt inadequate.

Lord, please give me the strength, I prayed.

"Hey . . . I'm Tomeka by the way," the female who didn't seem too bright introduced herself.

"I'm Falicia." I matched her smile.

"Hey . . ." another female said as she sat on the edge of the metal bench we all shared, "do you mind praying with us? With me? That maybe I won't hit rock bottom . . . you know?"

"Yeah, that I won't come back to a place like this," someone else stated.

I nodded in agreement and stood to my feet. My heart rejoiced because God had given them the courage to ask for what I was too afraid to offer—prayer. *God, I promise from this day forward, I will not allow an opportunity to pass me by. I promise.* Every woman in that cell joined me in the middle of that space. We bowed our heads once everyone's hands were joined together.

As I began to pray, I could see my grandmother Olivia smiling and telling me, "God has a purpose for your life, Falicia. He will use you if you allow him to."

Well, I was willing. I had given the devil my all and it left me with nothing to show for it but shame. I wanted to know what it felt like to do something that would impact the world for the better—to empower those around me. And this moment in this holding cell was the perfect time and place to begin.

CHAPTER 3

"Please press one for a collect call." I complied with the operator and waited for my grandmother to answer.

"Hello?" She sounded so beautiful, though her voice was filled with sleep.

"Hey, Ma!" I couldn't hide my excitement. "I'm sorry I woke you up."

"That's okay, suga. Where you calling me from? It sounded like they said a different place."

"I'm at Fulton County, Ma."

"Why?" I could hear the concern in her voice.

"Just some pending charges, nothing to worry about though. I need you to tell my mom, so she can contact Ken and let him know I'm here." I looked around and noticed a tall, handsome, dark chocolate dude with short locks. Dressed in a leather coat, jeans, a button down shirt and some leather boots, he stood at another set of phones staring at me. I smiled a little and looked away, continuing my phone conversation. A few minutes passed, and a male trustee practically walked up on me.

"He wants to know what you want out the vending machine," he stated as he walked by and went to go empty a trash bin nearby.

"Who is that?" my grandma questioned. I smiled, reminiscing on how nosy she was. I turned to face dude who was grinning. His beautiful white smile sent chills through me.

As a woman of God I should probably just ignore him. I really don't have any business flirting with this man. But he is cute as a fool! I reasoned. He smiled at me again.

"You can get me a juice and some chips or cookies," I said loud enough for him to hear me. All of my debating went out the door.

"Who you talking to?" Grandma inquired. I burst out laughing. "Chile, you hear me talking to you."

11

"Some dude, Momma. Calm down."

"What he want?"

"To buy me something."

"How in the hell he gon' buy you something? His ass in lockup just like you." I looked back in his direction.

"What's your name?" he mouthed.

"Falicia," I answered

"Falicia. Don't be telling him your name, he might be a damn lunatic. Put him on the phone!" she demanded.

"Put him on the phone? For what?" I burst out laughing. "Ma, I can't. That man can't come over here."

"I can't tell . . . He close enough for y'all to be talking." I couldn't help but laugh at her. "Stay away from him." She was so serious, and that's what made it funny. I watched as he walked over to the vending machine.

"You have one minute left," the operator announced.

"All right, Ma. I'll be careful." I didn't want her to worry.

"If they have you sitting there until the wee hours of the night, you can call me back if you need to talk. If I don't answer the first call, just call me back until I do. Okay, baby?"

"Okay, Momma. I love you."

"And I love you too. Stay away from them men. Don't no man in jail mean you any good!" she hurriedly stated before the phone hung up. "I'm praying for you!" she managed to say before the operated said good-bye. I noticed the guy approach the trustee and hand him the stuff, so I remained where I was standing, holding the phone to my ear as if I was still on it. It didn't take much longer for the trustee to come hand me an apple juice, a honey bun, and a bag of Ruffles sour cream and cheddar chips. I smiled because they were my favorites.

"He wants to know your full name," the trustee said as he practically threw the stuff in my hand and got the hell on. I looked over in the direction dude was, and he smiled one last time before going back into the holding cell. *How in the heck am I supposed to give him my name if he didn't stop long enough to get it?* I thought.

"Oh well . . ." I hung up the phone and went back where I had been sitting for over two hours.

Instead of complaining, I needed to thank God. I had received an opportunity to possibly make someone think twice about the life they were living, and then I was just blessed with something to eat. It could have been worse.

By the time some short, dark male officer came to get me and two other females who had arrived since the initial group of females had left, I had fallen asleep and wrote my info down on one of Ken's business cards.

I'll just slide it under the door as I walk by. I grabbed my Bible, the only thing they permitted me to bring with me and cuffed it with my left arm. Standing in front of the door, I held it open for those who were exiting, being courteous. Yet also wanting to be at the end so I could give this dude my information. I stood seconds away from the door I had seen him enter. As I stepped closer and closer, I slipped the card into my right hand, prepared to slide it. The officer walked just one person ahead of me. I looked inside the holding cell trying to locate the cutie who had been generous toward me. Several dudes started shouting and saying provocative things as we passed by. But despite their effort to grab my attention, I spotted that leather coat sitting on the floor not far from the door. It would have been perfect, but the sight of him with his head buried in the lap of another nigga took me by surprise! And the dude wasn't just some gay-looking dude. I would have respected that. He was fine as hell too! Corn rows braided in a design to the back, fresh tape, lined up, thick, buff nigga. Dope boy swag! The sight caused me to stop in my tracks!

"You'll be surprised!" the male officer addressed me with an expression I couldn't decide was either a smirk or disgust. Them dope boys . . . thugs . . . money over bitches . . . sworn to the streets kats be the ones in here stealing gloves and raping these boys. Damn shame, and they be sitting in visitation with they baby mommas like they so hard, so thorough with their undercover asses." He rolled his eyes as if he could see what I was looking at.

13

"Close your mouth, Falicia," I told myself as I made my feet keep walking. There was no sign of that man who had just been flirting with me hours ago. Not the way his body was positioned, and definitely not with the things he was doing. I couldn't believe my eyes, but I wasn't the one to judge. However, I was disappointed to say the least. He could have just let me be; I didn't ask for his info. He asked for mine!

My encounter with dude wasn't my only surprise at Rice Street. It just so happened they were doing some renovations on the jail, and whatever section Ms. Velvet was staying at had been moved to the dorm I had only been in for a couple of days, pod 400. I hadn't laid eyes on the broad since the day we had gotten arrested! The crazy part about the entire arrangement is the minute she saw me she seemed extremely uncomfortable. Me being as outspoken as I am, I approached her.

"You don't know me now?" I asked, sitting on the step next to her as we lined up to receive our trays for dinner. She didn't answer at first. I just stared at her. Not much had changed except she looked a little smaller than I remembered, and her hair was even longer than before. She looked all right; Velvet wasn't what I called pretty, but she wasn't an ugly girl either. I noticed one of her lymph nodes was swollen on the back of her neck. Slowly, she nodded.

"Oh, so you don't know me?" I asked, unsure if I should be offended or not.

"I just don't know who you became," she finally spoke. "Like, I don't know what happened to you."

"Are you serious?" I asked, sincerely taken aback. "Lord, help me!" I prayed, not wanting to flip on this broad.

"Yes," she admitted.

"Where were you? Did you miraculously disappear all the times I was getting my ass beat? As if he wasn't beating your ass too!"

"But you could handle him, Ma—Falicia," she corrected herself. Just hearing her almost say that made me uncomfortable.

"You sound like Smiley saying that. Same way I told her she was twice my size and you used to be. If she couldn't handle him, then what made you think I could?" She just nodded some. I took a good look at her. *This dumb bitch—excuse my language, Lord, is still brain washed. I think it's best I stay away from her.* I chuckled a little bit before I rose to my feet. "For some reason it doesn't surprise me that you can sit there acting clueless to all the hell that man put us through, but it's your life. I heard your mother got you a good attorney, and you'll be getting off easy, thanks to the cocaine addiction he introduced you to. I'll be praying for you." I stated my peace and walked away. I needed to be alone! I went to my cell and got on my knees.

It tore me up to see that she was once me, completely blindsided by reality. And it only further disturbed me that she chose to believe it was all me that did the things I did, or downplayed what he was doing to us. That revelation ripped my heart apart! It was a broken place to be, and it hurt to know she was still there. I cried until I found peace with our Creator that she was in His hands! I cried until I was encouraged! I cried until God reminded me I needed to take my eyes off my circumstances and put them on Him! Before I got off my knees I was determined that I would spend my days there bringing Him glory, nothing else would matter. So instead of concerning myself with wondering if Velvet was talking to Ike sometimes when she was on the phone watching me, I would go in someone's cell, or huddle in a corner and have Bible study with those that asked me. Or I would accept an invitation to go pray with someone.

People I didn't even know started coming up to me.

"Ms. Falicia, I owe you an apology. Because I didn't even know you, but I believed what someone said about you, and I have said some hateful things about you and I'm sorry . . ."

"I apologize because I allowed myself to judge you before I even knew you, and you're nothing like what I heard about you."

I give God glory for that! Because I felt to a certain degree I was living out something Jesus had taught. "How blessed you are when people insult you and persecute you and tell all kinds of vicious lies about you because you follow me!" Matthew 5:11. Though the things that were being said about me wasn't because I had chosen to put my trust and heart in His hand. It was quite the opposite, but God in His faithfulness was condemning the words that were spoken against me. I just told them, "You don't owe me nothing. It's the God in me."

As the days passed, some of the same people who came to apologize began asking me if Velvet was HIV-positive. One girl named Swole that she was having sex with at some point was under the impression that Velvet was "Momma" at home calling all the orders and not one of Ike's girls, as if Velvet and I had swapped roles . . . Swole expressed her concern because of Velvet's swollen lymph nodes and a rumor also surfaced that she was infected. It wasn't my business to tell, but I imagined the possibility of me doing so must have been a bit much for Velvet; she got her mother to have her moved out of that dorm in a matter of days. But just like I didn't feel the need to clarify the rumors Pumpkin spread about me, I wasn't about to be any different toward Velvet. They have to stand before God and give an account just like I do, and He knows everything! So, they could say whatever they wanted, to whomever. I'm responsible for me, and it's my obligation to be at peace with God. I have nothing to hide. Who I was in the past is just that, the past! So I refused to allow another individual to make me feel ashamed of who I am! HIV and all! Most people can't walk a day in my shoes, so why should I feel inferior to them?

CHAPTER 4

By the time I got back to DeKalb County, I was so relieved to get away from that filthy jail. I had a stack of mail waiting for me and enclosed was a letter from someone I didn't know, someone I'd never heard of or even knew existed, but somehow I played a significant role in this man named Kevin's life.

> *My Black Angel,*
>
> *I want you to know you have saved my life. I was scheduled to go to trial this year and Lemetrice Twitty was the key witness against me. As I'm sure you already know, he was a key witness against Ray Lewis as well, and his testimony was why they found Ray guilty.*
>
> *I hate the road that lies ahead of you, and I'm sure you don't see your situation as something to celebrate, but you are my angel. Because of you, I'm going home next month, and if you need anything I got you. Keep your head up, God knows all things. You'll be hearing from me.*

After reading that letter all I could do was get on my knees and cry out to God. One man's triumph was an entire family's devastation. How I wish I could have truly saved lives instead of taken them. This would be the first of three letters he would send me once he was released from the county jail.

The day I returned, I was sitting on the step waiting for the shower when this short, dark-skinned young lady approached me. "Oh my God! It's you!" she spoke boldly, stopping directly in front of me. "You don't remember me?" Looking her over, I hadn't the slightest idea. "Black Satin." I just stared at her, trying to recall. I didn't remember her.

"Nah, I'm sorry. I don't," I finally answered. *She's cute though*, I thought.

"We worked at Body Tapp together," she stated as she sat next to me. "I owe you an apology. The last time I saw you in the dressing room, God told me to tell you something and I didn't. You looked so burdened. But now . . ." She reached out for my hand. "Your nails are so long and pretty, your skin is clear, and your smile is bright!" She beamed. It felt a little awkward because I didn't know her.

"Thank you," I finally said, after she released my hand. I didn't want to seem rude.

"I know I'm coming off strong, it's just that I have wondered about you for so long," she confessed. I offered a slight smile. "I used to wear these thigh-high, black patent leather boots with a long wig. I can't believe you don't remember me." I tried to imagine what she looked like with a wig on.

"Oh! I got this birthmark directly down the middle of my body, one side of me is lighter than the rest."

Suddenly, I remembered her. I, along with some of my male clients, had been very intrigued by this fact.

"You didn't work that often?"

"Yeah, that's me. I'm her!" We both burst out laughing. "Omg! You don't know how burdened I have been since that day I didn't tell you what God said. Like it could have saved your life."

"It's okay. That was the past." I tried to comfort her because her eyes were welling up.

"No, it's not."

"Well, just tell me then. Tell me now." She bowed her head for a second, then looked up.

With tears in her eyes she stated, "He said to tell you 'I love you and you don't have to do it.'"

I just sat there quietly, wondering how would I have applied that to my life back then, or if I would have even been able to receive it at all. My dazed expression must have made her uncomfortable or something because she further explained, as tears ran down her face. "I was scared you would think I was crazy or lying or something." I understood how she felt, but for whatever reason I couldn't say so. I felt myself getting emotional, and I just wanted to be alone.

"Please, excuse me . . . I need to jump in this shower." I stood up, relieved one of the showers had just become available. I broke down crying once I finally made it in. *If I knew that God loved me back then, would it have made a difference? Or that I didn't have to do the things that was demanded of me?*

Black Satin, who I had grown to know as Dora, became a pillar for me. She taught me how to be myself and still love God! To have a voice and not be a doormat for anyone. The confidence I had lost as a result of finding out I was HIV-positive was regained as a result of our friendship. Likewise, I developed a passion for God's people. One of the male trustees took an interest in me, and he would send me a vegan tray with a letter wrapped up in plastic in the apple sauce or a meat patty of some sort beneath my beans. He also gave me extra everything, especially peanut butter. Which came in handy because those who didn't make store would often come ask me for something to eat not long after dinner because it was never filling.

Ken wasn't pleased with the District Attorney's decision not to prosecute Ike, and he arranged for me to do an interview with *Creative Loafing* so that my situation would be documented and not forgotten, or someone who had the ability to help might arise. He feels that Ike is a predator and a coward who needs to be off the street.

The morning arrived and I sat on my bed feeling as if it was one of those, 'only by the grace of God moments!' There I sat humbled by the fact that someone wanted to know and understand the misconception of what I *thought* was love. The tragedy that changed so many lives forever, and what actually led up to that day and why. That God saw fit for my voice to be heard. Not that I had done anything special or even amazing, but the quite the opposite. Taking the foolish things to shame the wise . . . as His word said He would do!

Once again I walked through the door of the multi-purpose room, and Ken rose to his feet. We hugged and a pretty, slim brunette stood to greet me as well.

"Mara Shalhoup." She extended her hand. We shook hands and they sat back down. I noticed a tray someone had picked over sitting on the table, so I excused myself and went to the door. I called out to a woman named Phyllis to come clean off the table, and she gladly complied. Often she volunteered to pass out and/or pick up trays.

I was very comfortable talking with Ken. Some of the things we had spoken on over the past nineteen months, I hadn't even addressed with my family. So him being present made everything flow, and Ms. Shalhoup seemed open and sympathetic. Not once did I feel she was being judgmental.

After two hours had passed, I had poured my heart out about the misfortunes that assaulted my life and the life I had come to know. I was the perfect, shocking example of poor choices, naivety, and what a young girl could become upon entering a den full of lions!

CHAPTER 5

I arrived at Diagnostics on April 4, 2004. This was it! I was with the *Big Dawgs* now! Diagnostics is the process an inmate begins once they enter state custody. A series of mental and physical tests are provided to determine the inmate's needs. This process can last a minimum of eight weeks to several months, depending on the outcome of the test results. Because certain inmates are a liability to the state, Diagnostics has a separate housing unit.

An organized task force of correctional officers dressed in all black and labeled as CERT (Critical Emergency Response Team) started yelling at us, demanding we get in a straight line side by side as we stood in the entrance of Metro State Prison. I thought they were a joke, but I knew better than to laugh. Immediately I saw what happened to those who did.

"You think something funny?" one of the two female correctional officers stood nose to nose with the girl who stood next to me, yelling in her face. The other female stood at her side, yelling in her ear, and the dude who was just as big as they were in height and statue stood behind her daring her to laugh again!

"You think you cute? Laugh again!" the man dared her.

"Do it! See how quick I put you on this ground!" the other female guard threatened. When she didn't take the challenge, they moved on to see if anyone else needed a reality check.

"You in my world now! You just a number from here on out! You do as I say! All that attitude will get your ass dropped!" one guard yelled in another girl's face. My heart raced! *Maybe these thick-built bitches ain't playing!* I thought as they bypassed me. I stood upright and looked straight ahead as instructed. It only seemed foolish to me to be defiant and subject myself to being yelled at.

"This is how it's going to be . . . From here on out, every time you're addressed, your answer will be 'yes ma'am, or no ma'am. Yes sir, or no sir.' Understood?"

"Yes, ma'am!" we all said in unison. It was about eight of us.

"Everything you got on is going in the trash, except your jewelry. You can mail that home. Anything you brought in with you and what you have on is to be set outside the curtain in front of you. When I say undress, you got one minute to do so, and wait until I approach your curtain. Then upon instruction, you will turn around, bend over, spread your booty cheeks apart and cough, then squat and do the same. Do I make myself clear?"

"Yes, ma'am!" we sounded off again. I waited for someone to give me the go ahead. *I hate that I put on this brand new shirt and boxers, when I'm just going to throw them away! Had I known that, I would have left it with Red like I did all my commissary,* I thought.

Red was this dominant lesbian I had known a little over a year during my county experience in DeKalb. After I got sentenced, she started pushing up on me again. This would be her second attempt to try to holla at me. I had just brushed off all her attempts in the past, but this last time I started entertaining her. Against my own religious beliefs, her presence seemed comforting.

"Look at this!" The lighter of the two female officers held up my son's picture as she opened the Bible I had brought with me, where his picture was secured. "Look at this beautiful baby!" she told her coworker. "Look at what God gave you, and you in here wasting time. You left this"—She stuck his picture close enough to my face for me to see him—"to come here! You better get your shit together, do what you got to do, and get home to him. God blessed you with him," she stated, and walked away to finish inspecting my belongings. Tears raced down my eyes for several reasons. One, because she was right. I had chosen the streets and Ike over Man. I always said I wouldn't be like my mother and grandmother, leaving their mothers to raise their children, and I did just that. And then the officer's disposition . . . She didn't yell at me or handle me aggressively. She spoke from a mother's perspective, and her kindness broke my heart! I wished I could just handle my business and get home to my baby, but that wasn't the case for me. Today was day one of the rest of my natural life.

CHAPTER 6

I found myself grateful that Bonnie (a girl I stayed in the pod with) was cool and left with me. Trying to keep her at ease prevented me from focusing on myself. After being sprayed (while butt naked) in all the places where lice could inhabit, we showered and had to dress out in these all white one-piece jumpsuits. It did absolutely nothing for my figure, but I suppose that was the purpose! And the boots they gave me were instantly uncomfortable, and kind of put me in mind of Jodeci boots. I looked around at the others who were with me and decided not to complain! Some of them looked a horrible mess with their stomachs sticking out further than their backside; the elastic in the waist clung to them, revealing flaws in their shape they probably hid. But I learned quickly the whole system was set in motion to degrade you. Finally, we had to stand in front of a camera and take a picture in an unattractive state no woman ever wants to be caught in. One of my eyes looked slightly shut because the guard sprayed me in the eye with some of the lice treatment solution. My hair was so matted and drawn up, it struggled to remain in a ponytail in the back of my head! My eyebrows were the only thing on point! I looked an ashy mess!

I really wasn't sure what to think about the different people, staff, and offenders peeking their heads out in the hallways as we passed Laundry and Intake.

"There she go! That's her!" I heard over and over as I locked eyes with strangers. I could only suspect they had been following my case on the news, until we finally made it in front of this building labeled G, and a girl dressed in a khaki button down shirt and pants called me by name.

"Hey! I'm Stacie!" She smiled hard, as if she was really excited to see me. "I read about you in *Creative Loafing*. If you need anything let me know!" And as soon as she appeared, she walked away. Our escorting officer began telling the other women to carry on. The women dressed in khaki uniforms were in General Population (GP), which simply means they completed Diagnostics and were not segregated from the rest of the prisoners. I watched as they all walked in one of the two directions that resembled a small road outlined in yellow paint.

The small institution was set up in an L-shape. The buildings that had a letter on them were dormitories. When you first step foot in a dorm there was an office to your immediate right, this was the counselor's officer. Each counselor was given a caseload to assist the inmates with rehabilitation through cognitive thinking and self-awareness groups. Each dorm had four ranges in them. A and B were downstairs, C and D upstairs. A bubble with a control panel to operate each range was stationed in the middle of each dorm, giving the officer visualization on each range. The range was set up with a section of four showers behind a shower curtain directly across from the TV room. The TV room was in the middle and shaped like a butterfly with cells on each side of the hallway resembling its wings.

The building that was marked with the letter B was the Business office. Administrative staff worked there, and other business like attorney visits and cosmetology were also conducted there. Beneath it was the Children's Center. Next to it was the dining hall, and on the opposite end, right before you got to the end of the L-shape was the mailroom, store, and a gym, where visitation was held. Finally at the end of the L was the church, school, and library. Directly behind all that was a huge yard with a few bars to exercise on and a track to walk in circles.

Bonnie and I were housed in the same dorm but on opposite ends of the hall. The first night was crazy because we didn't have the simple necessities that made living under these conditions easier (shower shoes, store brand soaps, such as Dove, Tone, or even Ivory). We had blue soap! A product of GCI (Georgia Correctional Industries), something one of the men prisons made. Along with state toothpaste and deodorant! So I showered in a pair of socks, not wanting my bare feet to touch the floor. I could only imagine the fungus and bacteria in those showers!

There was no such thing as privacy anymore! I shared a shower with three other women, a room and a toilet with five others and one of them had to show me the expected way to make my bed and set up my locker. We were all expected to wake up, stand up for count, eat, march, bathe, and go to bed *together*! This would take some getting used to, but it beat sitting in a cell or in a pod in front of a TV half the day, or even standing around doing someone's hair. Sure, it was far better than feeling like a trapped animal in a glass cage. Now, if I could only accept that this is the life I had chosen for myself, then I'd adjust just fine. As I stretched out on the thin mat considered as my bed and covered my head with the thin, cream-colored, superficial cotton blanket, I couldn't help but wonder how comfortable was Ike sleeping?

CHAPTER 7

"Line up for chow! Line up for chow!" a correctional officer yelled, scaring me from my sleep. I sat straight up in bed. I was in what they called 'the princess bed' because I didn't have a bunk over me. The two sets of bunk beds lined the wall next to the window. My bed was positioned directly across from one of those, next to a half wall that separated the bunks from the toilet and sink. Toward the foot of my bed there sat another princess bed a few feet away.

I looked over at one of my roommates who didn't seem phased by the abrupt disturbance. She stretched and yawned. "Time for breakfast." She looked at me and spoke as if she could read my mind.

"Breakfast? I'm not hungry . . . I'm going back to bed," I stated, and lay back down facing the wall.

"Baby girl, you don't have a choice."

"What do you mean?" I rolled over with the covers still pulled over my head.

"We have to go to every meal, regardless if we eat or not. And she'll be back in here to check in a few minutes. I advise you to go ahead and get up, brush your teeth and stuff before everybody else, because then we'll all be running circles around each other," she advised as she climbed off her bunk. My roommate then walked over to her locker that sat on top of her bunkmate's locker. I lay there considering what she said and thought it was best to take her advice.

No sooner than I had my teeth brushed and my face washed, my other bunkies got in line to use the toilet and gain access to the sink. It didn't take an entire day to pass in order to know I wasn't going to like this. *That's a lot of ass on the same toilet!* I thought. *Plus, one is trying to wash her hands while the other is trying to brush her teeth. They're spitting in the sink! Oh my God!* Just seeing it gave me the creeps! I got dressed and got out the way after locking my locker. I didn't need anyone to instruct me about that.

In the TV room, several others sat in the few chairs that decorated the small room with one circular table as well, while others stood. I noticed people crowding the bulletin board that hung from the wall. Several hold-ins were tacked on it. A hold-in is a small slip of paper that shows an inmate's full name, security level, date of birth, housing unit, and the location and time of any appointments. When the crowd dispersed, I approached the board and saw one with my name on it. I was to report to Medical to see the specialist at seven. It was a pass to see the HIV specialist. I looked around the room to see how many people were wondering who the person seeing the HIV specialist was? I locked eyes with a group of about eight girls staring and whispering to one another and looking at me. *Shit, I guess it's no such thing as privacy here,* I thought as I mentally prepared myself for the cruel criticism that was bound to come. I had already persevered through it in the county jail; now that I was in a new environment with new people, there would be new opinions and remarks!

I wasn't pleased to have to march everywhere we went yelling in cadence, but the fact that we would be going to the store immediately after lunch made everything seem minute. We gladly lined up in formation outside the dining hall, waiting for the demand to take off.

"Make a hole!" someone yelled as several people fell back out the way.

"Inmate Falicia Blakely!" the male sergeant on the Cert Team yelled out. I continued to stare at the four of them walking up checking IDs. I heard my name but didn't comprehend they were calling me.

"Inmate Falicia Blakely!" he yelled again.

"Falicia, he calling you," Bonnie, the girl that came with me informed me. But before I could answer, the tall, dark dude in front of me held an ID in his hand, looking from the picture on the ID then back to me.

"Falicia Blakely!" It sounded like more of a threat than a question. I was afraid to answer. I barely nodded.

"Let's go!" he instructed, and began walking. I glanced back at Bonnie, who pleaded with her eyes to know what was going on. I had no idea what to tell her as I was escorted to my room, instructed to pack up my property, and was monitored as I did so.

"Can somebody please explain to me what is going on?" I asked several times to all four Cert Team members at least twice. It seemed no one was willing to answer me. The sergeant grabbed my mattress, and then they walked me over to D building, which was lockdown. I stopped outside of the building.

"Why I got to go to the lockdown dorm?" I asked the sergeant.

"Come on," he advised. Tears poured from my eyes as I entered that building.

"Why am I being locked down?" I repeated, as they escorted me into this filthy one-man cell. "Why are y'all doing this to me? I already been sentenced." I couldn't hold back my tears. "Sir, please, please tell me something," I pleaded with the sergeant. Finally, when all my things were secured in the room, he looked at me through the window and told me I was in involuntary protective custody. But hell! I didn't know what that meant.

"Hey, kid. You gon' be all right, just don't forget God is with you," the sergeant said. I did believe God was present, but this wasn't the favor I was used to receiving. I sat on that metal bunk crying because I was being punished for a crime I had already been sentenced to pay with my life, and now this . . .

"Ma'am, I need a mattress!" I yelled at the correctional officer as she walked by doing her routine check. I didn't know what happened to the mattress I had been given. I had been sitting in this filthy room for over an hour looking at the paint chipping off the walls, rust eating away at the metal bed and window frames. The cracks in the dust covered windows and the various bugs that became prey to infested cobwebs! I dared not remove any of my property until someone had given me something to clean this allotted space.

Once it was clear that my concern wasn't the officer's, I decided I needed to turn up a bit. I leaned my back against the door and started kicking it with all that I had in me. Being civilized clearly didn't matter in this type of environment.

"Inmate! What is your problem?" the CO yelled from the opposite side of the door.

"I need to talk to somebody. I don't know why I'm back here. I haven't done anything. We were on our way to the store, and next thing I know I'm back here in this disgusting room. I need a mattress and some chemicals to wipe down." I felt myself wanting to cry. She walked away without saying a word. I looked out the cloudy window watching her for as long as I could.

"What did I do?" I asked God aloud as defeat hit me like a wave. I turned my back to the door and just slid to the floor crying uncontrollably!

"I can't do this! God, if this is how I'll have to live the rest of my life, I can't live it like this." I sat there giving up, overwhelmed with pity. About five minutes had passed when I heard a tap at the door. I was crying so loud I didn't hear the knocking at first.

"Hey! Where you at?" a female voice came from the opposite side. I jumped to my feet.

"I'm right here," I replied.

"Step over there." She pointed toward the metal bunk. I complied and she opened my door, tossed in a mat and a torn piece of towel that dripped a liquid. I assumed it was chemicals. She shut the door back and I picked the rag up and smelled bleach on it.

"I guess this is better than nothing," I reasoned. I squeezed the rag over the metal toilet seat, to allow the excess chemicals to clean the seat I would have to soon sit on. The Lord alone knows how many people had shared this same filthy-looking toilet. But before I wiped the toilet off, I walked over to my bed and used a sanitary napkin to remove the food crumbs that someone left on the bunk. Once that was cleared, I wiped down the bunk, the desk, the sink and the toilet. The room was far from being clean, but it was a start. I desperately tried to encourage myself, but when I took one look at the cloth, piss-stained mattress lying out on the bunk, fresh tears fell from my eyes. It wasn't plastic like the one I had previously. It took a few seconds of thinking, but then it dawned on me that I could use the trash bag the cert officer had given me to dump my bed linen in. So I split it the long way and spread it across the filthy mattress before I covered it with my sheets and blankets.

I rinsed out the rag and wiped out the locker so I could store my property, and then used another sanitary napkin to sweep and mop the floor. Once I was finished, I sat down on the bunk and took a deep breath. Somehow, I would have to find a way to be okay with this arrangement. I did my best not to think about what Bonnie and the rest of the women I had shared a room with were doing while I was locked away in this filthy cell, like a filthy animal.

"I just don't think I can do this, Lord," I confessed, as I realized I needed to pray. I knelt and began to cast my cares upon the Lord. I was determine not to get up until He had given me some form of peace.

Later that night someone slid an envelope under the door. Olivia Blakely was the returnee. *Thank you, Lord!* This woman always had a way of comforting me! I didn't know where I would be without my grandmother, and I hope that during my sentence I wouldn't have to find out.

April 28, 2004

Dear Falicia, (I.D. #1154104)

I don't know if you are able to receive mail yet. I know you cannot have visitation until (6) weeks. I hope that doesn't apply to mail.

I just wanted to let you know how much I love you. I am looking forward to seeing you when your six weeks are up. I know that I have not been writing like I should or like I want to, but all last month and this month I have been taking care of Teki and Lexy.

Tasha is buying a house and has taken a part time night job. I am here at her house from Sunday night until Friday night.

When I first started in March, she didn't have the night job, but she needed extra money to buy some things for the house.

I don't remember if I told you she was getting a divorce. She went to court this month. It should be final by June.

You know Lexy's birthday is coming up this weekend. I guess her dad is having a party at Chuckie Cheese. She'll be eleven.

Tony is not working but he is looking. He is happy to sit at home and draw unemployment. Did I tell you that Bill was buying a house on Franklin Street? Your old home! Genus moving this week!

I miss you so very much. I just cannot express in words what I feel, but I know you know how much I love you. I want to be strong for you, but sometimes it is hard.

Please, pray for me. I am praying for you. I want you to be strong and keep trusting in God. You know after all is said and done, God is all we have.

I love you, will write more soon.
Love Grandma

I studied my letter as I placed it back in its envelop. *God is all we have.* I reflected on her words. I honestly believed that He was the only reason I hadn't snapped! *Lord, I'm not in a place where I'm ready to say, 'Your will, not my will be done,' but I'm willing to trust You. The plans you have for my life. Please keep me.*

CHAPTER 8

"Ahhh! Leave me alone!" I was awakened to someone screaming at the top of her lungs. "Leave me alone!" she kept screaming. I jumped to my feet and ran to the door where I caught a strong whiff of doo-doo, but her screams didn't permit me much time to even consider where the smell was coming from.

Is someone messing with this lady? Is that the reason we are thrown back here in these cells, so people can come violate us throughout the night? My mind raced a million miles per hour. "Lord, please don't let no one come take my butt or jump on me," I prayed.

I heard all sorts of commotion in front of the cell that was two cells over to my right. Staff gathered on my range for whoever was screaming and now kicking the door. The individual who was housed directly across from me must have been startled from her sleep as well; she was now up and peeping out the window.

"Listen here, when I approach this flap you better not throw any of your shit at me, do you understand?" a female officer with a raspy voice demanded. It was quiet for a second.

"You better stop eating that shit! Your shit is what's going to kill you one day," that same officer said.

Her shit? Like, does she mean her shit or some other shit? I thought and couldn't reach a conclusion.

"Call and send for me an orderly. She smearing that shit all over the walls, eating it and she trying to flood the toilet," the same voice instructed someone.

Flood the toilet? Does that mean it's going to spill into my room? I wondered. But no sooner than the thought came to mind I heard the officer say, "Y'all better put something under the door. She been balling her shit into little balls, and she's trying to push them under her door."

Like, are you serious? What kind of person plays, eats, and decorates with her bowel movement? I felt myself getting angry. It had to be past midnight, and she was up with this BS. I couldn't think of anything I could use to put at my door. But the more I heard her toilet flushing and heard her screaming for a Lieutenant Williams, the more my mind worked. I ended up using my sanitary napkins to line them beneath my door. Hoping this would keep out the unwanted.

Possibly a half hour later she was escorted somewhere, and other inmates were sent into her room to clean it. I eventually fell asleep, but I heard someone complaining. "It's almost three in the morning, and she pulled this dumb shit!"

Tap! Tap! Tap! Tap!

Someone hit against the door with something metal. I rolled over and made eye contact with another unfamiliar face. "I just can't seem to get any sleep around here!" I complained.

"Here's your tray." She set it on my flap and carried on.

Well, at least I don't have to get up and march anywhere to eat, I thought as I grabbed my tray, ate what I wanted, and set it back on the flap and lay back down. It seemed as soon as I drifted off there was the tapping again.

"Get up and get ready for your shower," the unfamiliar female officer instructed.

"Ma'am, I don't mean to be a headache, but I don't have any soap or shower shoes."

"What you mean?" she asked. "Did you leave them by mistake, or were they not in your property?"

"Neither, ma'am. I just arrived yesterday, and my dorm was headed to the store when those people in black—"

"The CERT Team," she informed me.

"When the CERT Team came and got me out the line," I corrected my sentence. "So I didn't get a chance to purchase any hygiene products or shower shoes." She just stood there looking at me for a few seconds.

"Well . . . I'm not sure what to tell you, but let me see what I can do." Fifteen minutes later she came back with two small hotel distributed soaps, shampoo, and conditioner.

"This ain't much, but this is all I could get from Chaplaincy. Now, in reference to the shower shoes, I don't know what to tell you, other than I don't recommend you shower with your bare feet." I looked around the cell, trying to think of what I could use and quick. I didn't want to keep the officer waiting. She had shown me the most compassion so far. I looked down at my feet.

Bingo! I thought. *Just bathe with my socks on again.* It beat missing my shower all together! I wouldn't be able to take another one until Monday morning. Lockdown only bathed on Mondays, Wednesdays, and Fridays. I gathered my stuff and extended my arms through the flap, and she cuffed me so I could be escorted to the shower.

"Hey, Falicia!" a brunette Caucasian woman said as I was being escorted back to the cell. "I followed your story."

"Hey," I answered, feeling a little weird about being known for such a heartless crime. I looked over at the officer, trying to read her expression.

"That's Kelly Gissendaner," the CO offered.

"Kelly who?" I replied.

"Kelly Renee Gissendaner. The only woman on death row."

"Oh my goodness!" It was all I could say as I thought about how I had almost joined her! "Now that you've said that, I do recall reading about her. She is the only woman on death row, and I would have been the youngest woman," I told the officer as she opened the cell to let me in. "So, this is what she lives like. I can't imagine staying like this." She opened my flap and I stuck my arms in it, to get the handcuffs removed.

"No, ma'am. She has exercising equipment, a flat screen television, and video games in that room. She's living comfortably," the CO informed me.

"I guess," I said. *How does she feel being locked away all day like that?* She remained heavily on my mind for the rest of the day. Thinking about her situation made me reflect on how merciful God had been to me, even sitting here in this cell. At least I had something to look forward to. Her days were numbered. Somebody else decided when she would take her last breath. This reality made my present seem less stressful. I suddenly had the desire to journal, but didn't have anything to write with or on. I lay in bed staring at my Bible, lost in my thoughts. I opened my Bible and a bookmark fell out between the wall and bed. I got down on my knees to retrieve the bookmark and discovered a pen. I washed it off and opened the back of the Bible and began writing a letter.

My Heavenly Father,

The One who is, who was, and is to come. The One who vowed to never leave or forsake me, I'm crying out to You in this hour. What is going on, Father? Is this Your plan for my life? Your plan that you promised in Your word to be of good and not evil, to give me hope and an expected end? Is it Your will for me to suffer in this cell alone for the things You know I committed out of fear? If it is, I pray for Your grace to endure. I pray that You keep me from the spirit of suicide and guard my mind as I accept the consequences for my actions. Help me to find purpose in the present. But if this is not THE plan you have for me, please send someone to give me some form of understanding as to why I'm up here in lockdown. Above all this, help me get my focus back on You. In your son Jesus' name, I pray . . . Amen.

I closed the Bible and cried myself to sleep. I don't know how long I was asleep before I heard a tap on the door.

"Ms. Blakely, get inspection ready and prepare to see the Deputy Warden of Care and Treatment."

"What's inspection ready?" I asked, jumping up.

"Make sure your jumper is buttoned up, hair off your collar, and your bed is made properly. If you have your boots, your boots should be laced up." I speedily carried out her orders, completely oblivious that God had answered my prayer that fast.

CHAPTER 9

I may not have known everything, but I knew Jheri curls were out of style, but somebody must have forgotten to tell the individual that stood before me. I thought I was about to see a scene from *Miami Vice* play out before me as I was escorted to a metal table and a connected stool that was nailed to the floor.

"What is it you have to say?" The individual removed some sunglasses, and I discovered I was talking to a woman.

"I'm not sure I understand your question," I confessed. "I'm trying to figure out why I'm in lockdown?"

"You're in segregation. This is your seventy-two-hour hearing."

"But I've only been here a little over twenty-four hours . . . and what did I do to be sent to lockdown?" She tilted her head slightly to the left, took a deep breath, and her brows narrowed. Instead of answering my question, she looked at me as if I was wasting her time or missing the point. She was beginning to make me angry.

"Ma'am, check it . . ." My attitude was shifting. "I don't have nothing that I need. Shower shoes, soap, deodorant, or food because you, or *somebody else* made this call for me to be brought up here right before we were headed to the store. All I'm asking is for some understanding! If this is where I got to do my time, say that. If not, say that, but don't sit there staring at me like a bump on a log. This mess is not fair!"

"I advise you to lower your tone talking to me," she calmly replied. I didn't realize I was yelling, but once she made that remark I looked around and noticed the officer was looking a little surprised, and a family a few tables over were staring in shock. I couldn't see the inmate they were visiting at first, but she turned around. It was Kelly. She waved and gave me the biggest smile.

Damn, I thought. *This woman is on death row and she's smiling and*

39

I'm sitting here showing my behind. I looked back at this Jheri-curl-wearing woman in front of me.

"Ma'am, I apologize. It's just . . . I've never been through this process, and I'm confused, even with the terms you use."

"You were pulled from the compound and housed in Segregation, which means you are not in trouble but were removed to make sure you aren't a threat to anyone, and no one is a threat to you," she explained, after standing next to the table in silence for a few seconds.

"A threat!" I couldn't wrap my mind around it.

"The compound was in an uproar because of you. Offenders were leaving their details, dorms, and stopping on the walk trying to see you. It's just procedure. Eventually, you'll be able to go back on the compound. Once our investigation is over." With that, she walked away.

Now to my shame, I didn't see God merely moving for my sake. I had just had my seventy-two-hour hearing, which meant the prison had up to seventy-two hours to see me. I didn't realize God was trying to show me it wasn't His will for me to do my time in lockdown, or that His plans are for good and this little time could be used as an opportunity to rekindle my desire for the Lord. Instead, I was offended that I had been treated with a lack of concern and the officer and her Jheri curl became many things that a child of God dare not speak openly. I was mad I didn't get any immediate results. I stomped my lil' ungrateful behind back to the cell.

By mid-week I had developed my lil' routine. Wake up when my breakfast tray arrived, shower on the days we were permitted to bathe, clean my room, make my bed, read my Bible and sit at the desk watching the people who went outside to the recreation yard that looked more like fenced cages for wild animals.

This morning I wasn't prepared for the sight before me. I sat in disbelief as one inmate stood outside in one of the cages undressing like she was an old whore from the sixties. She ripped her panties off and unfasten her bra and slung it between her legs as she attempted to dance seductively, like it was a bull.

I couldn't believe my eyes! No one in their right mind would possibly be getting naked outside, but what happened next as the officers rushed to the gate confirmed my speculations. She lowered her body into a squat position, placed her hand beneath her butt and released her bowels. She motioned for the officers to move away from her and when they didn't, she tossed a handful of shit at them.

This is the woman who was eating her stool the other night, I thought. I couldn't stop watching as she continued to poop in her hand and spread it over her body. What could possibly have gone wrong in her mind to do such a thing? My heart ached at the reality that this butt naked woman had lost her mind! I couldn't watch any longer. I got down on my knees and prayed. I didn't know what took possession of her, but I did not want to become her.

CHAPTER 10

"Ms. Blakely, what are you doing in handcuffs?" Mr. Morning, the Diagnostics unit manager asked. I stood in the hallway of Medical waiting to be seen by a nurse practitioner to complete the routine examination. "Did you get in trouble?" The handsome, six foot, brown-skinned, middle-age man stood before me giving a simple tie and linen pants a new label.

"No, sir. I was only told it was for my safety."

"Your safety?" Frustration covered his face. "How long you been back there?"

"Sir, at least two weeks." Suddenly a brick was pressing against my chest, slightly choking me as I fought to refrain from crying. I knew I was standing, but my body didn't feel like my own—but controlled by someone else. I was on the verge of breaking down. "I haven't made store. I don't have shower shoes, or a real bar of soap, or deodorant." I could no longer hold my tears back.

"Don't cry . . . I'm going to take care of it. Just do what they tell you to do," he stated, and walked away. It was apparent he was pissed. I hadn't been on the compound long enough to know if he honored his word or not, but in my heart I felt he was a good man, fair and consistent. To everyone's surprise but mine, by one o'clock that day I was told to pack up my property, and I was being moved back into G building, a range one of the six ranges for Diagnostics. Where I had come from. I had God to thank for sending His servant down that hallway at the exact time I was standing there! I was just beginning to see His hand in my present environment.

It didn't take long for me to get into the swing of things. The prison only permitted Diagnostics to receive a care package from home consisting of three pairs of panties, bras and socks each. That was it, but

43

I didn't make a fuss about it because some of the girls in General Population had given me T-shirts and lip gloss. Simple stuff like that made the daily routine go by smoother. On the other hand, the Georgia Department of Corrections provided three meals a day, Monday through Friday. On Saturday and Sunday we were served breakfast and dinner. Therefore, if we wanted to eat lunch on the weekends, we would either have to be at visitation, or get some commissary from our locker.

It didn't take long to see the epidemic in prison is that a lot of people go without financial support from their family and/or friends. As a result, a lot of heterosexual women change roles and become dominant bisexual as a means of surviving. They cut their hair off or keep it braided in styles that give off the resemblance of men, or what we call 'studs' in prison. Many are labeled the distasteful name 'gay for the state.' Why? Because a lot of women still want a man, and a stud is the closest thing to one. The ratio is about one stud to every twenty women, so this puts them in high demand! To their shame, most of these broads will compete with one another. Trying to buy love, just like some of us have done at home and therefore, a stud normally doesn't want for anything. Whether someone is giving them their $60 weekly store bag, or putting money on their books, they aren't going without! I considered myself blessed because my mother and son came to see me every weekend, so I wasn't concerned about lunch.

One afternoon I was outside the dormitory at the end of the ramp that led up to the lobby, picking up my range laundry. Twice a week we sent out our jumpsuits with the option of sending out a net bag with our underclothes and pajamas in it. A bunch of new intakes were arriving and were in front of our building separating their property from the Diagnostics that were going to H building. Two studs were amongst them, both no taller than five six, one slim, cute, and dark skinned. While the other was heavier, kind of cute, and brown skinned with good hair. I noticed the heavier one checking for me, but I wasn't looking for that type of attention, so I kept to my purpose of being outside in the first place.

44

Forty-eight hours hadn't passed before someone came up to me to inform me that Niko thought I was the prettiest black girl she had laid eyes on.

"Tell her I said thank you for the compliment, but I'm not interested," I told the messenger and didn't give it much more thought. I figured as soon as somebody told her I was HIV-positive, she would lose interest. Most people fear what they don't understand, and in this environment some people treated those that are HIV-positive as if they have the plague.

The next morning while we were lining up to march to breakfast, Niko made an attempt to get my attention. I smiled and got in line with my range. She was on B range and almost ended up in line next to me and was making her presence known, along with the other stud I first saw her with. Now known as her cousin. By the time breakfast was over, we were having a conversation.

"Well, I appreciate you making my morning pleasurable," I confessed, in reference to her humorous presence in the chow hall, where she made it her business to sit with me.

"Pleasure was all mine." Niko grinned seductively. I couldn't help but notice her teeth weren't as white as I preferred, but they weren't rotted out, and she had all of them. It made me wonder what type of life she lived at home.

"If they call something, I want you to come out," she suggested as she walked me to medical for pill call. She was referring to the couple of minutes they made throughout the day for smoke break and Pavilion, where the entire institution went outside behind the dorms to this huge field and track, where a lot of people jogged or power walked. Some came out for the fresh air, or to use the little bit of exercise equipment. The area also had a baseball field and a basketball court.

"Look. I don't want to waste your time, nor do I want you to be blind about the fact I have HIV," I blurted, before I lost the courage to do so. For some reason I was a little apprehensive about telling her, slightly feeling she would shun my presence. But I couldn't focus on that. I had to remain true to myself, and if people wanted to treat me different because of it, then that would be their loss and not mine.

"Damn!" she quickly replied. "I would have never thought that." She took one step back and looked me over. "You don't look sick . . . I mean . . . you don't look like you got the package."

"Most people don't," I retorted, feeling slightly uncomfortable.

"If you don't mind me asking, how did you contract it?" I stared at the individual whom I claimed not to be interested in. She was a few inches shorter than me, not my normal attraction features-wise, but she seemed genuine.

"My ex-boyfriend sodomized me." I watched as her expression went from curious to shocked.

"Are you saying he . . ."

"Yes, I'm saying he raped me in my butt. For various reasons I was no longer sexually active with him, and one day during a fight, he folded me up and raped me. We were both bleeding, and that's the day I believe I contracted it."

"Damn, I'm sorry." She reached out for my hand.

"It's cool. You don't have to pity me. My past is molding me into the woman I am becoming." I didn't remove my hand from her grasp.

"Well, if you permit me to, I want to still be a part of your life. I think you're even more beautiful now." She smiled at me until my smile matched hers.

As days passed, I embraced the attention I received from her. It was a welcomed distraction, but I couldn't open myself up to being her girlfriend because I really didn't know her, and I wasn't confident she could handle not staying in the dorm with me and upholding our relationship. Then, the subject of her wanting to have sex came up rather quickly. After discovering she didn't know much about HIV, her willingness to engage in sexual activities made me paranoid about her health and lack of concern for risky behavior. Just because I love myself and believe it's unfair to take someone's choice away from them is inhumane, I recognize that some people just don't give a fuck, and so where I desire to educate and enlighten anyone, someone else would subject people to whatever they carried, with no intentions of coming clean about it. When it was all said and done, I wasn't trying to catch something, simply trying to bust a nut.

Over the next couple weeks, we got to know each other a little better, the type of home setting she had and the life she lived that led to prison. She also was enlightened about my health status and desired to satisfy me sexually. Against my better judgment, one evening after dinner when they called smoke break, I snuck off my range, crawled across the floor past the officers' bubble and into her range. She was about six rooms down from the front door. Her five roommates were gone, and she was waiting for me. Swiftly, I removed my jumpsuit and was down to my panties, bra, and socks. My heart raced as my spiritual mind told me this was a bad idea. Mentally, I wrestled with the thought of contracting something else. Niko looked around the room trying to decide where she wanted me. She slept on a top bunk, so the two of us climbing up there wasn't the best idea. I took my panties off as she covered the window with some paper and told me to get up on the sink. I did so and she got down on her knees. As soon as she took me into her mouth, I heard what sounded like the front door opening.

"I think I hear the police," I told her as I pushed her head away and got off the sink. The sound of a walkie-talkie got closer. I grabbed my jumper and ran on the opposite side of the wall and crawled beneath the bed. She sat on the toilet as if she was using it. As soon as she flushed, someone knocked on the door.

"I'm on the toilet!" Niko yelled.

"Anybody in there with you?" a female officer questioned. I could hear Niko turning the water on, and then opening the door.

"No ma'am. I'm just using the toilet." My heart raced as I hoped like hell that woman wouldn't come looking beneath the bed.

"Okay . . . I'm looking for somebody. Someone told the lieutenant somebody is over here unauthorized."

"Word! Well, she ain't in here," Niko stated, and closed the door. I was so scared I could have pissed on myself. I got from beneath that bed and slipped into my jumpsuit so quickly, Niko didn't have time to look out the window to see if we were in the clear and look back at me.

· "I knew I shouldn't have brought my ass over here," I spoke aloud as I buttoned up. "Who the fuck went and told the police I'm in here, Niko?" I got in her face once I was dressed.

"I don't know."

"I should have asked which one of your 'hos would have went and told the police I'm over here." She could say whatever she wanted, only a broad who felt I was stepping on her toes would go put the police on me. "Get me out of here!" I demanded, wanting to slap the spit out her mouth.

"Baby, before you leave I need you to believe I'm not doing shit." She tried to embrace me.

"Get me the fuck out this room!" I was already convinced. There was nothing she could say. I reached in my back pocket and felt my panties tucked away in it. "Hold these. I don't want to get caught with these on me." Niko smiled like I had just said I forgave her. When she told me the coast was clear, I ran across the hall to a two-man cell and hid behind the door.

Niko's cousin walked back in from smoke break looking for me, trying to get to me before the police did. She was standing nearby when the broad went up to Lieutenant Williams and told her I had crawled out of my dorm, passed the officer's bubble, and went down the steps of my neighboring range. I couldn't believe I slipped up like that and hadn't paid attention to her watching my every move. Plus, knowing some random chick thought it was okay to hate on me like that! The thought made me want to fight. I looked at Niko like I was going to kick her behind, but before I even had time to act on it, the front door opened and that same officer came directly down the hall and went into Niko's room.

"Where is she?" I heard the officer question. Niko walked up the hall and into the TV room like she didn't know what was going on. Niko's cousin stood in the doorway like she was just being nosy, as I hid behind her door.

48

God, please! Help me get out of this, I prayed, barely expecting Him to get me out of the mess I created. The officer looked into each room, but not behind the doors. Once she was off the range, I jetted out too. I made it past the officer's booth and had opened my range door. I couldn't believe I actually made it back without getting caught! I took my first step down the steps when I heard someone say, "Hey! Where are you coming from?"

Damn! I thought, pretending I didn't hear her.

"Hey! I said where are you coming from?" She yanked the door back open.

"Smoke break," I barely whispered.

"Nah . . . come here," she instructed. I looked at my roommate as she stood in the middle of the hallway looking like she had been on pins and needles.

"It is what it is," I told her and turned around. She had told me she didn't have a good feeling about me going. The officer cuffed me up and escorted me outside where the Lieutenant was standing.

"Where you find her?" The Lieutenant asked.

"Sneaking back on her range."

"Lock her down!"

"Lock down!" I repeated in disbelief. "She can't prove I was sneaking back on my range."

"You claim you were coming from smoke break, your smoke break was over five minutes ago." I just looked at her. What could I say?

"Carry on . . ." The Lieutenant rolled her eyes, and I was escorted back to D building. Only this time, a Disciplinary Report was slid under the door. I didn't have to wonder; I knew exactly why I was placed in this filthy cell.

CHAPTER 11

I had my seventy-two-hour hearing and was back on the compound. This time I was being housed in H building on C range. I had four roommates instead of six and was in the princess bed again. I sent word to Alicia, my previous roommate that I was cool with, to tell ol' girl to send me my stuff. I hadn't heard anything negative about Niko, but I had already decided I was done before I left her range. And after sitting three days, I most definitely had come to my conclusion: I only wanted to see her to get my panties back! I only wore the three pair from home! The ones the state provided was a girl's version of tighty whiteys!

That night when we went to dinner, she waited for my building and was acting like she missed me, but I stopped that immediately. As far as I was concerned, God had spared me of *something* and whatever it was, I was steering away from it! Likewise, the broad that put the police on me hadn't made it to lockdown, and therefore, there was a problem! Niko clearly hadn't put her in her place! She claimed she checked the bitch, but it didn't matter because it should have never taken place.

There was an elder lady, Ms. Elaine that was my roommate whom I took to. This wasn't her first time in prison, and the sentence she was serving was a result of her taking her grandson's drug charges. Other than the many nights we would sit in the room and read the Bible together, she didn't do a lot of talking. But when she did, whoever was in the room listened. She was the ideal Mom Dukes to me. Lovable, wise, and enlightening every time her lips parted. Old enough to be respected by all, but sassy enough to handle the younger breed. Aging, but apparently, she was hell in her younger days. Always cooking something that smelled so good you wish you were about to enjoy some!

One afternoon, not long after I had gotten out of lockdown, I was taking a nap and someone came on my range and started yelling my name.

"What in the world?" I sat up looking around the room. My roommates appeared just as surprised. Before my feet could hit the floor, a beautiful black woman draped in a hijab that matched her attire, stood in the threshold of our cell.

"Ms. Blakely, you must need something to do, lying around." The smile she wore was the only evidence I had that she wasn't being hostile.

"I need to get out of Diagnostic so I can get a detail," I responded as I slipped into my shower shoes, wondering who this woman was.

"See, I knew you needed something to do. You can come with me." She was only about five feet six, but she stood tall, straight backed, and confident. She even glowed, and it puzzled me because she was obviously a Muslim. I knew from experience that those who had a self-denying relationship with the Lord, glowed. *So did this mean that Allah was God too?* I wondered, as I looked around the room. Ms. Elaine gave me a look like she was encouraging me to go with her.

"Ma'am, I don't know who you are, so I definitely don't know where you're taking me."

"I'm Chaplain Kahmear, and you will be accompanying me to my youth group, so get yourself together so we can go."

"How did you even know I was here?" I questioned, still trying to understand what made her pay me this visit. She pulled me out into the hallway.

"This is for you." She handed me a burgundy leather-covered Bible with my name engraved in gold.

"Oh my God! This is mine?" I couldn't hide my excitement! It was my first leather Bible and personal engraved one!

"Do you recognize this ministry?" I looked at the name she pointed to as soon as we opened it, where they had signed it personally to me. I nodded no.

"They called me and asked if they could send you this. Said they had been following your case and wanted you to know that God was with

52

you. So this is yours." She smiled so lovingly. "Now come on, we have somewhere to go."

I ran back in my room, put my boots on, and placed my new Bible in my locker. Then headed out the door with her. Headed to the Programs area made me wonder where I had been because everyone greeted her, or ran over to get hugs from her. She seemed like the inspiration to practically everyone we passed.

She escorted me into this area where two beautiful red velvet love seats and chair sat. Two women who were in General Population sat waiting for her. The room led to her office and another office. I was told this was the Chaplaincy Department. One of the two women was nicknamed S'vyn. She was pretty with long hair, and as soon as she opened her mouth, I knew she was blunt. The other girl seemed a little more passive and quiet. Chaplain Kahmear told them to give her a minute as she directed me to follow her into her office.

"Do you believe in a higher power?" she asked as soon as she closed her office door.

"Yes, ma'am. I have received Jesus Christ as my Lord and Savior." I picked up on the fact she either didn't have time to waste, or didn't beat around the bush. "If you don't mind me inquiring, why do you ask?"

"Because I have been speaking with a young lady who has been at war with herself concerning you. She was the girlfriend of one of your victims, and she doesn't understand why she can't hate you. Some of the things she has been feeling regarding you, makes it clear to see that Allah is watching over you." I wasn't sure I heard her correctly.

"Is she here?" It was the only question I could form my mouth to speak, as I looked back in the direction I had seen the two women sitting.

"She's housed here, but she isn't out there. Those are my group aides. Anyways, she wants to sit down and talk with you. How do you feel about that?"

"I'm more than willing. I imagine she needs closure or an explanation."

"Well, I'm sure she'll be relieved to hear that. I'll let her know, see what I can arrange. I also want you to know that I am here for you. If you need anything, to talk or call home, I'm here for you."

"Well, thank you." My response was short. For whatever reason, I believed her. I was just distracted, thinking about this girlfriend on the same compound with me, and even more so about her faith.

"My daughter works at DeKalb County, and she asked me to look out for you." I looked around the room and spotted a photo hanging on the wall.

"This is your daughter? Oh my goodness, I love her!" I exclaimed, recalling the beautiful, thick redbone. "She always checked on me! Very kind!"

"I know . . . She's been asking me about you since you arrived."

"Tell her I said thank you for her kindness, please."

"I will. Now come on. We got to get to group."

"May I ask you something?" I couldn't miss the opportunity.

"Yes, what is it?" She sat back in her chair.

"Do you feel Jesus was Allah's son?"

"No I do not," she answered politely.

"Who is Jesus to you?" I further inquired.

"He is a messenger of God."

"A prophet of God," I added.

"Yes."

"But not the son of God, or a ransom for our souls?"

"Correct."

"Then what do you feel the purpose of the cross was?"

"His own people crucified him, the crucifixion has a different meaning than what we have time to discuss right now." I respected she had somewhere to be. I didn't say another word as I rose to my feet and waited for her to escort me out. I wouldn't deny her relationship with God, but neither could I deny that God revealed Himself to me, through Jesus Christ, and for that reason I had to stand firm on my faith.

I wasn't sure what to think of this youth group that I sat in a circle with many others that were my age or close to it, openly discussing the things that some dreaded, or were concerned about inside the gym. Maybe if I knew the group of people better, I would have been less reluctant, but all I could do was listen.

That weekend came, and Alicia (my previous roommate) begged me to come outside so I went to Pavilion. We were walking around the track, and several people had been stopping us. A couple offered me some encouraging words, and after expressing how they followed my case, promised to keep me in their prayers. But there were a few that reminded me why I didn't care to be out when the whole compound was out. They wanted to know what clubs I danced at, desiring to hear details about my crime, claiming I had lured some NFL football players to a hotel room and robbed them with a knife and all kinds of fabricated stories. I personally didn't care to clarify any of the rumors and was trying to govern my disposition and enjoy my time with someone I had taken to as a friend. We were approximately on our third lap and were considering sitting down so we could have a private conversation. Normally, we would sit down anyway, but I had on a medium jumpsuit and called myself being cute, wanting to parade around my shape.

"Falicia, can I holla at you for a minute?" a brown-skinned girl in GP, who I had seen shake dancing before, called out as we passed.

"Honey, what you want to talk about?" I failed to hide my frustration, thinking she was about to ask me to do something ratchet.

"Closure . . . I just want closure," a pretty, short redbone with natural hair answered. I was almost in shock because I had made eye contact with her several times on the compound. My first thoughts of her was that she was beautiful and shaped like a stripper. Immediately, I felt remorse and wished I hadn't answered them like that.

"I apologize for my attitude, people just keep asking me ignorant questions, but I'm most definitely willing to answer whatever questions you may have. Do you mind?" I asked Alicia as the girl stood and descended from the rock she was sitting on.

"Not at all," she spoke aloud. "I'll be sitting over there just in case some shit jumps off." She spoke into my ear as we hugged. She was from Miami and always ready for the cause, if necessary. I followed as the girl walked us away from her friend and to another set of rocks.

"I'm Juice. Dre was my boyfriend." I couldn't help but stare in disbelief because I had found out during court proceedings that Dre was the only one who was married out of my three victims.

"I was his mistress. I knew all about his wife and family. I took this charge for him." She enlightened me about the day she was arrested and why she made the decision to take the charge because he had already done Fed time for drugs. "Dre has taken care of me since the beginning. I stopped stripping a long time ago. I still got money on my books from him. But because of you I'll have to work again. I want to hate you, but for some reason I can't. I thought about paying somebody to take your life, but that wouldn't bring Dre back." She looked me in the eyes as she spoke. I sat there just thinking how God looks out for His people, even when we didn't even know it. I was humbled! I didn't even know danger awaited me!

"I just know I'm going home in June, and my family would want to know if I talked to you or something since I'm in here with you. They probably have so many questions." She looked away for the first time. I could feel the burden she was bearing.

"Listen, whatever you want to know I'll tell you. I can imagine how hard this must be to sit here next to me, when I'm responsible for altering your life and causing you and your family such pain."

"I told Dre he was going to get killed behind some pussy. I just didn't think it would be like this." I sat silently watching her as she wrapped her mind around the present. "My cousin was bunkmates with your co-defendant. I asked her what happened, but I didn't get any peace from her letter. It was as if she was hiding something."

"That's because she wasn't keeping it 100, but I'm going to tell you everything." I took a deep breath and began telling her the unfortunate fate I had caused her man.

CHAPTER 12

What should have been a six-week process at the most, turned into months because I had an abnormal pap. There were some cells that could lead to cancer on my ovaries, and I couldn't get medically cleared, which was required to be processed into General Population. So I began volunteering to work AM Kitchen, filling up the compounds ice coolers and stripping and waxing floors.

There was a woman named Bike who was in Diagnostic with me, and she had been back and forth, in and out of prison her entire adult life and had become an expert with the maintenance of the floors. She must have been good at what she did because a Unit Manager, Ms. Oubly, authorized her to obtain a group of about five other offenders, including myself, to tend to the floors. Bike saw that I worked hard and asked me to assist her. During that time she had become like an uncle as she taught me the trade and took the time to tell me the do's and don'ts of doing time

"You pretty and you got a lil shape on you; that alone is going to bring you some attention. Don't be no thirst bucket, running around craving attention. Women like that ain't respected. You a young lady, remember that! Keep your legs closed. You hear me?" she said one night while we sat on the step waiting on a coat of wax to dry. Many nights we would be up until the wee hours of the morning doing floors after lockdown.

"Do you hear me?" she asked again when I didn't answer right away.

"Yeah, unc. I hear you," I answered, looking into the face of a woman who didn't look like one at all, not even with her hair slicked back into a long ponytail. Her tall, slim physique only added to her dominant persona. "You know I ain't trying to be had."

"That's right. Let me tell you about this girl who wanted to be. I was at Washington, and this young girl 'bout your age, was always running around showing her shape. She pretty too, but always had her butt out, coming on to folk. That ain't cute! Anyway, she kept on. Several of us old heads told her to cover up and quit throwing herself on folk. You think she listened? She ain't listen. This one dude who had been telling her to stop got the girl moved into her room. She told that girl, 'you want to be had so bad; I'm going to treat you as such.' Niecy, let me tell you! She would lock that girl in their room and shove broom sticks up that girl! Beat her ass and take all her store. That girl was too scared to even tell what he was doing to her in that room. You could hear her screaming sometimes."

"Are you serious! Did anybody help her?" I asked in disbelief, almost wondering if she was lying!

"As a heart attack . . . No, ain't nobody get in that. Prison a different world, baby girl. People turn their head in here. That's why I want you to just stay away from situations like that. Don't be so quick to trust anybody."

One day we were stripping and re-waxing the handicap range. The residents had to go to the gym because the floor stripper let off some strong fumes that caused many to have an asthma attack, so we had to move quickly! A female named Peaches was one of the girls Bike added to the crew to speed up the process. She was kind of cute and thick like a video vixen. I took note that she stared at me a lot, but I really didn't make much of it because I stayed up under Bike, and no one made any advances toward me. We were at a stopping point, and I chose to post up on a step and eat my sandwich from my pack out.

"You mind if I join you?" Peaches asked. I gestured with my hand to come on. I had seen a lot of bad broads in my profession, but her backside was big. I wondered what type of lifestyle she lived prior to prison.

"Your name Falicia, right?" she asked, once she finally sat down next to me.

"Yeah." I finished my lunch.

"I know some of the same people you know," she stated. I looked at her, anticipating her calling out some names. When she didn't, I just stared at her briefly. Something about her presence began disturbing me. I had an uneasiness in the pit of my stomach.

"You do, huh?"' I stated, after an awkward silence.

"Yeah . . . You're a pretty black girl, too." Her voice was inviting, but the look in her eyes stated something different.

"'Preciate the compliment. Don't mean to be rude, but I have to excuse myself." I stood to my feet, stretched, and walked back on the range where Bike was. So many things went through my mind. If she knew my ex, had I robbed somebody significant to her? Or had somebody put a mark on my head or what? What I did know was I most definitely was going to watch my back.

By the time we were finished for the day, I was still disturbed so I sat down with Ms. Elaine and recollected my day.

"Stay away from Peaches. She told this other girl at Washington the same thing, right before she splashed hot water and floor stripper in the girl's face. The girl ended up having to get plastic surgery to reconstruct her face."

I was speechless.

"I mean it, Falicia. Stay away from her envious behind, you hear me? Stay away! That child evil!" Ms. Elaine warned me. I really was enjoying doing floors, but I wasn't trying to find myself in the hospital from third-degree burns.

CHAPTER 13

Sometimes you can be so caught up in what you got going on that you neglect to pay attention to your surroundings, which in some cases can be dangerous, and being aware can prevent you from having a lot of unnecessary heartache and drama. I'm not saying sit around watching people, but take note of who is always in your space and question why people are trying to make conversation. I didn't do either as my final weeks of Diagnostics were coming to an end.

This woman named April who was in her early forties, and a dominant lesbian, often stopped by my room to chop it up with Ms. Elaine. Normally I would be gone all day doing floors, and by the time I got off work, all I wanted to do was shower and go to bed. So I hadn't noticed the long haired, sexy woman, who was of Cherokee Indian heritage. Until she was sitting on my roommate's bed checking for me. This particular night it was a little hot in our room, which made it hard for me to fall asleep. I stood up in bed and began yanking on the window that appeared to have been installed in the early eighties! Paying little attention to the company in the room, I looked back just to see if someone was willing to give me a hand because the window was jammed. April was sitting a few feet across from me on Ms. Elaine's bed and was bent over as if she was trying to look between my legs.

"What you looking at?" I asked, wondering what she expected to see through the white pajama pants that had tiny blue circles all over them. A pattern every female inmate in the state of Georgia wore for our night attire.

"Huh?" she responded, caught off guard, slowly raising her eyes, looking embarrassed.

"Ain't nothing down there for you," I retorted nonchalantly, enjoying seeing the grown woman intimidated. I turned my attention back to the window, determined to open it since I had an audience now, feeling I had something to prove. Once my mission was accomplished, I lay back down without saying another word. Just like the young girl that I was, the idea that this cutie was smitten by me, humored me. At some point after I had drifted off to sleep, April came and kneeled down next to me.

"Falicia, if you can find time tomorrow, I would like to chop it up with you," she whispered, peeling my blanket back from over my head. I didn't respond right away as I stared into her hazel eyes.

After a few seconds I answered with a grin, "I'll think about it." Her face lit up.

"You're so beautiful. That's my first time seeing you smile."

What's sad is just like that, she had my attention. I don't know if it was because she was the most sought after, or because I was craving companionship. Whichever one, I found myself letting down my guard way faster than I should have, and her well-being became a part of my daily routine. What started out as a welcomed distraction, turned into something more. I actually enjoyed her company and felt if we continued to hang out, I needed to tell her I was HIV-positive. I was a little nervous, but I sat April down and explained my HIV status, the risks, statistics, and the lifestyle I previously lived. She wasn't judgmental at all. Though I feared she would treat me different after being made aware, but she didn't. As a result, I started walking to the opposite end of the hall where she stayed just as much as she came to my room. If I cooked, she ate too. I made both of our beds, fixed our lockers, and filled out her store sheet.

Still dominated by my street mentality, I wasn't impressed with the way her hair was being braided. It was taking away from her swag. Everything else about her stood out, and I felt her hair should too! Especially if I was going to entertain her. I didn't know how to braid, but I was willing to try, and I murked it! I couldn't part straight, so I ended up putting some designs in her hair. I had her hair so fly, I became in high demand; everybody wanted me to do their hair!

Many nights we were in one of our rooms exchanging memories. One thing that compelled me to engage in sexual activity with her was knowing she had been staying with this woman she referred to as 'wife' for years, and this woman had never rolled over and attempted to satisfy April. Her 'wife' didn't even try! April was the provider, satisfier, and problem solver! All this wife did was spend money and cook! They adopted the wife's granddaughter from her son and were raising her as their own. I couldn't believe April was a lesbian and had so little knowledge and experience with her sexuality. Here I was, twenty years old, about to turn this forty-one-year-old woman out! It's no point in mentioning the things I did to her and the pleasure it brought me knowing I had given her something she never had.

This 'wife' of hers was making it easy for me with all the drama and arguments she seemed to ignite over the phone and during visitation. In which my mother and I witnessed when the slimmer version of the heavier Star Jones lookalike came in with a beautiful little girl, both dressed in pink Baby Phat outfits. She made it easy for April to turn to me. I was her calm after the storm and means of relaxation after a fight. I became what she looked forward to and wifey was what she dreaded.

April's birthday came around, and outside of making her a cookie cake, I wasn't sure what I would do. I already made her time as comfortable as possible, which was the role most girlfriends played in this environment. I went to visitation to see my mother and son, like I did every weekend, when Red, this lesbian who had chased me a year in the county and ended up being my roommate some months before I left, walked in looking like a cute ass little Fat Joe in jeans, button down shirt, and a low haircut with golds. I had put her on my visitation as my sister, and here she was, unannounced! My mother took one look at her as I stood to hug her and knew what time it was. After I introduced them, she sat next to me. My son didn't like that and came and stood between my legs. Whenever Red reached out for me, addressed me, or expressed how much she missed me, Man would say, "That's *my* mother."

At some point Red went to the vending machine to get me something to eat. My mother decided to leave early so we could visit. In my son's eyes, he saw a man trying to steal his mother's attention. Red came back, sat down next to me, and addressed me in a very hushed tone.

"I just realized I still got some weed in my pocket."

"What? How?" I asked, surprised.

"You know how jeans have those small pockets inside pockets?"

"Yeah . . ."

"It's in there. I honestly forgot about it."

"I can't believe you brought that in here." I started looking around, trying to make sure no one knew what we were talking about.

"Do you want it?" Her next question took me by surprise.

"How am I going to get it?" My heart started racing.

"We will figure that out, just tell me if you want it."

I considered it for a few seconds. "I may as well." It was so close and available. "Yeah."

We looked at each other briefly. I knew she was thinking the same thing I was thinking. "Go to the machine, buy a bag of chips, and open them," I advised. "At some point take it out of your pocket and just drop it in the chips." She got right up and did as I told her. She came back with an open bag of Doritos and some white powder donuts. I sat there eating those chips and thinking about that sack of weed, anticipating the smoke in my lungs and the relaxed feeling I hadn't had in a long time. When I finished eating all the chips, I threw my head back like I was finishing off the crumbs until the sack was secure in my mouth. I knew April and I were about to get lit for her birthday. Now all I had to do was excuse myself to the rest room and make enough conversation with the CERT Team member that towered over me as I squatted over the toilet to slip the bag of weed into my vagina.

My heart was beating the entire time as I sped walked back to the dorm and signed in with the officer.

"Hey, baby! How was your visit?" April greeted me as soon as I walked into her room.

"My room right now," I instructed her and headed to my room before she had a chance to respond.

"May I have a second please?" I asked Chanelle, the youngest of my roommates as I walked in the door. She came off as a very sweet girl, but she was sneaky.

"Yeah," she responded as she set the notepad down that was in her hand. "Can you come get me when you're done?"

"I will," I replied as I stood in front of the toilet like I was waiting on her to leave so I could use it. Right as she was leaving, April walked in.

"What's the matter? Is everything all right with your family? Are you about to tell me some crazy shit, Falicia?" She asked one question after the other before I had time to answer. I didn't say a word; I just washed my hands and squatted over the toilet to retrieve my prize possession.

"Falicia, you don't hear me talking to you?" she continued. I went back to the sink and rinsed off the bag. I took a piece of tissue, dried it off, and tossed it to her as I went to the door to make sure no one was standing outside of it listening.

"Happy Birthday!" I said proudly as I stood in front of her and began undressing so I could put on something more comfortable.

"What the fuck! How did you manage to do this?"

"What you mean? It's your birthday! You should have known I was going to do something special." I made it seem as if my coming up was intentional. It just sounded better.

"Girl! Now *this* how a muhfuh want to spend her birthday in prison!" She seemed so pleased with me and I loved it. She laid me on the bed, then got on top of me and kissed me. Taking time to stare into my eyes. "It amazes me that my days only seem to get better with you. I really don't know how I would be handling all of this if you weren't in my life."

I didn't say a thing. I could only smile. I took pride in knowing my companion was pleased with my ability to cater to her needs, giving her new sexual encounters, and being willing to take dangerous risks just to add something spontaneous to her life. To go the extra mile and do what the next female couldn't! This made me feel as if I had a purpose in 'her' life. That I was most definitely making an impression that wouldn't be easily forgotten. What I didn't realize then was that I wasn't with her because I was codependent and needed to fulfill these attributes in someone's life. Nor was it because I was lonely. I was with her because making her mine was a challenge, and I found pleasure in making her choose me instead of the rest. I was intrigued by captivating the mind of this woman who was twice my age, and this truth about myself was the very thing that led to my dealings with grown men as a child.

Later that evening we went outside to pavilion. April had used the tampon wrapper paper to roll our joint. She took some Brillo and batteries to light it, and we stood away from everyone and smoked. We didn't get a chance to enjoy the entire thing because we kept hearing people say that they smelled weed. So in our paranoia, we put it out after we had smoked three-fourths of it. I decided I would just give the rest to Alicia, but she wasn't outside, so I would have to hide it until the opportunity presented itself.

By the time we made it back to the dorm, we were two red-eyed, laughing at everything, paranoid fools!

"Mmm, it smells like weed," Chanelle informed about twenty women as we all mounted the stairs that led to our range.

"You heard that?" April asked, looking like she had seen a ghost.

"Yeah, but stop looking like that," I said. She gazed at me for a second, and then we burst into laughter. Scared we might smell like weed smoke, we agreed to get straight into the shower.

I stood in front of my locker getting undressed as fast as my limbs would allow, laughing at myself.

"What's so funny?" Chanelle asked, eyeing me suspiciously as she squatted down next to me. Her locker was next to mine. I ignored her question as I knelt down to get my soap dish and state-provided robe to take to the shower. My towel and face cloth were hanging on the bed rail. I placed my hygiene products on my bed, along with my fresh linen. Pulling my locker door up, I hooked the combination lock on it and walked over to the toilet area like I had to use it so I could wrap the rest of the joint up. When I finished, I tucked it in one of the corners, locked my locker, and stood upright. Chanelle was still in front of her locker. Something about the way she kept watching my every move made me feel she was up to something. I didn't say a word as I left the room. I can't explain it, but something about marijuana in my system makes me aware of everything. I can sense when something is suspicious, and I knew exactly what Chanelle called herself doing. I stepped into the shower where April was already, and I saw Chanelle walking out the room and headed to the TV room as I pulled the curtain back.

"Baby, what took you so long?" April asked.

"I'll be right back. This lil' bitch thinks I'm stupid," I replied as I set my soap and stuff down and walked back to my room. I tried to open my lock, but it would not unlock. I put my combination in two more times, and then leaned over and put my combination number in on the lock that was on Chanelle's lock. Just like that it opened! On the first try!

"This lil' bitch think she slick!" I spoke aloud. She thought she was going to wait until I was good in the shower and come back and open my locker and see what she could find. It took everything in me not to go yank her behind out that chair she sat in. So I sat on my bed and waited for her. Seconds passed, and just like clockwork, she burst in our door but came to a halt when she saw me sitting there with her locker open.

"Bitch, get your lock off my locker!" I got straight to the point.

"What? What are you talking about?" She tried to play dumb.

"You're beginning to piss me off, acting dumb. You thought I was dumb, and that is pissing me off too! Now get your shit off my locker!"

"I don't know what you're talking about," she mumbled, bending down and putting her combination in. It opened on the first try. "I don't know how that happened," she lied, standing to her feet.

Before I had time to think, I grabbed her by her neck and pinned her to the lockers.

"Lil bitch, don't ever touch my shit! I'm not playing with you!"

CHAPTER 14

I was knocked out sleep when my cell door swung open.

"Blakely, pack up!" the female CO demanded and went on to inform others that they too would be leaving. It was around four in the morning. *Dang! Just like that . . .*

My stomach suddenly filled with dread as I walked to the opposite end of the hall. I barely tapped on April's window; she jumped up from her princess bed looking tired. With sad eyes she gazed at me through the window. I told her I was leaving.

"Remember what I said: no girlfriends and stay focused." I pressed my lips against my fingers and placed them on the window. April did the same.

Those of us who were getting transferred anxiously gathered in the chow hall to eat breakfast before shipment. We ate and waited. Waited and got counted and waited . . . Something was wrong because those that got transferred previously were out of the facility before five o'clock count. When count cleared, we were told to go back to the dorm, our transfer was canceled.

Now, ain't that some BS? I thought as I walked back to my dorm with my property. My roommates were so excited to see me when I walked back into our cell that one of them started crying. I was so disappointed to be back, until I saw their reaction.

"Chile, you ought to see that April. She look so pathetic," Ms. Elaine declared as she shook her head.

"Don't nobody tell her I'm back," I instructed my roommates who were headed to the day area that was positioned in the center of the range. We gathered there to check for hold-in passes to go anywhere and waited to be called out for meals. I rounded the corner, and April was sitting in the corner looking like the world was falling apart. Her face was red, eyes puffy, and sadness was all over her. Somebody was rubbing her shoulder telling her it would get better. I didn't say a word as I stepped into the TV room.

"Fe?" one of the girls whose hair I braided called my name, surprised to see me. I smiled and hoped April hadn't heard her or several others say my name, but she did. April looked in the direction that the commotion was brewing and made eye contact with me and looked away. Immediately, she did a double take. In seconds she was on her feet and holding me.

"I was just sitting here wishing I could see you at least one more time." She beamed. "What's going on? Did you leave something and had to come back for it?"

"No, they just sent us back. Said our transfer was cancelled."

"I don't mean to be selfish, but you have no idea how relieved I am to see you right now!" She pulled me into her embrace and casually began to guide me toward the exit. Although everyone seemed happy for us, one female in particular, didn't try to hide her displeasure. The same hand that she'd just used to rub April's back was stuck in the air, along with the sour expression on her face. Baby girl must've had some choice words for me, yet I kept smiling as April pulled me into her again.

"Whenever you want it," I told ol' girl, right before we made our exit from the TV room.

"What, baby? You trying to give me some?" April asked.

"Woman!" I play slapped her. "You're always thinking nasty."

"How could I not?" Her tone was serious, and we locked eyes.

"Hmm . . ." I dropped my head to shake off the energy she was sending. "I was actually talking to your 'ho," I confessed, as we got closer to my cell.

"My 'ho?" April's brows kissed, showing her confusion.

"Yeah, that broad who was in the TV room caressing you!"

CHAPTER 15

I had about two more weeks with April, and then she got transferred. I wasn't upset to see her leave. To a certain degree I felt her place in my life was seasonal, and it was cool because I learned something from the experience. I had discovered something I didn't know I could do with hair. She made sure I had everything I needed when my mother wasn't in a position to send me money, and she chased away many lonely nights.

A couple of weeks passed, and I was told to pack it up again. I thought for sure I was out this time, but instead of getting woke up to get dressed and report to the chow hall, I was awakened to be informed the transferred was cancelled due to the weather.

Now, ain't this a bitch! I thought as I lay back down, unable to go back to sleep. I was past the point of frustrated! I had been in Diagnostics for four months. The thrill was gone! The next morning I spoke with Mr. Morning.

"Blakely, what are you still doing here?" he asked, after seeing my face. I stood outside sweeping off the vamp that led to our dormitory door.

"That's what I wanted to ask you?" I replied. "I have packed up twice, but . . ." I threw my hands in the air.

"I'm going to handle it. I got to get you out of here; your co-defendant is on the way," he stated, and then walked on about his business.

"Thank you, sir!" I yelled behind him, wondering if I would get the chance to see Pumpkin. *Was she on her way as in today? Or was she preparing to come now that she went ahead and pleaded out?*

Naturally, after speaking with Mr. Morning, I expected to leave right away. From my previous experiences with him, he had always made things happen ASAP. But that wasn't the case in this situation, and unfortunately for me, I was getting discouraged. That night I received a letter from my grandmother that was dated April 28, 2004. I couldn't even be mad at the fact my letter had just arrived, and it was postmarked months ago because it was right on time! My grandmother always had a way of soothing me. Yes, still being in Diagnostics was frustrating because I wanted to move forward and begin making the necessary adjustments to get accustomed to the life that was set before me, but maybe God had another reason why I hadn't left yet. Maybe the people I would have ended up in the room/cell with wasn't a part of his purpose. Maybe those transfer vans would not have made it safely to my destination. Whatever the reason, I had to know God was in control, and if I believed that, there was no room for the negative feelings.

The next day, Saturday, September 4, 2004 arrived and as I opened my eyes I thought, *I made it!* It was my twenty-first birthday. It felt surreal to a certain degree because I never thought I would live long enough to see this day. I tossed the covers back, swung my legs to the floor, and got out of bed. After stretching, I positioned my shower shoes side by side and kneeled down to balance my knees on each one. I needed to pray. This was something I hadn't really done in a while, and with my roommates still asleep it was perfect. Fifteen minutes passed before I concluded my thanks to God for blessing me and taking the time to spare my life. I got up, took a shower, and got dressed for visitation.

When I arrived, my mom and son sat at the miniature circular table with a chocolate cupcake and a Butterfinger bite stuck in the center like a candle, singing Happy Birthday. It was a really cute gesture. My mother looked so happy and youthful!

"This is for you, baby!" she sang as she handed it to me. "You know if I could bring you a real cake, I would have brought you one, possibly an ice cream cake." My son, almost four years old, stood about the same height as the chair next to me. He stared at my cupcake like he was ready for us to eat it.

"You want some?" I asked, holding it in his direction.

"No, that's Momma's," my mother stated. He looked from her to me, and then at the cupcake and touched the Butterfinger bite with his index finger and placed his finger in his mouth.

"You can have some if you want some." I normally didn't go against my mother's instructions.

"Birt—day," he said.

"Yeah, it's Momma's birthday!" I smiled, and he started clapping.

"Birt—day!" he said again and touched the Butterfinger once more.

"Get it," I said, smiling. My mother sucked her teeth.

"Boo Boo, it's a whole bag right here. He can have one of these. That's yours," she whined.

"Good, he can have this one and you can just give me another one and what's mine is his." I smiled as we watched his face light up. He leaned closer to the cupcake and pulled out the Butterfinger with his thumb and index finger.

"Birt—day!" he sang as he danced, putting it in his mouth. Eyes wide.

Spending the day with my family was a gift from God. Alongside that feeling though, I was a little disappointed I hadn't heard from anyone else other than my grandma and my previous Public Defender, Ken. Red had made so many promises she hadn't upheld, mainly about sending me money. It was hard for me to accept that she would suddenly fall off the face of the earth after we had spent so much time together and obtained such a strong bond. I hadn't seen my stepsister Mylena since before I got sentenced, and I couldn't help but think how all those people I looked out for were around when I was on the up and up, but they seemed to have forgotten about me now that I was down.

Later that night, I sat on my bunk with practically a new set of roommates (Ms. Elaine and two others had been transferred out), trying not to think of what my birthday would be like if I was home. My roommate and a few other females on the range whose hair I did every week burst in my room with some Bombay. Bombay is an excessive amount of coffee, Kool-Aid, fruity sodas, or juice mixed together. A combination that the average offender loves to drink during special occasions. Some choose to crush up various medicines in it, in the name of getting fucked up. I personally preferred the virgin kind.

Before I had a chance to protest, somebody was making a beat, and everybody in the room was dancing. I couldn't help thinking about home and if I'd still be in somebody's strip club busting it for a dollar. Or would I even be alive to see twenty-one?

CHAPTER 16

Five days after my twenty-first birthday I was finally leaving Metro State Prison. It had taken me three times to pack up to actually leave the premises! Naturally, I was relieved to leave that chapter behind me, but as I watched the city fade in the distance, a concern for the unknown gave birth. Silently, I sat looking out the window just thinking of how I was about to come face to face with real criminals! As if I hadn't committed the unthinkable myself. Some of the horror stories I had heard about prison were possibly about to be my life! Daycare was over!

"Oh, my God! These people are taking me someplace where ain't nobody going to be able to find me!" My wholehearted confession spilled from my lips as I sat looking out the window. Everybody on the van started laughing, but to me, it was no laughing matter.

I was a city girl! I had never seen goats, cows, and sheep! Somebody had to point out which one was what! I fought back my tears just thinking of how far away I was from my family and the road that I had chosen to travel on! Silence engulfed me a few more miles until something else caught my attention. The van slowed and came to a halt as we neared a stop sign. Fields of tall grass about four or five-feet high stood on both sides of the road, and on the side of the road that was visible, this white, fluffy-looking stuff blossomed from bristles. It was rows and rows of the stuff.

"What is that?" I asked no one in particular.

"That's cotton," an older lady answered.

"Like . . . like the cotton my ancestors used to pick?" I don't know what I thought cotton looked like or how it was made, but I most definitely didn't think it grew out the ground like this.

"Yes, our ancestors picked plants like these," the older woman answered, but looked off in the distance as if she had experienced her own share of picking cotton, or memories of forced labor. Looking at her check out made me reflect on my own life.

Without question I didn't want to be headed to prison, but it was better than some of those times when I had gotten off work and just wanted to go to sleep, but Ike had other plans for me. Like the repetitive nights he forced his penis down my throat and I vomited. During that stage in our relationship, I didn't want his private parts in my mouth. And I felt as if I was in a sex boot camp. Nor did I understand his random change of plans. For example, one night I thought Ike and I were going to a sport's bar, but we ended up on Metropolitan Avenue also known as Stewart Avenue. I was told to stand out in the cold until some pervert pulled over and propositioned me. After comparing all those past incidents to my current situation, I just sucked it up and decided I would trust God for strength to get through the journey that awaited me.

My heart pounded as we pulled up into the prison. Except for the barbed wire outlining the top of the gates that surrounded the prison, it kind of didn't look like a prison. It was sort of inviting and not dreadful like: 'I'm surely going to die in this place.' We pulled up into the U-shape driveway and climbed out the van, stepping immediately into a building that was labeled: INTAKE.

With much patience and anxiety, I sat on the third row in a chair that was connected to others like a bench. I tried not to concern myself with what's next as I waited for everyone I arrived with to take another picture, receive a new identification badge, replace the white jumpsuit with a pair of pale turquoise pants and a short-sleeve shirt, with a pale turquoise collar. We received two more sets of uniforms, two T-shirts, a raincoat, a new mattress, pillow, and two blankets. Along with the DOC-made toiletries and sanitary items. We piled all our stuff in buggies and followed the officer who was escorting us to our assigned housing units.

The first thing I noticed was the officer pressing the button on the intercom that was attached to the gate. She identified herself, and someone in a control room unlocked the gate for us to pass through. I took note that a building classified as Medical was to our immediate right. It seemed all movement ceased as our presence became known. A girl named Sherika, someone whom I was cool with in the county jail, stood amongst those who stopped walking. I felt like a fish in an aquarium, or a monkey at the zoo as everyone stood in the windows and along the sides of the pathway to stare.

Across from Medical was the Security building, where all the shift supervisors, sergeants and lieutenants, the captain and deputy warden of security offices were. We walked around the building and headed toward the right side of the compound. The first buildings I saw had E6 and E7 painted on them. They were one level and sat directly across the pavement from each other. Beautiful, well-maintained lawns stretched out in front of each with assorted flowers outlining the pavement that led up the porch, which led to the front door that led to the sally port. Picnic tables sat on each side of the lawns. Several women sat on those benches staring at us as we walked by. I tried not to look at anyone in particular, but couldn't help but notice that women inside the building were popping up in the big open windows above the porch on both sides of the dormitory. These dorms were broken down by two sides. A/B side and C/D side. It was structured like an X, and the officer sat in the middle. The open space where the officer sat in front of the control panel was called the day area. A TV room was off to the side. Next to each hall was the laundry room with two washing machines and two dryers, a janitor's closet, storage room, an ice machine, a fountain with hot and cold water, and a few tables with chairs all made up the day area.

Each hall was assigned a letter and had twelve cells and housed twenty-four women. Six cells were on one side and the other six on the opposite side. At the entrance of each hall was a door just to the right of A and D halls and to the left of B and C halls. There was a door that led to the shower area which was equipped with three shower stalls and a closed-in tub area. Across from these doors on the opposite side of the hall was an ironing board and an iron.

We pushed our buggies past the two small dormitories until the pavement split in two directions. Two huge dorms stood parallel to each other. E8 to the right and E9 to the left. The barbed wire gates outlined these dorms which had broader lawns with more picnic tables. It resembled the county jail from outside. As we made a right to approach the dorm, I saw more women staring at us through a back door of E7. I noticed about four tables positioned within each hall. I didn't know much about the arrangement, but it just seemed the smaller dorms would have been more suitable for the adjustment I was about to make. Less women to deal with at one time.

We finally made it to the door, but I couldn't see inside. Someone popped the door, and as soon as we stepped in the sally port, women popped up at the windows next to the front doors. To the left was E8-A, and to the right was E8-B. I was instructed to go to E8-B. I helped unload everyone's property and grabbed my stuff. As soon as I heard the door pop to my new housing unit, my heart began to pound. I opened the door and everyone's eyes were on me and the other girl who was moving in with me as well. *I wish I was anywhere but here.*

Once inside, my thoughts were confirmed. This prison resembled the county jail I was in previously! It was very identical, only bigger! Cells outlined the two-level open dorm building in the shape of a U. Two-man cells housed ninety-eight women in total. Six square tables sat in the center of the floor where mostly everyone present was engaged in a card game, or putting together a jigsaw puzzle, or preparing a meal. Further away from the door, toward the back of the dorm were about four rows of bench chairs lined up in front of the TV. I pretended I didn't notice all of the attention as I located my room and stepped inside.

"Hello, I'm Crystal!" a Caucasian woman greeted me as soon as I stepped into the cell that was on the bottom level.

"Hello, I'm Falicia." I tried not to appear nervous, and then I looked at the other Caucasian woman sitting on her bed.

"This is my friend . . . Sherry." She smiled too.

"Nice to meet you," I replied politely.

"You're pretty," Sherry commented. I wasn't sure how to take her compliment. So I just smiled, but felt awkward when she kept staring at me.

"Can you give me a second, please?" I addressed Sherry, wondering why she didn't think to excuse herself once I came in. The cell was only so big, and the bunk bed dominated majority of the room. The wall locker and desk took up the rest of the space on the opposite side of the cell.

"Of course," she stated and stood to her feet. Squeezing beside me, making an effort not to step on my belongings that I set down on the floor next to the door. "Just come by my room when you finish," she told Crystal.

"She doesn't mean any harm. She wasn't trying to come on to you." Crystal cleared the air as soon as her friend left the cell.

"That's good to know." I wanted to be clear where I stood right off top. A few seconds went by before she spoke. I opened what would be my locker. There were food crumbs in the cracks and dried up Kool-Aid throughout.

"Is this your first time?" Crystal stretched out on her bunk. "Coming to prison?"

"Yes." I took a deep breath. I was slick getting an attitude that my locker was so nasty. "If you don't mind, may I ask you something?"

"Sure!" She sat up and crossed her legs Indian style, perking up.

"How long have you stayed in this room?"

"My entire sentence."

"And how long has that been?" I furthered inquired.

"Almost a year."

"How long has it been since you've had a bunkmate?"

"She went to lockdown yesterday."

I'm going to have to school this woman on how to keep our living space clean, I thought.

"Do you have any chemicals and a clean cleaning rag I can use to wipe down?" What she didn't know was, I wanted to know if she had time to wipe this locker out. And she did. The fact that it was filthy was a reflection of her. I bet if I looked around in the corners of her bed and underneath the bed, I would find trash and/or crumbs. I knew she was going to be a problem sooner rather than later.

CHAPTER 17

They were calling us out to dinner before I had cleaned up my area and stored away all my property. I stuffed the rest of my things in the second locker we had beneath the beds, locked it up and lined up with my dorm to go eat. I wish I had some commissary because I knew I didn't look my best and honestly preferred to stay in.

As I entered the dining hall and saw the other general population with their hair relaxed, braided, or dreaded up and some with a face full of makeup, I knew I must've looked like a bum. I wasn't into makeup, but my eyebrows most definitely needed to be arched, and my hair wasn't in its best state.

The first familiar face I saw was Niko. She looked away shyly as we locked eyes. I scanned the other three chairs that were bolted to her table and peeped out a thick, brown-skinned girl sizing me up. *Must be her girlfriend*, I thought. I didn't want her, but since it was apparent I posed a threat, even in my present state, I decided I might as well get under somebody's skin. The serving line slowed, and it positioned me directly in front of their table. I waited for Niko to look up at me.

"Your girl don't permit you to speak?" I asked.

"Nah, it ain't like that," Niko replied, her eyes pleading with me not to start.

"Let's hope not because I would hate to be considered disrespectful. Especially, the way you claim you would always be a part of my life." Niko grinned a little as she looked away. Her girlfriend didn't say a word, but eyed Niko. "There's no reason to feel indifferent about me. She was just a friend," I stated, and moved up in the line. She probably didn't know it, but Niko was the last thing on my mind. As quickly as she pushed up on me, I knew anyone could have her, and her present girlfriend didn't need to feel special.

I sat down and was a little impressed with the salt and pepper shakers on the table. The food wasn't the best, but it would do until I could get my locker straight. After I had consumed all that I was able to eat, I didn't wait for my dorm to head back. As I approached the end of the pathway that separated, I spotted April coming out of E-9. It took me by surprise. I didn't even know she was here. A part of me felt I wouldn't see her again. She looked like she was adjusting well. Her hair was braided, white tennis shoes, clothes creased. I looked down at my clothes and decided not to get her attention. I turned on my heels and made a break toward my dorm, but before I could get out of sight, someone recognized me.

"Falicia? Is that you?" I heard the voice call after me. "Falicia!" someone continued. I stopped and turned around. It was Sherika.

"Girl! What's up? I miss the hell out of you!" she exclaimed as she ran to close in the space between us.

It felt nice seeing a familiar face, especially one that was glad to see me. I could see April approaching. I looked away because I really wasn't ready to face her, but as I glanced upward, I caught her avoiding my eyes. Call me paranoid, but you would expect someone to recognize the person they were just laid up with weeks ago! Now I ain't gon' lie—that tugged at my feelings a little, but I didn't want to jump to conclusions. However, a part of me felt she had just switched up in a matter of weeks, but I was not about to let it show. She didn't deserve to know my actual feelings. It was my first lesson that everybody in prison had a motive, and it was my responsibility to know what type of people I was dealing with.

Later that evening, the institution called pavilion, and Sherika was outside my dorm telling anyone who would listen to tell me to come out. I went to someone's cell that faced the yard so I could tell her I wasn't coming out.

"Girl, I got somebody I want you to shut down!" She was turned up on the opposite side of the window. Using her hands and arms to stress her point.

"What, Sherika? I just got here, plus I don't have any shorts. I'm not going."

"You got to come! This broad always out here dancing! You got to shut her down."

"I hear what you saying, but I'm not going. I just got here. I'm tired, and I got a lot on my mind." I needed to sort through my feelings and put everything in its proper perspective.

"Okay, but if I send you some shorts, will come out tomorrow and dance?"

"I'll think about it."

"Run it! I'm cool with that!" I watched as she walked away and headed in the direction that everyone else was walking. I was relieved my roommate had left as well because it gave me some time to be alone, pray, and clean everything without causing offense. Then I put some twists in my hair.

The next day Sherika was waiting for me when they called my dorm to dinner and gave me some white shorts.

"I'll see you tonight!" She handed them to me and ran to her dorm. I was really indecisive about going around all these strangers just to dance. Especially, considering she was the one who talked so much mess about not believing I really could dance when we were in the county. After taking her words as a direct challenge, I put on a pair of boxers, got on a table, and showed out then. And now here I was being persuaded by the same person to do it all over again in a new environment. I got dressed, feeling a little country with my boots on and a pair of shorts, but I sucked it up, signed out, and followed the crowd that led to the pavilion. As I approached Sherika's dorm, I didn't see her anywhere in sight, so I stopped in front of it and asked a couple of polite faces if they knew who she was. Someone told me she stayed in E9-B but didn't know if she was coming or not. The crowd narrowed, and a few stragglers were coming out.

"Excuse me, do you know Sherika in E9-B?" I asked this stud with a low haircut who was the last one to come out. She sported a mean mug, like the world needed to pay for her unhappiness. Her hands were tucked away in the pockets of her long gray shirt. I could tell by the way her tennis shoes were laced she was from up North. She didn't say a word as she approached me. It was as if she didn't even notice me standing at the gate's entrance because she bumped into me.

"Dang! You didn't see me standing here?" She didn't say anything. "I don't understand why people have to be so rude in this prison," I spoke aloud.

"What's your name?" she asked, after she had taken a few steps away from me.

"Why? You should be apologizing for bumping me." My frustration was rising quickly. I wanted to slap her cocky butt. Instead I started walking back in the direction of my dorm. *I didn't want to be outside anyways!*

"Are you Falicia?" she asked, ignoring my statement. I stopped in my tracks and turned to face her.

"Yes, why do you ask?" Looking at her only made me more upset because of the dumb grin she donned.

"Sherika said she coming. Don't go back in," she stated, and then turned and headed toward the pavilion. Her wide steps with her feet turned outward reminded me of Tupac's swag in the movie *Juice*.

I really wanted to slap her then. She could have said that off top. Something was seriously wrong with the people down here in these back woods. But before I had a chance to curse her out or take another step, Sherika came out the door.

"Hey, boo! I'm so glad you didn't go back in. I didn't mean to keep you waiting. Did you get my message?" she yelled as we walked toward each other.

"Girl, don't ever send me a message by that rude SOB again!"

"What happened?"

"What should have happened was her picking herself up off the ground!" I was so angry.

"Girl, that's Jayden. You can't pay him any mind." Sherika made an attempt to lighten the mood as she walked through the gate that led to the pavilion.

"*Her*," I corrected her choice of gender.

"Her. Him. Around here we call the boys 'him.' You'll see."

"I already know that, but she's a bitch to me." I looked around and noticed the yard was smaller than Metro, but it was cleaner and better equipped. I was impressed. There was a track that made a massive circle around the pavilion which had several picnic tables and benches. A volleyball net stretched across a wide section that was positioned in plenty of sand. Beautiful green grass lay on the outskirts of the sand and around the basketball court that had several people engaged in a full-court game. All within the track. To the left outside of the track was a huge baseball field. About two and a half acres of land stretched out. Beautiful green grass demanded your attention, and directly across from the baseball field was a gym with an indoor basketball court with bleachers lining the left side of the wall. Classrooms lined the right side. Vocational classes for Culinary Arts and Plumbing were held in this area. Likewise, there was a class for SAGE (Student Assessment of Growth and Excellence) and TABE (Test of Adult Basic Education) testing and a restroom. Church was also held in this area on the weekends.

Sherika led me to a place beneath the pavilion where a bunch of people sat on benches and tables and some just stood around.

"This the girl I was telling you about," Sherika told someone, and then watched as several people crowded around. I learned a long time ago I couldn't bank on Sherika's word, but the broad had a mouth piece on her. And as I sat there acting oblivious to the crowd that navigated toward us, I witnessed firsthand her ability to convince people. *If only she put her mind to something productive, she could get the unthinkable accomplished,* I thought.

I watched as this super-thick red bone walked over to the table. "Hi, I'm Yellow," she introduced herself, and then sat on the bench next to me. Her aura came off like she was a sweet person, not arrogant like you would expect because of her looks. She was soft spoken, pretty, with long hair and video vixen thick. I could tell all her assets were hers. Plus it was 2004, body injections and Botox weren't a big deal like they are in 2018.

For a moment I got nervous because this broad had a lot of ass! A female officer walked over to see what was going on because such a huge crowd was forming, and after talking a lil' smack with a few girls, she disappeared. Somebody asked if I had a particular song I wanted to dance to, holding their CD player and head phones in hand. My favorite song was "Let Me See It" by UGK, but I didn't expect them to have that so I told her, "I'm good with whatever she wants to dance to."

"You wanna dance first?" she asked.

I told her, "Nah. Go ahead, this your house."

Somebody started making a beat on the table, and I watched as she began to make her butt bounce. I sat on the bench waiting for her to do something impressive with all that behind, and after she didn't deliver, I stood up while she was still dancing and just turned up. Bouncing my behind, making my cheeks jump individually and rolled this thing in circles! Everyone standing around started hooting and hollering. It only encouraged my madness! I got up on the table, popping everything thing below the waist and was considering getting on my back when that same female officer broke through the cranked-up crowd and snatched me off the table.

"No, ma'am!" I heard her say once I realized why I was being pulled from behind. "Get down! Get down! You are not permitted to cause these type of uproars."

For the first time since I had started dropping it low, I felt ashamed. Several people were telling her to leave me alone, chill out, or not to be petty, but it seemed none of that really mattered now that I was being instructed to see her after pavilion was over.

The girl Yellow must have stopped dancing, or just blended into the crowd once the officer busted up the commotion, and that was cool. I wasn't about to point out who I had been dancing against. Sherika tried to come to my rescue, but the lady who now identified herself as Sergeant Cantrell was adamant about penalizing me for causing an uproar. She reached in her pocket and pulled out a pair of latex gloves.

"Ma'am, I cannot express how sorry I am," I said sincerely as I took the gloves and put them on.

"If you're not, you will be if you try that mess again." She rolled her eyes. I stopped in my tracks and stared at her momentarily. She was giving off all the signs of being a bitch. The snappy tone, her hands on her hips, the twisting of her neck as she addressed me, even the way her lips and nose curled up, but her eyes said something else. And I couldn't quite put my finger on it.

"You can't just stand there staring at me. I got stuff to do. Get with it!" She made a sharp turn with her feet and stomped away. The CO was a super-thick woman. I was convinced she was raised in the country eating cornbread, fatback, and greens all her life.

"What's your name again?" I asked as I jogged to catch up to her quick steps.

"Why, you want to grieve me? Write me up for not locking your ass down?" She shifted her weight as she rolled her neck, gesturing with her free hand.

"No, I just want to thank the woman who thought enough of me to extend some grace, instead of penalizing me." I looked her straight in the eyes. It bothered me that I couldn't read her. She took one step back like I had caught her off guard. Then she blinked.

"Sergeant Cantrell," she finally said. That's when I saw past her tough CO façade. She was really a sweetheart.

"Sergeant Cantrell, thank you for caring." I took off running toward the field to handle my business. I didn't look back because I knew the impression I left her with, and I was grateful for the one she had made on me, despite being a correctional officer.

Ten minutes into my assignment, she produced a small clear trash bag. Ten more minutes later, she was satisfied with my work on the pavilion and instead of permitting me to go back to my housing unit, I was instructed to follow her. We went through the back of the gym and came out the front where I discovered another side of the compound. There was a long sidewalk and the programs area, where a chapel for Bible studies and various groups was available. There was a chaplaincy department, cosmetology, and some counselors' offices. Also, there was a pantry where we had the privilege of spending up to sixty dollars on commissary a week. The education department offered Adult Basic Education (ABE) classes, General Education Diploma (GED) classes, and Title One, which is a program for those under twenty-one without a diploma or GED. To the right of the strip, a beautiful landscape stretched out into what reminded me of a college campus.

"What are these five small dorms that are shaped like a fancy L?" I asked, intrigued by the architecture.

"This is E1 where they have the RSAT program," she said. "Mostly people with drug charges are required by the courts to take this program. You got any drug offenses?"

"No, ma'am."

"So you don't have to worry about that. The one right across from E1 is E3, it's the AM Kitchen dorm." We walked past E1 and E3 and at the end of the walk was a dorm in the cut to our left. "This is E2, the Honor Dorm. In order to stay here you can't have any DRs. That means no disciplinary reports for a year." We kept it moving and she quickly pointed out E2 and E4 and told me that anyone could stay there. At the very end of that walkway was E5. "That's our Outside Detail Dorm," she stated.

"What's that?" I asked.

"Our details are contracted out to surrounding counties. Your security level has to be minimum in order to leave the institution." *Dang! Mine is close maximum security!* I knew I would never obtain a detail like that. *Heck, I'll be lucky to get my security level dropped to medium because of my sentence.*

"So what do they do? Clean? Like I used to see some of those men doing on the side of the road?"

"Yeah, landscaping, picking up trash and tree branches . . . stuff like that. If you're interested, we also have an Inside Grounds Detail."

"No, ma'am. After today, I am not." I held up my clear bag full of trash. We both laughed.

Sergeant Cantrell didn't make me go pick up trash on the small side, but I did have to make sure there was no trash in front of the dining hall or the library. Then she escorted me to every dorm on the big side until I finally made it back to my dorm.

"Don't let me catch you on nan 'nother table, you hear?" she threatened, as we both walked into the sally port of my dorm.

"Yes, ma'am," I responded politely, ashamed that I had barely been here twenty-four hours and made such a name for myself. But I could only hope that I carried out the goals I set for myself. This place had a way of provoking you to do things you swore to yourself that you would never do.

CHAPTER 18

I went through Classification and got assigned to Prison Industrials for my work assignment. Which is this huge warehouse with rows of sewing machines that serve a variety of purposes. It had various rows of material in multiple colors, a forklift, and a cutting table. A modern day sweat shop, to say the least. The jumpsuits we wore in Diagnostics and in some county jails were made here. The men's uniform and release pants were also made here. Likewise, we assembled all the shoes and boots (the state of Georgia provided them), with the exception of attaching the soles. The State had most definitely found a way to save money with several GCI (Georgia Correctional Industries) 'sweat shops' in various institutions. Producing everything from the milk we drank, the soap DOC provided us, to the eyeglasses someone wore. And if we were good girls and worked like slaves Monday through Thursday and on Fridays (during some seasons) to meet our daily quota, we were rewarded once a quarter with a chicken box (from Zaxby's, Chick Fil A, or KFC).

I was blessed and got chosen to be a side seamstress, and it was my obligation to seam two hundred jumpsuits daily! It didn't take long for me to get into the flow of things. My bunkie turned out to be a really cool older white chick who believed the weekends were meant for her to take a bunch of pain killers and get high. And she made several attempts to get me to join her. I always declined—popping pills hadn't ever been my thing.

My mind was still accustomed to the street life. All I was stressing about was my appearance, and I didn't want to wait to get approved to order some new shoes, so in the meantime I bought a pair of white Reebok's from a girl in my dorm. I started dreading my hair, which I discovered I could do while sitting on my bed one afternoon while reading a book. I held the book in one hand and just twisted my hair with my free hand.

At this point, my mother had long ago proven she was riding this sentence out with me, and permitted me to send home for a package to receive panties, bras, T-shirts, a watch, necklace, and my mother's old wedding band, CDs, and miscellaneous stuff. My mother did simple things like purchased T-shirts from Walmart and sprayed them with her perfume. Those little gestures made my time easier, and it meant so much to me and made me feel as if she was near.

My routine pretty much consisted of getting up at four in the morning, taking a shower, and then getting ready for work. Once I made sure my living quarters was inspection ready, I reported out as soon as five o'clock count cleared. I'd eat breakfast and afterward, go to work. Once lunchtime was over, it was back to work until sometime after two, that's if I was lucky. I'd come in, shower, go eat dinner and call it a night. During the week I'd be so exhausted, but it seemed as if somebody always wanted to come in my cell and talk. Whether it was to get my opinion, or just laugh about nothing. Many nights, I fell asleep reading an urban novel. I avoided going to pavilion as much as possible because I didn't want to be persuaded to turn up; some people even went as far as propositioning me with commissary.

On Friday mornings I went to get my commissary from the pantry. Also, I had the option of going to the library with my detail on Wednesday nights.

One morning my entire detail (which was about 200 of us) was standing outside the dining hall waiting to eat breakfast. Jayden walked by talking loud, making her presence known. My skin grew itchy, and with no effort of my own, I rolled my eyes. A girl named Lyric had become my work buddy and was standing next to me. "What's wrong, Falicia?" she asked, noticing the difference in my disposition.

"Her! She was rude to me. She makes my skin crawl," I retorted, still watching Jayden, who had just skipped the line and was about five people in front of me.

"Who, Jay?" Lyric asked in disbelief.

"Yes, her! Why you seem so surprised? She just skipped past us like we were not even standing in line!" I felt myself getting pissed all over again.

"That's my brother. You might not believe it, but he has a really good heart." Lyric wrapped her arm in mine and pulled on it, trying to make me get out of my funk. She was a very intelligent, 'easy on the eyes' kind of girl. She wore her big beautiful curls pulled up into a puff when natural hair wasn't so popular, so her five feet five inches tall physique stood out. She reminded me of a slimmer Jill Scott with a touch of Janet Jackson in *Poetic Justice*.

"Girl, I really don't care because she moved me the wrong way, day one." Suddenly as if Jayden heard us discussing her, she turned on her heels, and with that same stride I recalled from the first day I met her, she walked the short distance between us.

"What's up, sis?" She threw her arm over Lyric's shoulder, being loud and obnoxious! Not only did I not care to be in her presence, I was offended by the volume of her tone so early in the morning. Without saying a word, I stepped away from the breakfast line and walked over to the gate that led to my work area and waited for it to be popped. I could still hear her big mouth.

"Sis, that's your lil' friend?" I was convinced she wanted to be heard. "I wasn't trying to run her off."

Later that week, Lyric and I met up for lunch as we had grown accustomed to doing over the previous few weeks. I had gotten into the habit of going to sit at her station for about thirty minutes every day. She worked on the assembly line next to me but further toward the back of the building, side seaming the male release pants. This particular day as we had just lifted our heads from blessing our meal, which was a pack out (two sandwiches and fruit), Jayden grabbed a chair from the vacated sewing machine behind Lyric's and sat down next to her. Instead of getting up, I decided to engage in a conversation on our normal topic, before Jayden had a chance to say a word.

"So what did you read last night?" I asked, referring to Bible passages.

"What did you read?" Jayden invited herself into the conversation. I looked from her to Lyric, but didn't respond, trying my best not to display my attitude. "What did you read? A Bible, a Qur'an, Watch Tower?" Jayden asked. I considered if I wanted to answer.

"Falicia . . ." Lyric whined, as if she wanted me to call a truce.

"The Bible," I answered nonchalantly.

"Oh, so you believe that white man's religion," Jayden retorted.

"That's what you call it?" I snapped back.

"Yeah! It's what the slave masters used to teach their slaves. You should study your Qur'an."

"So you're Muslim." It was more of a statement than a question.

"Yeah . . ." she answered proudly.

"Well, from what I know about your religion, a Muslim is supposed to read both the Bible and the Qur'an."

"Where did you receive that information?"

"My dad is Muslim. Actually, he's what they call a Chris-lim. He lives according to the Qur'an and wholeheartedly follows its way of life, but he also believes that Yeshua's death was to reconcile all mankind back to God and not just the Hebrew people." I glanced over at Lyric, who seemed to be pleased that we were engaging in a civilized conversation.

"Well, if your dad is Muslim, how come you aren't?"

"I have my reasons, but to make a long story short. I have had some very personal encounters, supernatural things that have happened to me by faith in Jesus' name. Now had God not revealed himself to me through Christ, I would probably be a Muslim because judging from the outside looking in, y'all got the message: Honor God first and love your neighbor as yourself. But I cannot deny how God revealed Himself to me."

"I feel ya," Jayden finally responded after a few seconds of silence. "Well, just know you are always welcome to come to Jumah on Fridays at one, if you're ever interested."

That day was the 'breaking the ice' encounter for Jayden and me. Even though I still had my reservations about her, she allowed me to see someone other than a cocky young woman with a slick mouth. What I didn't know was that something greater than ourselves was at hand. I had no idea just how much her presence in my life would affect me.

CHAPTER 19

One Friday afternoon, I was lying on my bunk reading an urban novel and suddenly this urgency to go to church came over me. I tried to ignore it, but it got to the point it became almost nagging. I didn't have to concern myself with how I would wear my hair because I was in the beginning stage of locking it up. So I kept it in neat coils, twisted down to my scalp. I kept a clean uniform ironed, and I didn't wear makeup. So, all I had to do was take a shower, and I would be ready in no time.

Sometime that evening, close to seven o'clock I walked through the gym door and was a little taken aback. The gym was jam packed and reminded me of an actual church service. Upbeat gospel music blasted from speakers that were positioned in various places throughout the gym. Approximately ten residents, five on each side of the pulpit, stood behind two altar benches openly praising God, appearing to be the praise and worship team. At least two hundred residents filled the multiple rows of chairs and bleachers that outlined the gym. In between the columns of chairs, several women that I had seen on the compound stood in these sections of the floor where no chairs were, creating the impression of aisles. They fulfilled the role of ushers with their cloth lace pieces on the crown of their heads, escorting us to our seats and holding rolls of tissue, just in case someone was in need.

I ended up sitting in the section of chairs on the left side of the gym in between two people I didn't know nor had I ever seen before. But I didn't mind being amidst strangers because I didn't have to concern myself with how I was being viewed in the presence of my associates or friends. Plus, I knew God had sent me here for a purpose. However, as I looked around at my surroundings, the individual who sat on my left must have read the curiosity on my face and decided to enlighten me.

"This is your first time here?" the woman asked. I nodded yes.

"This is Minister Gray's service. All these woman are her choir members.

"Oh, okay," I said as I leaned down and put my Bible underneath my chair. "Are all the services like this?" So far I was impressed!

"Oh, no . . ." She nodded. "But there are some other services that are good too. This is just Minister Gray's. She has been in prison ministry for years." She pointed out a brown-skinned woman with shoulder-length hair, with a smile as bright as the lights in the gym, walking around to every bleacher and each row just to hug every individual. "She has a love for us that you can feel. You know what I mean?" the woman asked, smiling like she was proud of the minister.

"No, but I can imagine," I replied and stood to my feet to join in with the congregation, hoping God would extend an invitation for me to be in His presence. What I loved about praising God was that as you forgot about yourself and lifted Him up in His Majesty and acknowledged the blessings He has extended in your life, you naturally just began to feel better.

It didn't take long before Minister Gray was standing in front of me with her arms extended, waiting for me to accept her embrace.

"Hey, boo!" she said as she wrapped her arms around me like a mother would a child. For some reason, I immediately felt I loved this woman. I stood there watching as she made her way down the row to the others that sat next to me. Some she seemed more acquainted with than others, but she didn't bypass anyone. I took a deep breath and lifted my hands to continue worshipping, and I just couldn't deny feeling so much more sensitive to the spirit realm. I looked over in the direction of where Minister Gray was. "Was it her hug?" I asked myself, feeling as if I had been marked by God, but I didn't want to spend much time contemplating on the matter.

Shortly after, the minister was standing behind the pulpit with the microphone and began her service. I watched attentively as one of the residents led us in prayer, then two others read a passage from either the

Old or New Testaments. The minister gave a few words of encouragement, then dismissed her praise team, who joined the remainder of the choir in the corner of the room by a set of bleachers.

"Next, we will have a praise dance by Miss Windy Bradley!" the minister announced. Several people abandoned their chairs and sat on the floor in front of the front row and the ones who sat in the back bleachers piled up in the aisles. I stood to my feet and watched as a beautiful young girl came to the middle of the floor and began to gracefully dance to, "Still I Rise," by Yolanda Adams.

"Oh my God!" I exclaimed! I had never seen anything like this before. I couldn't move, nor did I want to blink. Her expressions matched her movements, and it all went along with the song. I raised my hand as a form of worship to God, feeling as if I was being ushered into His presence and He was only a few feet away from me. Suddenly, my heart began racing, and I struggled to breathe. I didn't want to sit down, but I feared I might be having a heart attack.

"Lord God, I plead the blood of Jesus over me," I spoke aloud, placing both hands on my heart as I sat down. A couple seconds passed, and my shortness of breath only increased! "I don't wanna die," I prayed to God as I considered what I should do next. *I need to pray. Like really pray!* I told myself as I took another look around. No one was paying me any mind, everyone was still engrossed in the dance. For a split second I considered how awkward I might look bowing down in my chair, but it didn't last long as the fear of dying overtook me. I kneeled down with my face in the chair and just began to plead with God for my life.

"Lord, I'm only asking that you don't allow Satan to get the victory over me," I pleaded with tears as what seemed like a weight was placed on my chest. "God, please . . . in Jesus' name," I continued.

"You shall dance for me," a deep voice spoke softly in my ear. I looked to the left and right, to see if someone was talking to me. No one's attention was directed toward me.

I must be tripping! I thought as I bowed my head again to pray, and then I heard it again.

"You shall dance for me." This time the voice was a little louder than before, and as if someone had flicked on the light switch, the realization popped in my head. God had just spoken to me! Fresh tears poured from my eyes, and the weight lifted from my chest. God Himself, was summoning *me* to use my temple to dance for Him. I had already yielded my body to glorify Satan by dancing to seduce, entice, and profit for my own selfish gain. Now I was being called to usher people into the presence of God! But I didn't understand completely what was being asked of me, and I only had one response: "Yeah, when I go home."

CHAPTER 20

"Girl, I'm telling you that mess liked to have freaked me out!" I recollected my encounter from church with Lyric as we ate lunch that following Monday.

"I wish I had been there!" She beamed, seeming equally as excited.

"I don't think I'll ever forget what His voice sounds like."

"I feel you. So, what are you going to do?" Lyric asked, changing the tone of our conversation.

"What do you mean?" I finally picked up my sandwich.

"When are you going to dance?"

"Girl, I ain't doing that! Maybe if I go home or something I might . . . but I ain't doing that here."

"Falicia!" Lyric stared at me with disappointment in her eyes.

"What? Why you looking at me like that? I don't know nothing about that. For one, I've never done it before. I don't have no gospel music to even try to find a song to dance to, and I haven't the slightest idea how to even get permission to do that at church."

"Well, don't you think if God told you to do something He would handle the rest?" Lyric had a point, but she was beginning to get on my nerves. Had I known she would make a big deal about this, I would have kept it to myself. I just looked at her. "Don't worry about it. I'll handle it."

"Lyric, don't do that! I'm not ready for all that," I whined, hoping she'd change her mind.

"Falicia, I'm your friend and I'm going to do what any real friend would do." Just as she stated that, I noticed Jayden heading our way.

"We're not finish discussing this," I warned her. "And please, don't tell anybody." I looked in the direction Jayden was approaching.

She looked back. "Of course not!" I wasn't sure why I didn't want

Falicia Rose Blakely

anyone to know. For some reason I noticed that most people who believe in God are ashamed of the things of God, but when it came to the things of this world, we are wide open and downright trifling.

"Of course not, what?" Jayden asked, pulling out a chair to sit in.

"Of course not, whatever I was talking to Falicia about, nosy!" Lyric checked Jayden, and the two of us shared a laugh.

"Whatever." Jayden brushed us off. "So, I was wondering if you would dread my hair, Falicia?" she asked, once we stopped laughing. "I've tried with a couple people, and none of their locks seem to stay."

"That would be impossible for me to do, being that we don't stay in the same dorm."

"I figured you could do it here."

"Jayden, I don't have that kind of time at work to get my quota and do your hair."

"I'm going to pay you."

"That's not the point."

"I just want you to know that I don't mind looking out for you." Jayden stared me straight in the eyes. I didn't answer right away because it seemed there was an underlying message going on. I hadn't mentioned money, and the fact she so freely put it out there that she didn't mind looking out for me. Those things told me she had other intentions besides just getting her hair done. Especially, when she had a reputation of just dating females who had that check, or were financially straight.

"I'll tell you what I will do. I can't make you any promises, but I will keep you in mind."

"That sounds fair to me." Jayden smiled from ear to ear, and for the first time since she was rude, I thought she was kind of cute.

The next couple of weeks consisted of Jayden invading on all Lyric's and my personal space. Every time she saw us together she would come and chill with us.

It took me two weeks before I finally made an attempt to do her hair, and then two afternoons after I finished my quota to twist her entire head.

102

"What's your favorite meal?" she asked that Thursday as we finished our lunch.

"I really don't know yet. I'm still figuring out how to cook prison meals," I answered, honestly.

"Oh, I got so many recipes. I'm going to have to make sure you try all of them." She smiled, pleased with herself. "Are you going to the store tomorrow?"

I looked at her and considered if I wanted to answer because I felt this was one of those questions that people asked when trying to find out if you were financially stable. I wasn't indigent, but I didn't go every week either.

"Why are you asking me that?"

"I just wanted you to meet me so I could pay you for doing my hair."

"Oh." I was only half convinced. "I'm not sure yet."

"Oh . . . okay. Either way I'll get it to you."

The next day I was in the dorm playing cards when somebody walked up to me and handed me a note with the instructions on how to prepare the tuna meal I was receiving. I thought the gesture was really cute and decided to stop being so hard on her. She began to go out of her way to spend time with me at work, even when Lyric and I weren't together. It also became routine for someone to come in from the store on Fridays with an extra net bag filled with food and snacks from Jayden for me. Personally, I didn't give much thought to why she was taking care of me. In my naive mind, I just wrote it off as she recognized real and knew better than to expect me to be like the flunkies who took care of her.

Jayden and I began to flirt with each other, and her friendly gestures swiftly led up to the point of her asking to be with me, and against my better judgment, I said yes. It wasn't wise of me to do so for several reasons: one being I had barely been on the compound a month, and that wasn't enough time to really get to know someone. Plus, I had heard rumors she hit on her girlfriends, used people for money, and she was a hot head. But because I didn't see any of those characteristics, however,

I assumed she was different with me, like I brought the best out of her. But above all of that, I didn't take into account that God had spared my life, set me aside in this place so that He could do a work in my heart. Strip me of what I identified with in hopes of me realizing who I was created to be, for His sole purpose.

What I couldn't see is what so many of us don't realize: I needed to heal. I needed time to discover who I was outside of who I identified myself as in my previous relationship. Take time to learn things about myself, such as what 'I' enjoyed doing aside from a relationship. What it was like to wake up every day and love the person looking back at me in the mirror. To fall in love with myself for who 'I' was, not what my ex or other people said I was. But I skipped this very vital aspect, and in less than two weeks into our relationship, I began to see things I would have seen had I just taken a little longer to get to know Jayden.

Every morning when we arrived to work, the detail had the option of going on the back dock to smoke a cigarette. Lyric and I decided to go get some fresh air this particular morning. The first thing we noticed was Jayden had this Mexican girl name Kayla pinned up against the gate. Out of all the weeks I had worked here I had never seen her before.

"Who is that?" I asked Lyric, who didn't respond, but just looked at me sympathetically. When I saw Kayla push Jayden, I walked a little closer because I wanted to know why someone was pushing my girlfriend.

"You lie!" Kayla yelled. Jayden spoke in a hushed tone so I couldn't hear what she was saying.

"Falicia, let's just go." Lyric grabbed my arm. I pulled away.

"Are you missing the fact that, that's *my* girlfriend over there with this broad?" I began to think of all the times Jayden would get up and go to smoke break, probably out here with this chick.

"Falicia, *please*," she pleaded as I walked closer. I had no intentions of making a scene. I just wanted Jayden to know I was present so she could get her lies straight.

"You lie, Jay! Just get out my face!" Kayla yelled and attempted to storm away, but Jayden grabbed her arm. At the same time, she turned and made eye contact with me. She released Kayla. I turned on my heels and walked back into the building.

Minutes later, Jayden was at my work station trying to explain. "It's not what it looks like."

"Get out of my face, Jayden! I don't want to talk to you right now." I was trying to remain calm, stay in a lady's place, and her wack ass excuses were rubbing me the wrong way.

"It's just, she mad because I chose you over her."

"Well, when did she become a possibility because you told me you weren't interested in anyone. So what gave her the idea she was next in line." I was sharper than she thought.

"I . . . I kind of . . ." she stuttered.

"Let me tell you something right now. The only way this"—I pointed from me to her— "is going to work is if you keep it 100 with me. Nobody should be able to come tell you anything about me that you don't know and vice versa. Do you feel where I'm going from?" She nodded yes.

"Now, I feel not only do you owe me a better explanation, but you owe her one as well. And for the moment, I don't want to look at you, so maybe you should go set the record straight with her."

"But—"

"Jayden, I'm trying to handle this shit the right way, give me some space," I interrupted her. She dropped her head, defeated, then slowly got up and walked away. I sat there fuming just thinking about how both Jayden and Lyric had played on my intelligence. I couldn't wait until our lunch break to confront Lyric about not telling me Kayla was in the picture.

A week later, Jayden and I were leaving work and somebody walked up to Jayden to give her a message from MeMe. I didn't know who MeMe was, but after hearing her send the message, "I'm done with you. You play too many games." I figured she was another potential interest. I didn't expect the messenger to be mindful of my presence, because I was new on the compound, and no one knew we were together. But before I even had a chance to even check her about MeMe, this dark-skinned girl name Zakemma walked up and started yelling at Jayden.

"You told me the only reason you weren't with me was because I'm infected!" I looked from Jayden to her and wondered if it was about to be a fight. It was clear to me that this girl was in her feelings because Jayden used the fact she was HIV-positive as the reason they couldn't be together. And now she was faced with an ugly truth that couldn't be the case because she was with me.

"You promised me that if you ever dated someone infected it would be me!" she continued to yell.

At this point, I was over it! I had taken all I could in one day. The Mexicans were now beefing with me like I had just wrecked a happy home because Jayden couldn't keep it real with all parties and now this? I didn't even say a word, just sped up my pace and walked to my dorm. I didn't care anything about Jayden calling after me, or the confrontation Zakemma was initiating with her. She could go to hell as far as I was concerned.

The following morning I lied to my supervisor about being up all night with an upset stomach and she bought it. I was back in my dorm with an excuse to miss work before Jayden had even reported out. I didn't want to see, much less hear anything she had to say. That Friday as usual, somebody brought me a net bag full of food from her. I told the girl to take it back. She did, and somebody else brought me an even bigger bag later that day.

Later that night Jayden came to the window looking for me, and I told several people to tell her I was in the shower. I figured if I ignored her long enough, she would just move on. I mean, hey, she had enough women lined up willing to be with her, so why waste time chasing me? But like all bad attachments, they don't just go away. You have to close a door if you want it to be shut. Unfortunately for me, I left it wide open.

CHAPTER 21

It didn't take me long to discover this broad was just like some of the dudes I dated at home. Once it became clear to Jayden that she was on her way out the door, she got creative with trying to find ways to get out of the dog house and back into good standing with me. She was on time for work every morning, showering me with gifts and asking me to meet up with her outside of work.

Because we worked together, I assumed that was a significant amount of time together. So, I really hadn't noticed that we didn't do anything as a couple until she began asking me to wait until they called her dorm for meals so we could eat together, or to meet her at the library. It amazed me that she wanted us to partake in every outside recreational activity and go to all of the church services. I should have questioned who she had been chilling with prior to us hanging out. I never thought twice about what she was doing when I inquired about her previous night's activities. But I most definitely didn't care now! I felt like I wasn't even being pursued by the same person. This was someone new, and I loved it! Straight up! In a matter of weeks I had fallen for the suave, intelligent, bad ass. I actually thought I had accomplished something major and snatched up the stud everyone wanted, but in actuality, I looked like another one that bit the dust. The next dumb-dumb.

Jayden liked to throw the word "loyalty" around a lot, and who else was better to fill those shoes than me? Misses Ride or Die! I mean hey, I'm in prison because I swore loyalty to a monster who clearly didn't give two fucks about my son's life nor mine! Surely, I can hold my bitch down inside these confined walls. What would it cost me to prove to this broad that I'd be by her side no matter what? My integrity? A little embarrassment? Ignoring my intuition? Some sleepless nights? Or a few altercations with people I called friends because my girlfriend was beefing with them? Her name tatted on my rib cage? I mean, what's that? That's not that big of a deal; I'm only denying who I am, and who God has called me to be for the sake of companionship!

You know how that is, right? Ignoring the slight conviction constantly nagging in your heart or mind that you're better than the things you're doing, or that feeling when you're forcing yourself to walk with your head high when you'd rather run and hide because you know everybody else probably knows how dumb you look, but keeping this persona was the most important thing at that moment. So you grin and bear it until you're so miserable and unhappy, you long for the strength to walk away. To simply keep it real and politely say, "I don't want to do this anymore." But for some reason that courage never comes, so instead you just pray for God to remove the obstacle, but you make no effort to remove yourself or address the real issue when you get into a disagreement.

In the meantime, Lyric took it upon herself to speak with Minister Gray's secretary about me dancing at church. But she didn't just mention to the lady that I was interested, she scheduled a date for me to dance! I almost lost my mind when she told me I had to minister through dance the first Friday in November!

"I'm not dancing at church, Lyric! I told you . . . I told God I wasn't doing that until I got out of prison!" I yelled, as I considered leaving my lunch at her work station and then stormed back to my own station.

"Falicia, you are not being logical." Lyric maintained her composure. "Sis, you got a life sentence. God is calling you to dance now. Think about what I'm saying." I sat quietly for a minute as I looked her square in the face.

"You have a purpose to fulfill in your present life, in your current situation. You never know what God has planned for you, but it's better to be obedient and walking in God's covering than to be disobedient and possibly forcing God's wrath against you." *God's wrath?* I pondered what Lyric had said to me. Was it possible that if I wasn't living life the way God's word stated we should, I could cause God to raise His hand against me for my harm or to be cursed, instead of being blessed? If so, then that meant I was already in the wrong because I was dating a woman, and for reasons beyond my own comprehension, I didn't want to leave her. Maybe it was loneliness, the unconscious decision to adapt to the environment, or maybe it was something deeper. Like, was I attracted to a certain *type* of person because of my soul ties to men in my past? Whatever the reason, I was now confronted with a new reality. Could I force God to curse me?

I sat there staring at Lyric. Alongside my new realization, a question that had been plaguing me for some time crossed my mind. As a friend, why didn't she tell me anything about Jayden and Kayla? I parted my lips to ask, but decided against it. Maybe she felt the need to be loyal to Jaden as well.

Meisha stayed in the dorm with me. We just started hanging out partly because of our resemblance. Both dark skinned, slim, tall, big smiles and pretty. I suggested she dance with me, and she was so supportive about it. She directed me to people who most likely had Christian music. Jayden brought me a CD player, but I couldn't find a song. I listened to like fifty songs. This lady that worked with me that everybody pretty much viewed like an aunt, heard what I was trying to do.

"Falicia, I got this song by Yolanda Adams that I just love. I would love it if you danced to it. Do you mind listening to it to see if you like it?" I can't remember the name of the song, but I did listen to it. I think the album is titled *Believe*. Yolanda Adams had this blue dress on the cover. It was a cassette tape, however, so the lady had to loan me her cassette player as well. I ended up loving the song, and after spending some time in prayer, I started making up the routine for the song.

"What can I do to describe the words of this song?" I found myself asking continuously, as Meisha and I strived to complete the dance. The closer we got to finishing it, the more Meisha seemed disinterested.

"Meisha, are we going to practice after count tonight?" I asked as she sat in the quiet room watching TV.

"I don't know if I'm getting back up after count," she replied, never taking her eyes off the screen.

"Well, if you want, we can do it now. I just got off work, but I don't mind."

"No, I'm not up for it right now. It's too many people up. I'll pass today," was her typical response, and as time progressed and I started telling her time was drawing near she would say, "Don't trip. We got time." We did finally finish the dance, and the day arrived for us to do it. I was a nervous wreck as I got ready for church. I went upstairs to check on Meisha, and do you know that heifer was in the bed!

"Meisha, you need to get up! We got church in less than an hour!" I couldn't hide my frustration.

"I'm not going," she said casually.

"You not going! What you mean you not going? We dancing! I know you not going to bail on me like this!"

"I'm not going, Falicia. I can't dance in front of all those people." I stood there for a second trying to have some form of sympathy for her, but the way she went about the whole situation was killing any opportunity to even take her feelings into consideration.

"You are a dumb 'ho!" I blurted out. "You could have told me a long time ago you didn't want to dance, and I could have prepared to do it by myself! You don't wait till the night of to decide to bail!" With that, I stormed out her cell and slammed her door shut. But as I dismounted the stairs, I realized she had shown me she didn't want to dance. I just chose to overlook the signs. Had I taken things at face value, I wouldn't have been surprised at her decision. From that moment, I determined within myself to pay attention to what people were not saying, as well as what their actions said to me about their character.

I went to church that night, but not with the mind to dance. My feelings were hurt that Meisha had done me like that, but Jayden and Lyric wouldn't hear of it. They reminded me that God could use me, and I was the one who came up with the dance to begin with. So, when the program started and my name was called, I went to the center of the floor and I stood there shaking like a leaf as the music began to play. I looked up toward the ceiling as I danced because there was absolutely too many people looking at me. Very shortly after I began dancing, something came over me and it wasn't about anyone in the room, and before I knew it, the song was ending. I heard a round of applause and I smiled, thanking God for literally allowing me to do such a thing. It wasn't until people stood to hug me with tears in their eyes, confessing that the dance was so encouraging that I began to consider that maybe God was really calling me to do something that was greater than my understanding. Because I didn't understand 'what' was so encouraging.

CHAPTER 22

Have you ever just sat in the middle of a park, possibly on a swing or in the middle of a basketball court and the sun seemed to be just the right temperature as it kissed your face, and the wind danced through your hair? The birds seemed to sing as they played in the sky and for a few seconds the serenity of it all took you far away from whatever issues awaited you back at home? That's the best way I can described the kind of peace I had after I ministered through dance.

Every day I woke up hoping that peace would govern my day, but I had to learn that hoping wasn't enough. I needed to make some adjustments in my life beginning with my attitude and the type of people I associated with. One evening, I was going to dinner and I had slowed down to give Jayden's dorm time to come out. Jayden and I were walking up the walkway with her dorm, and a Sergeant I had never paid much attention, or held a conversation with before sought my attention.

"Hey . . . you. Stand right here." The heavyset man pointed at me, his finger only inches away from my face as we were approaching him.

"Can you watch where you're pointing your hand?" I retorted, pissed off that his hand was in my face. "That's rude!"

"I said stand right here!" He ignored my comment.

"For what?" My blood pressure spiked as I stopped walking, inches from his face.

"What the fuck this nig' want?" Jayden asked aloud.

"I don't know," I answered, and started back walking.

"Hey! Inmate, I told you to stand here!" he yelled, coming up behind me.

"Dude, don't run up behind my girl!" I could tell by the look in her eyes, Jayden was about to flip. I saw this going sour, so I just stopped walking and leaned up against the wall.

"Go eat," I told Jayden. She didn't want to, but I was persistent.

"Why you stopping me?" I snapped at the sergeant once Jayden was out of sight.

"You need to be careful who you hang with," he stated, standing in my face as if he was challenging me.

"You need to mind your business. Ain't nobody fucking with you!"

"You don't seem like the type to follow up behind somebody's mess. Some people can get you in trouble just because of who they are," he warned, but his body language had me on the defensive. His entire approach made it hard for me to comprehend that he was trying to look out for me.

"You don't know shit about me!" I stood upright, hoping he would give me a reason to swing on his big ass. He just looked at me. "Are you done, because I'm ready to go eat?" We never broke eye contact. I wanted him to know he didn't intimidate me.

"You can go . . . just remember what I said." He stepped aside so I could walk away.

"Whatever!" I rolled my eyes as I bent the corner and locked eyes with Jayden.

"What the fuck was that about?" she asked.

"Fuck if I know!" I snapped back as we walked into the dining hall. I couldn't understand why I was so angry, and though I couldn't see it then, just being affiliated with Jayden would get me in a lot of shit. It had already begun, but one thing he was wrong about: I *was* the type to follow up behind somebody's mess. I was in prison because I was too afraid to lead with my own mind, and it would be a bumpy path before I realized it.

Not long afterward, Jayden formed the habit of sitting at my work station throughout the day as I worked. For whatever reason it became a problem to my supervisor, Mrs. Marvin. Oftentimes when she addressed Jayden about it, she would mouth off at the lady. Her silver hair complimented her tall, slim frame and her soft spoken demeanor made you want to respect her. Even protect her like you would defend your granny, so at times I would reprimand Jayden. But as the weeks turned into months, and she began to complain about her being up under me, she had started to piss me off. This particular day we were eating lunch, and Mrs. Marvin walked by and frowned. I didn't bring it to Jayden or Lyric's attention. I just watched as she walked over to the officer's desk and asked what I assumed was for them to remove Jayden from area.

Now this broad has gone too far! I thought as Ms. Wheels got up and started in our direction.

"Jayden, no matter what is said, keep your composure," I warned as Ms. Wheels walked up.

"Frick and Frack, how many times this woman gonna have to tell you to remain at *your* work stations?" she asked, playfully.

"Well, I didn't think that applied to lunch," I said, before Jayden had a chance to. Her mouth was lethal.

"I have asked her to stay from over here, period," Mrs. Marvin retorted.

"Well, what's the problem as long as I'm meeting my daily quota?"

"The problem is you're working, and she needs to be doing the same thing. Not socializing."

"You ain't my supervisor . . . Fuck wrong with you?" Jayden blurted out. I snapped my head around and glared at her. I had enough sense to know nothing would get resolved like this. Officer Wheels looked just as taken aback as Mrs. Marvin did, but Jayden was only getting started. "Y'all kill me with that prejudice shit! You don't say shit to the white people who fucking sit around all day, but my girl not only do her job, she kiss your ass and you still got a problem." Mrs. Marvin held her hand to her mouth as if she was appalled.

"Now, I think it's best you come from over here," Officer Wheels instructed in her usual playful manner. She always put me in mind of a thick, country Patty LaBelle.

"Jayden, please be quiet," I began my plea in vain.

"Nah, this *trash* . . ." She stood and was waving her arms and using her hands to emphasize her point. "Gon' go put the police on us, like we over here doing something wrong! We're fucking eating lunch like the rest of these motherfuckers!" Ms. Wheels looked at me, pleading with me to get Jayden before it turned into something else. Several people began to take notice that something was transpiring.

"See, this is the reason I don't want her over here," Mrs. Marvin stated, in a matter of fact tone. Jayden wasn't intimidated in the least.

"Who gives a fuck what you want?" she snapped back.

"Jayden, chill with all that." I got in between the two of them. I never knew what Jayden would or wouldn't do.

"Ms. Wheels, don't nobody be fucking with her!"

"Everybody calm down, please. This can be handled better." I tried to gain control of the situation.

"No. Ms. Blakely, I will not be disrespected!" Mrs. Marvin was the one talking with her hands now. "I'm sorry, but I'm asking that you tell her to leave from over here and not to return." I looked into Jayden's eyes, wishing she would have just walked away, but she was too stubborn for that.

"With all due respect, Mrs. Marvin. I feel it's a little extreme to ask that she never come in your area, especially because we eat lunch together."

"I don't want her over here, period." Mrs. Marvin was unrelenting.

"This my woman! Wherever she is, I'm there!" Jayden clearly wasn't considering the position she put me in.

"Well, if that's the case, you can leave too." I was taken aback by Mrs. Marvin's response.

"I work my behind off over here!" She looked around the room as I began to protest her conclusion, giving me the impression she wasn't interested in what I had to say.

"Fuck her!" Jayden spoke barely over a whisper. I thought about the fact I was doing OJT (on job training) as a Machine Operator, so I really didn't want to sacrifice what I had been striving to achieve.

"Mrs. Marvin—"

"Ms. Blakely, I don't want to hear it. I just want her gone," she interrupted me.

"You're being rude now . . . interrupting me." I was losing my cool. I looked at Officer Wheels, who was staring at Mrs. Marvin standing there looking like a hateful old lady.

"Baby, you don't have to put up wit' this shit," Jayden instigated.

"Mrs. Marvin . . ." I made one last attempt. I just wanted her to understand where I was coming from. She rolled her eyes.

"Fuck it!" I said calmly, and began clearing out my station.

"You leave, just know you're not coming back." She stood wide legged with her hands on her hips.

"Who gives a fuck? You need her!" Jayden only added fuel to the fire as she helped me get my stuff. Mrs. Marvin turned on her heels and stormed away.

"Jayden, shut the hell up sometimes!" Officer Wheels blurted out.

"Fuck that! You know my baby don't bother nobody!" she retorted.

"You're right, but this wasn't about her. It was about you!"

Jayden either wasn't in a place to comprehend her role in the chaos, or didn't care because she got what she wanted. And it was the first time I'd seen Ike in her. The outcome really didn't matter as long as he was straight. Forget about what I feel, or how I ended up feeling that way. Just make life comfortable for him, but in this case, *for her*. But it didn't do me any good to recognize such things and do absolutely nothing about it.

That afternoon once I was away from her, I couldn't stop thinking about how Jayden had been a little inconsiderate and could have handled the situation better for my sake because I would have taken into account how my actions would affect her. But truth be told, I couldn't think of anyone I had been with that had ever considered how their actions affected me. *Maybe people just don't know how to love the way I love?* I thought.

I ended up on Sanitation after that, and I think it was what Jayden really wanted because she pretty much got all my attention, unless I was cleaning up, and even then she managed to become a part of that too. She started talking about getting moved so that we could stay together.

I called myself being in love and did what everyone does in prison to prove it. I got her name tattooed on me. Some of these women are like walking canvases. You don't even have to ask who they've been with, just sit or stand next to them. You'll see the names on their necks, arms, legs, face, and hands. I put Jayden's name on my upper stomach, on my ribcage.

Yes, I lay stretched out, positioned on my back on top of a trash bag, as this young girl who was well known for drawing, took a needle that I purchased from work and some waterproof mascara, and with a pair of gloves on her hands, she proceeded to prick Jayden's first name on one side and her last name on the other. Even as I was getting it done I had second thoughts because we had only been together a few months, but I had a point to prove. I was riding with her no matter what. The tat would also silence all the broads who couldn't understand "why me." I was letting it be known wifey was home. I didn't need anyone to tell me how dumb I was being! Every time Jayden would lift my shirt to show off my tat featuring her name, I was reminded of how dumb I looked! Some of her friends praised the declaration and some simply asked, "How long y'all been together?"

But prison is a world inside of the world. We operate to our own set of rules. Some things we do in here would be frowned upon in society or labeled differently but overlooked in here. A day is as a month in here. Some of these people have monthly anniversaries, whereas it's normal to celebrate yearly anniversaries. If a relationship lasts six months, you are viewed as being in love. A year, you must be getting married, and anything longer than that, it's understood that no matter if that couple breaks up, they will always be together and will eventually navigate back together because they are most definitely wives or husband and wife for some.

It only took a few weeks on Sanitation detail for me to begin losing sight of myself and begin adapting to the conditions of prison. Jayden would often come into the restroom area whenever she realized I was going to clean them or use it. The flimsy, eight wooden stalls did little to provide the privacy one would be used to in a public restroom. But filth was just the same, so I made it my business to bring the sanitation up, the restroom being a main target.

"You need some help?" Jayden asked, walking up behind me as I scrubbed one of six sinks out.

"No, I'm almost finish. Thank you, though," I answered sweetly, loving when she held me from behind. Well, loving when she was affectionate period.

"Okay." She kissed my neck and walked into a stall. That simple gesture made my womanhood awaken. I entertained the idea of going to peek at her, but decided against it, not wanting to start something I couldn't finish. I could hear her peeing, and then she flushed the toilet. She walked up to the sink that was next to the last one I was cleaning and washed her hands. I glanced over at her and couldn't help but adore her chocolate skin. Her locks were growing and resembled fresh grass sprouting from the ground. Her crisp, tapered line made the beauty of her cheekbones and lips cause envy. Her brown eyes appeared to be filled with love for only me. Her physique, a few inches taller than mine, forced me to feel vulnerable every time she stood over me.

"Give me a kiss," she instructed as she cut the water off.

"What?" I replied, trying to buy some time. She knew I wasn't a kisser. I just really didn't understand the purpose until the day I kissed her.

"Give me a kiss," she repeated calmly as she watched me drop the chemicals I was cleaning with in the tray and remove my gloves.

"Jay, why you trying to start with me?" I couldn't contain the smile that was plastered across my face, as I picked up the tray and walked toward the exit.

"Where you going?" She grabbed me by the waist with one arm and pulled me into her embrace, staring into my eyes. "So, you don't want to kiss me?" she asked, but no other words were exchanged as I got lost in the increase of my heartbeat and the throbbing of my vagina. Slowly, she leaned in and our lips met. One of her hands caressed the small of my back and gradually my butt. I pulled away, but she took the other hand and placed it behind my head, forcing us even closer as she slipped her tongue into my mouth. A soft moan released itself somewhere in between her shifting her head to kiss me deeper. Every nerve in my body seemed to be stimulated, as I took her lead and rolled my tongue around hers. Slowly, she pulled away.

"Put that down," she instructed. I looked around, trying to figure out what would happen next. I walked to the entrance and set the chemical tray on the floor outside the restroom just to get a glimpse if anyone was coming or looking in the direction of where we were. Nobody.

I turned and immediately approached a sink to wash my hands. Jayden was standing in the frame of the last stall. My heart began to pound because I knew where this was headed.

"Come here," she instructed and disappeared inside of it.

"Bae, you trippin'," I commented nervously.

"Girl, come here!" she retorted. A part of me was aroused that she could handle me and another part of me was very uncomfortable with the idea of being in this toilet stall.

"Jayden, what if somebody comes in here?" I whispered, hoping to change her mind. She didn't respond, instead she came out and took me by the hand and walked me into the stall and closed the door. My nerves were shot. I stood there trying to listen for footsteps or the police to call my name. Jayden, on the other hand, didn't seemed concerned as she swallowed my mouth again. At first, I couldn't focus and wished she would just get out of the way so I could get out, but as her hands caressed my breasts and her lips graced my neck, my body began to yearn for her. I closed my eyes so I could go where she was taking me. I felt her hand trying to pull my pants and panties down at the same time.

"Jay!" I called her that whenever I was serious and grabbed my pants so she couldn't pull them any further. "We can't do this, not here," I whispered.

"Please, baby. I have fantasized about this a long time." She hastily began kissing me again and released her grip on my clothes and slipped her hands into my vagina. I gasped for air in utter surprise that she was touching me in this nature, but she didn't give me much time to think before I could hear moans flowing from her mouth and her whispering her pleasures about me being so wet. I didn't want to be in that stall, but the satisfaction that she was getting from merely touching me made me overlook the things I didn't care for.

"You gon' cum for me?" Jayden asked in between kisses as she stimulated my clit.

"If that's what you want, then get it." I took her mouth into mine and propped one leg up on the toilet.

CHAPTER 23

Jayden and I had several places we designated as our kissing and touching encounters, but it never went any further. I believe it didn't go to the next level because we weren't in a position to do so. Had we lived together, I'm sure it would have went down. And to be quite honest with you, the way she used to leave me so aroused, I began to wonder how was she relieving herself? I guess you could call it my intuition, but I wasn't even surprised when she came to work with scratches on her neck.

"Jay, help me understand why in the hell you got scratches on your neck." My pressure was boiling. What began as my pleasant morning was swiftly becoming a curve ball, and her ass was about to strike out!

"I got a scratch on my neck?" She hit me with the foolishness.

"No, not *a* scratch, *scratches*."

"What?" she asked, eyes wide, brows wrinkled. Looking like she hadn't the slightest idea as she touched her neck with her fingertips.

"Jay, stop playing with me! Ain't no way you didn't know them fucking scratches are on both sides of your neck! If nothing else, it would have stung when you took a shower." I wanted to get up and leave her behind, sitting in the back of the warehouse by herself, but my desire to know who put them there was greater. "So, what bitch you been . . ." My chest tightened. It's one thing to suspect something, but a different ball game when it becomes a reality! I struggled a few seconds as I mustered up the courage to say it. "Who . . . who you fucking, Jay?" I sat silently, doing my best to keep my poker face, watching every move she made.

"Fucking?" she retorted quickly. "Nah, ma." She reached out for my hand and took it into both of hers. "I wouldn't do you like that; I wouldn't do us like that." She looked me straight in the eyes, with an expression that seemed genuine. She was good, or I was dumb. "Now, Cuppie and I have been wrestling. So it's a possibility I got them that way."

Cuppie! I thought. She was this Caucasian chick that was about five years older than us and was known for being a THOT! I didn't even have to say a word for her to know I wasn't buying it.

"You can ask her if you don't believe me." Rule number one, I didn't go ask a broad nothing about mine because then they knew I was feeling some kind of way, and it's mostly perceived as an insecurity. Instead, I wait! People got comfortable and started being messy, or they forgot the lies they told and tell on themselves. I had nothing but time. I would wait.

"I'm not about to go ask her nothing. 'Ho just going to lie anyway. But straight up, if you on the BS, out of respect for me, you need to close this door before you open another one. I don't take well to people playing with my feelings." With that, I got up and walked away. I didn't want to hear her lies because in my heart I felt she was doing something inappropriate. Unfortunately for me, I was too weak to just deaden the entire situation. So, since I couldn't just walk away, I began to refrain from our lil' hot and steamy encounters, claiming we needed to chill before we ended up in jail like this other couple. I advised Jayden to wait until we moved in together. In the meantime, I just avoided being in situations that we normally would use as an opportunity, even to kiss.

Early one morning, while most of the detail was at breakfast, this older couple had decided to skip breakfast and ducked off into the restroom area. Officer Chun, one of three officers we had supervising us, had snuck in behind them and went to the stall next to the one they were in, stood on the toilet and peered over and caught old daddy giving his lady the time of her life, as she stood up on the toilet. I could imagine her looking up and seeing Officer Chun staring at them. Lord have mercy! I probably would have started peeing! Rumor had it she watched them for a minute before she even said a word.

It saddened me that though I still held true to my feelings regarding

Jayden, I couldn't bring myself to break up with her. In the beginning, when we spent most of the days talking, getting to know one another, exchanging childhood memories and such, she had expressed how she often felt people always abandoned her. Like most women, I wanted to be that one who was different. Whose love she knew she could depend on. But I had yet to recognize not everybody deserves the best of you. Some people don't know how to love themselves, or even be honest with themselves. So how can they love and value you? For two years I somehow loved a man through fear, regardless if he beat my ass, asked or demanded I disrespect myself, or purposely destroyed my life and my hope for this life. And here I was again. Signing up to be mistreated and taken for granted! The only life I should have been this dedicated to was my son's.

December rolled around, and I was having my first visit since I left Atlanta. Man would soon be five years old, and when I walked into the visitation area, he took off running into my arms. He was the cutest thing I had ever laid eyes on.

"Hey, Momma!" he sang as I scooped him into my arms. He wrapped his tiny arms around my neck. I scanned the room and spotted my mother in an all-black sweater dress with gold embroidery on it. She wore a pair of knee-high black leather boots and some micro braids pulled back into a French braid. She looked so well put together. I was surprised! Momma usually dressed country. We locked eyes, and her face lit up. I blew her a kiss.

"Oh, Momma misses you so much!" I admitted as I took my attention off my mother and placed it back on the bundle of joy in my arms.

We approached the long, narrow fold-up wooden stained table. Two officers sat near the entrance signing visitors in and instructing them which table to sit at.

"Hey, Miss Blakely," the high-yellow, heavyset, female correctional officer exclaimed.

"Good morning, Ms. Smith," I replied.

"Who is this handsome fellow?" I looked over at my son, who I held on my hip. He was dressed in his three-piece suit.

"This is my son . . . Man."

"Hello, Man." She smiled at him politely. He smiled back, and then laid his head on my shoulder as if he was a little shy. I humored her a few more seconds with his presence, and then hurried to the table with my mother. We embraced, and the three of us hugged like our lives depended on it. I had grown accustomed to seeing them every weekend, and in the couple of months that had passed, my baby had grown so much it made me emotional. But I dared not allow a tear to fall from my eyes and possibly upset my son like that.

"You look so beautiful," my mother cooed as we released each other and sat down.

"Thank you," I replied, but only partially agreeing with the compliment.

"You've lost some weight." It was more of a statement than a question. I nodded yes as I stared at her beautiful face. I knew exactly where her thoughts shifted to.

"It's not because of my health. I been taking my medicine . . ." She didn't look convinced. "I just been stressing a little. Ma. I promise that's the only reason."

She eyed me warily for a second, then shifted her weight in the chair. It was as if God whispered in her ear that I was fine because the smile returned to her face, and she turned her attention to the food on the table.

"What you want to eat first? Is there something else you want?"

"Ma, I want sum shicken!" Man jumped out of the chair he was sitting in and grabbed a pack of buffalo hot wings off the table, bypassing the cheeseburger, BBQ rib sandwich and various bags of chips.

"I want sum shicken," he repeated, looking between my mother and me as if we weren't listening.

"Okay, baby." I took the pack out of his hands and gave it to my mother. He smiled, pleased with me. Hot wings had become a regular for him whenever he visited with me. But I had to remove the skin and the meat from the bone in order for him to eat it. I didn't mind; it gave me a sense of purpose. It was an opportunity to know what it felt like to feed my child, in some sense, fix him something to eat.

Outside of taking a picture, the next four or five hours were spent sitting at that table watching Man's every move, recognizing how he had grown, the sentences he made, how much money he knew how to count and discovering if there was anything else that little mind wanted to know. As I looked over at the clock and realized that time was swiftly approaching for visitation to end, a slight heaviness mounted my shoulders.

"So, baby, what does Momma's big boy want for Christmas?" I asked as Man sat in my lap facing me.

"I want you to see my presents under the tree." His handsome face lit up.

"I wish I could," I sang, smiling back to meet his excitement, but emotion gripped my throat.

"Momma, there go the police right there." He pointed toward the correctional officer who had been walking around the room periodically. "If you ask, she may let you come spend the night at my house." He swiftly turned his head to face my mother. "Right, Nana? Momma can come spend the night? She can sleep in my bed." My mother gave him a gentle smile and looked at me. He rushed back around to face me. "Momma, you don't want to come to my house?" Confusion slowly crept across his face.

"Baby, I would give my life just to lay next to you for one night."

"Well, let's go then!" He grabbed my shoulders and attempted to get down.

"Man, look at me." I picked him up and placed him comfortably back on my lap. Held his precious face in my hands. My heart gradually sunk to my stomach as my insides began to ache. "Look at me," I gently instructed, again. He searched my face for answers. "Do you know that I love you with everything that I am?" He nodded yes. "Good, and I need

127

you to try to understand that Momma has been a bad girl, and my actions had nothing to do with you. It's not your fault, okay?"

"O . . . okay," he spoke, barely over a whisper.

"And Momma being a bad girl is the reason I can't see your presents under the tree, or hold you at night." I sat there staring in his face trying to prepare myself for whatever he might ask.

Silence.

"Okay, Momma. I understand. We just pray, like you tell me." He leaned up and kissed me. I wrapped him into my embrace and held him for as long as he allowed. I didn't want him to see the tear that managed to escape my eye. *Lord, how long will it be before he wants to know exactly what I did to be a bad girl?*

CHAPTER 24

The month of December seemed to be the best time of the year in prison. Various prison ministries made the most of the Christmas season. Gay Hatcher, this elderly, very wealthy widow had a prison ministry named after herself, and she faithfully donated to all 1,300 women. The gift bags contained lotion, shampoo and conditioner, baby powder, toothpaste and toothbrush, some emery boards, greeting cards or stationary and envelopes. A pen and a pencil. We received the gift bag after we sat through a brief program of someone explaining the birth of Jesus and joined the minister in singing a few traditional Christmas songs

Another ministry gave us a few bars of soap and a Bible. Joyce Myers' ministry gave us a bottle of shampoo, but I received one of her books, *Me and My Big Mouth*. It was very encouraging knowing that even though we were locked up, God had touched the hearts of His people and used them to remind us that He loves us, and we are not forgotten.

Even the warden gave the entire compound a bag of common snacks. For some, these gift bags were all that they would receive. But for those of us who had financial support, we were able to receive a package from home, and Ken maxed out everything I was able to receive, just as I asked. For those who may have forgotten who Ken is, he was my Public Defender and the reason I wasn't indigent, like most Lifers. He sent me four bars of Lever 2000 soap, a pack of T-shirts, panties, socks, thermal set, white sweater, Clinique Happy Hearts perfume, dry shampoo and leave-in conditioner for my locks, three bars of Secret gel deodorant. Cashews, smoked almonds, and two five-pound bags of candy (Jolly Ranchers and peppermint candy). Yeah, I'm an old lady! And how can I forget unlimited cookies! I'm not even sure of the variety of all the cookies, but I know Famous Amos oatmeal and raisin. Chips-Ahoy chewy chocolate chip are my favorite and I had plenty of them. Oreos were Jayden's favorite, so I gave her some for a Christmas present. Being that Jayden and I worked together, we ended up going to pick up our package on the same day, and it just so happened that whoever sent her a package didn't have her cookies, so I was like her cookie monster hero. The cookies I didn't eat, I gave to people who didn't receive a package.

The moment I walked in the door to my dormitory, I could feel the shift in the atmosphere. It was extremely loud! Grown women were running back and forth across the dorm showing off their new clothes, comparing hygiene products, and trying to bargain each other out of their perfume cream. It resembled a playground to say the least. I was relieved to see them excited instead of fussing and fighting, but I wondered how a child would view their mother if they could see her demeanor when she's at her worst.

A week hadn't passed by when we suddenly got the news that our warden, Nay Nickman was leaving, and we were getting a new warden. I didn't know much about the man, but I respected him, especially being a successful black man because he seemed to be about his business. Handling your concerns on the spot and not procrastinating. But I was most impressed that if you wrote him a letter, he would tell you to personally give it to him and not his staff because then he may not get it. Every day he walked the compound in a three-piece suit with a bottle of water, and someone held an umbrella over him. A lot of us used to tease that he carried himself like a pimp. So, it was a little sad seeing him go. The warden's impending absence created a lot of anxiety, especially not knowing who you would get next, but at times like that you have to trust God, keeping in mind that He knows the plans He has for you.

Nate Nickman's replacement, Mr. Tim Chipman came from a men's prison, and in his first week it was obvious this man was being used by God. All the things that Mr. Nickman wouldn't approve for us to have in our December package, Warden Chipman did. He permitted us to order a second package to receive a housecoat, face cloths, towels, and electric clippers. I couldn't put myself up to ask Ken, being that he had already been such a blessing, so I prayed about it and took a chance by asking my mother.

"Ma!" I couldn't hide my excitement as she answered the phone.

"Hey, Boo! Did you get the stuff Ken sent you? It should be there by now. I took it to the post office weeks ago."

"Yes, ma'am. Thank you." I could have kicked myself. I was becoming so consumed with the 'prison life,' I neglected to tell my mother I received my package. "I apologize for not calling and letting you know."

"Well, did you at least write Ken and tell him thank you?"

"Most definitely!"

"So, what's going on? Why you sound so excited?" I was elated that she asked.

"Well . . . you remember I told you about the new warden coming and what not?"

"Yeah." It was apparent I had her on edge.

"He just approved for us to get another package.

"Okay. So does that mean I can send you something, too?" *See, stuff like this is the reason I love this lady! Always on standby,* I thought.

"Well, if it's not too much to ask, I would like a housecoat, a towel, face cloth and some electric clippers."

"I would love to!" Her tone met my excitement.

"Really, Momma, that's not too much?" I didn't ask her to begin with because I felt the responsibility of having my son was enough. I wasn't about to ask her to spend close to two hundred dollars or more on me, especially when she solely had to get his Christmas presents.

"Too much? Is it possible I can throw you a bag of candy in there too?"

"I don't see why you can't try!" We both laughed. I got off the phone feeling like my mother's baby!

Two weeks later, I was at the mailroom picking up a long lavender cloth robe, electric leg trimmers, and a bag of Welch's candy. Ma had picked me out a face cloth and towel to match my robe, and I couldn't receive it because it had to be white or beige. So I sent it to my grandmother for Christmas.

The incentive we received during this holiday season are items that aren't normally sold in the commissary but are available to order. This particular year, Ms. Forest, our pantry supervisor, managed to satisfy the entire compound! She added jalapeno squeeze cheese, tortilla chips, tortilla wraps, salsa, salami summer sausage, pound cake, Christmas cookies, Zest body wash, Dark and Lovely shampoo and conditioner. Jayden helped me understand the importance of stacking up on these items so I would still have them during the months to come. So, that's what I did, but making poor decisions seemed to be my MO.

This particular evening on the weekend, I decided I would take Jayden a few bottles of cheese and salsa for her to store in her locker. I stuffed the four bottles in the lining of my pants and panties and reported to dinner when my dorm was called. Her dorm hadn't been called yet, so I stalled and went to go stand in the pill call line until I spotted Jayden, then hurried to get in line with her. She spotted me and started smiling, extending her arms for a hug. We met up a couple feet away from her dorm.

"Girl, I miss you!" she proclaimed as she maintained her embrace, never breaking eye contact.

"Yeah, you better!" I teased, soaking up the attention.

"What is all this I feel?" she inquired, rubbing my waist.

"Just some stuff for you." I smiled, pleased with myself. She reached out for it. "You can wait till we on our way back to get it." She nodded like she agreed, took my hand, and we fell in line with the rest of the dorm. We were laughing and talking about nothing in particular as we entered the chow hall. "Why weren't you in line with your dorm?" the short, butchy, dark-skinned lieutenant walked up to me and asked.

"I was in the pill call line," I answered her directly, yet respectfully.

I wasn't looking for a fight. Not today. I just wanted to eat dinner with my boo thang and go back to the dorm and miss her some more. Hoping they called some kind of outside activity. She didn't say anything else, just mugged me as I proceeded to get my tray and followed the line to the next available table. Once she gave permission for my table to put our trays in the dish room window, she called out for me.

"Blakely!" I looked across the chow hall and stared at her. "Come sit right here. You going with me." I looked at Jayden and rolled my eyes. That quickly, all the happiness I felt left my body. This broad was picking with me, and I wasn't taking it too kindly.

"I love you," Jayden said as I went to go sit in the chair the lieutenant pointed out.

The last dorm she had to feed was already coming in the door. I felt myself getting agitated as I observed other people who stayed in other dorms walk in the door with their folks, and even more so when people kept asking me why this broad had me just sitting there.

Once the chow hall was clear, she walked me over to Medical where I spotted my roommate in the pill call line.

"What the fuck?" she mouthed as I walked in behind the lieutenant.

"Did this inmate come in here to take medicine?" she asked the male officer who ran Medical. I chuckled to myself, already predicting how this was about to go down. I wished I would have passed off this stuff to Jayden. *Lord, please keep me*, I prayed.

He looked over at me and reluctantly answered, "No, ma'am."

"Oh, so you lied to me!" Her lil' short round ass started screaming.

"Actually, I didn't. I said I was 'in' the pill call line," I stated as I stepped backward toward the door. Her tone was rubbing me the wrong way.

"You know what, inmate—" She stopped short on her threat and glared at me with such hatred, I couldn't help but feel her pressure with me was personal. *Was one of my victims her loved ones?* I thought.

"Let's go!" she yelled as she turned on her heels and burst through the door we had just entered, almost bumping into me! She was so enraged, the other lieutenant that sat in security came running out to meet her as she approached their office door.

"Cuff that inmate!" she yelled at him as soon as the door swung open, before he had a chance to ask what was going on. He looked around, I assumed looking for a commotion, someone showing signs of hostility, anything. There was none. I stood opposite them, still in front of medical trying to keep my composure. Slowly, the time bomb began ticking within.

"That one right there!" she screamed as she pointed at me. Everything seemed to move in slow motion as officers just began to appear from everywhere, male officers at that. For some reason, in my mind it was a set-up! This minor issue was being blown out of proportion and was obviously being used as an opportunity to cause me harm.

"Lord, keep me!" I prayed over and over as I stood there in silence. The medical officer approached me from behind and began to cuff one of my wrists.

"Bring her in here!" The Smurf made her last request before she snatched open the door to security.

"Nah! Whatever you gon' do, do out here!" I flipped! I wasn't about to be restrained and jumped behind closed doors. They would have to take me down right here outside in the open, so I could have witnesses to what happened to me. "If I'm going to jail, let's go because I'm not going in there!" I didn't even realize it, but I was yelling just as loud as the lieutenant. Somehow, amongst all the chaos, I managed to hear my roommate begging me to corporate.

"I'm not going in there cuffed up! I haven't done shit!" I continued to rant in my defense.

"Please, young lady, just comply before I have to use force," the male officer spoke calmly in my ear.

"Do what you got to do! Jump me out here!" Slowly a crowd was forming. People stopped walking down the walk. No one was getting their meds anymore, and everything around me was becoming a blur. All I can remember is screaming, being shoved into the security building, and another officer joining the medical officer to finish cuffing me.

"Take your hands off me! Fight me outside! Y'all like fucking with people, fight me outside where everyone can see!" I was losing my mind and couldn't see I was making the situation worse! Somehow I ended up on the floor, and the first thing I did was sit on my butt and slide my arms underneath me, so my cuffs could be in the front. Just in case I needed to swing and adjust my bottles of cheese and salsa. The lieutenant stood opposite her desk, a few feet away looking like she would pounce on me any second.

"Bring that inmate in here!" she demanded. I refused to get up, sitting right outside her office.

"Come get me!" I demanded. I had long lost my ability to be logical. I was being treated unfairly, and there was no way I was going to cooperate.

"I said bring her in here!" Smurf slammed her hand down on the desk, a clear sign she was losing her cool too.

"I need you to get up." The medical officer looked down at me with empathy in his eyes. "Please, don't make this worse than what it is."

"Y'all can go—" As I was about to curse them out, I spotted Jayden in the window. Somebody must have told him what the deal was.

"Please!" was all I could make of what she was saying. "Please!"

Please what? Don't show my behind? Don't let them beat me up? Don't go to lockdown? I pondered.

"Don't do it!" she yelled through the door. I didn't give a damn about what she saying either, but the desperation in her eyes sent chills through me and wrapped itself around some of my hostility.

It was a few days short of Christmas and just a few more before her birthday; she didn't want to spend it without me, I assumed. I looked back in the direction of the door where she was standing. Her watery eyes appeared as if she was about to cry any second. Slowly I stood to my feet and reluctantly walked over to the threshold.

"Inmate, I'm writing you up for lying! And if you don't settle down, your ass going to lockdown!" She glared at me like she wanted to come across the desk and cut my throat. I matched her stare. Without breaking eye contact with her, I sized up everyone in the room. Four dudes and her, they'd probably beat me into a pool of blood, but a part of me didn't care. I didn't appreciate being called a liar. I had done many things in my life, and as a result was labeled many things, but my mouth hadn't uttered a lie, and for that reason I wanted to be vindicated.

"It's not my fault you wasn't listening when I answered you." I was getting tired of saying the same thing, and now Jayden and my roommate were at another window staring at me, pleading with me to comply.

"Your mouth is going to get you in a lot trouble," she retorted. I rolled my eyes. I was over this. Whatever they were going to do, they would do. I just stood there looking at Smurf as if she was wasting my time.

About twenty minutes later, I was leaving with a disciplinary report. My charge was for lying, but the offense said I was unauthorized. Jayden took one look at it and told me it was written wrong, and it would get dismissed! I couldn't help but wonder if she wrote it wrong on purpose, or if God was intervening on my behalf?

CHAPTER 25

You know how a bootlegger posts up on the block always selling something? During my youth he would walk around with a trench coat on, and when he opened it, he had everything you could possibly want! Rolls and rolls of pockets with merchandise in them. This white girl named Jen was like that when it came to jewelry. Her family owned a jewelry shop, and she would keep plenty of rings, necklaces, and earrings. So for Jayden's birthday, my dumb behind decided to purchase a wedding set and gave it to her. She put the ring with the stone on my hand and wore the band. You couldn't tell me I wasn't wifey now! Proud to wear the title of a broad who was most likely cheating on me! And another thing, that wifey mess ain't cute! It means you bear the characteristics of a wife, you do everything a wife should do, but you're not enough to actually *be* the wife; your spouse just *enjoys* the *benefits* of *you*, but isn't quite ready to actually make you the wife. So do yourself a favor and stop grinning when your spouse says, "This is my wifey."

My miserable behind flashed the biggest smile whenever we were together. People often commented about how cute and loving of a couple we were. From the outside looking in, we had something real! The kind of thing that was rare in prison, and I would have believed it myself, but I couldn't ignore my gut feeling.

Valentine's Day had swiftly approached, and we were setting records because we had been together five months! Surely, we were in love, or that's the lie women in prison like to believe. As if time equaled substance! Time meant motive. In here, a lot of people have their own personal agendas, and they have their selfish reasons for being with you. It's wise if you take out the time to discover why, so you won't be under false pretenses.

"Baby, I need you to meet me outside when count clear tonight,"

Jayden said as we walked from work, referring to seven o'clock count that evening.

"Why? You got me something for Valentine's?" I beamed, gripping her hand that was already intertwined with mine.

"Just make sure you meet me." She smiled and leaned over to peck my lips. My heartbeat sped up, but not from her touch; I didn't know if any police were standing somewhere watching as she kissed me. I was always on the lookout of my surroundings, especially when I was with her because Jayden had a mouth on her, and she didn't mind pissing people off. I never wanted to give someone the opportunity to catch me nor her slipping.

Count cleared that night, and I somehow convinced the officer to let me out the door. The sun was setting and the walk was pretty much empty, so I could clearly see if Jayden was anywhere walking around. I managed to get someone's attention who looked in her room and told me she wasn't in the building. I looked for her in the library, the dining hall, and security. I couldn't find her anywhere. Church would have to be the only other place she could be, but that didn't make sense. She wasn't a Christian.

"Why would she tell me to meet her out here and not show up?" I asked aloud as I headed to church. After I walked in, it only took a few seconds to spot Jayden sitting on the fourth row next to MeMe with her arm draped across the back of MeMe's chair. For some strange reason my feelings weren't even hurt. I could only laugh to myself. *This nigga told me to meet him after count to assure I wouldn't come to church!* I entertained the idea of walking up and punching Jayden in the face on the strength of principle, but I respected the Lord's house. I sat on the bleachers in the back of the gym, centered in between the rows of chairs, so when he got up to leave he would see that I had been able to see him.

The service ended and my adrenaline began to pump. Some people formed a line to speak personally with the outside volunteers and minister who had delivered the message. Others got up and greeted their friends, while a few couples made their way toward the exit. Jayden was in the latter and had her head down as she eased out of the row behind her date. I stayed put with my leg crossed, mugging her like the scum on the bottom of my shoe, willing her to look up and face me. Slowly she raised her head, it appeared that shame rested across her face until she locked eyes with me. Her eyebrows immediately kissed in horror as her mouth opened to say something, but she lost her footing and stumbled a few steps, but caught her balance before she hit the floor. Her less than five feet Asian date stumbled forward but was saved by a bystander. Nonchalantly, I got up and walked over to speak with a volunteer hoping to blend in, where I stayed until the gym was cleared, and I was almost the last person to leave the gym. I knew better than to believe Jayden would have just gone on to the dorm, but I did hope so. I didn't want to talk to her. I had been on the compound long enough to know that MeMe was a check. She was known for spoiling the studs she was with and that was cool, but all Jayden had to do was tell me what was up, and I could have walked her through it. And established what boundaries she couldn't cross. That was the previous lifestyle I had grown accustomed to. I respected her need to make sure we both ate. She would have had her wifey and her money too. But she tried to play me, and that's where our problem lied.

Something about the cool night air, the sound of crickets, and the way the stars decorated the sky had always given me a peace. Quietly, I walked down the walk, past the Programs building and Education. Instead of turning in front of Education to head toward the big side of the compound, I kept walking straight ahead toward Medical to go take my medicine.

"Falicia." I heard Jayden call me as I passed Education. I wasn't surprised she was still out here lurking around. Nor did I have to look behind me to know she was following me.

I busted a sharp left, but instead of stopping in the pill call line, I sped past Security and tried to rush down the walk. A few seconds passed before I heard my name again. I had no intentions of stopping, and for some absurd reason my heart was racing. I bypassed her dorm and was about to make a right and take off running to my dorm when Jayden grabbed me from behind.

"So, you just going to act like you don't hear me calling you?"

"Leave me alone, Jay." I pulled at her arms in an attempt to free myself from her grip. "What's already understood don't have to be explained."

"What the fuck that mean?" she questioned, refusing to release me.

"It's done. That's where you want to be, leave me alone." For the first time all night I felt myself getting emotional.

"Everything ain't what it look like . . ."

"I don't care!" I was losing my composure. "It's Valentine's Day and you sitting up in church with another bitch, when you should've been with me! Leave me alone." I dug my nails into her arm until she released me.

"Falicia . . ." She ran in front of me. "Please, at least hear me out. Baby, it's not what it looks like!" She stood in front of me looking pitiful, one hand extended to my chest trying to keep me from walking away and the other hand on her chest, like she was in some form of pain.

"Baby, you got to understand I love you." She reached in her pants and began pulling out a card and something else out. I slapped it out of her hand and walked away. I refused to let her see me cry. She had proven to me what I suspected all along. It wouldn't be the last time I let her hurt me though.

I heard the dorm next door, E8-A didn't have a dorm wash orderly next door, and I immediately stepped to the counselor. Not only did I apply for the position, I signed up for the Faith and Character program. Which is a program set in motion by the Department of Corrections for the purpose of enlightening offenders of all religious backgrounds and providing them with the skills necessary to not only enable them to live out their fullest potential by walking in character and transformation of their personal life, but also equip others with the same skills. I was convinced one of the two had to set me free. By nobody's grace other than God's, I was throwing up the deuces to Satan's advocate.

CHAPTER 26

My roommate tried everything possible to get me to tell her what happened, but I wouldn't budge. Instead, I just lay in bed with my head covered and cried. I suppose after she concluded I had cried long enough, she would intervene. I felt her tapping my shoulder.

"Here . . ." She extended her hand as she stroked my back with the opposite hand. Slowly, I sat up and faced her. She had two small purple pills in her hand and my cup filled with water. "Take these, they'll make you feel better."

"What is this?" I questioned. I hadn't taken anything since I had first gotten locked up in the county jail.

"Take it." She extended her hand some more. I didn't consider my options, instead I took them from her hand and tossed them in my mouth, then chased it with some water. She took the cup from me, handed me a cassette player, headphones and a Donnie McClurkin tape, *Live in London* and more, *The Rebirth of Kirk Franklin*, then cut the light back off and left out the room.

I put the Donnie tape in and pressed play. Immediately the song "Didn't You Know" began playing. Something about the lyrics of the song made me feel God was sitting right there on the bunk with me, bearing the burden that I was carrying too. As if He had dethroned Himself and picked me up from the rut I had willingly climbed in. Tears soaked my pillow, but this time it was because I was beginning to realize I wasn't alone. God had seen everything that I was enduring, and He wasn't judging me. He wanted to help me. He loved me. I lay there for an hour listening to that song. By now, my lips had begun to feel numb, and everything was tingling. I got down to pee, and even my feet felt foreign against the floor. Simply sitting on the toilet and trying to climb back on my bunk several times before I was successful, brought me much humor. I wasn't sure what I had taken, but sadness was the furthest thing on my mind.

The next day came and went without me. I only got up once to use the bathroom and to eat a Lil Debbie cake. That simple snack cake made me feel like I had taken those pills all over again. I was oblivious to the fact Jayden had come looking for me, and sent me lunch and dinner. It didn't matter. I hadn't taken a shower all day or brushed my teeth. All that mattered was that my body demanded sleep, and I was a slave to its command.

The following day came and I was still in bed. My roommate was concerned and she woke me up to eat. I was definitely still under the influence of whatever psychiatric medication I had taken, but I knew I needed to shower. It took a lot of effort to do simple things like lift my arms or turn over in bed. My body was tired, and everything seemed to move in slow motion. It wasn't an easy task, but I gathered my things and headed to the shower.

Not long after I had slipped into a fresh T-shirt and shorts, someone came knocking on my door like they were the police.

"Fe!" the female voice yelled as if she had been running. "Fe!"

"What?" I screamed from the inside as I pushed the button that unlocked my door. Slowly, it slid back.

"Jay told me to run down here and get you. He's at church waiting for you!" The young girl spoke hastily, as if her life depended on it.

"Oh well." I grabbed my door in an attempt to close it.

"Fe, she's worried about you. She has been coming over here all weekend looking for you, bringing you something to eat, and Meat tells her you're in bed every time. If you don't go to church, she'll probably come up in here unauthorized," the girl concluded, holding my door open. I was too weak to snatch it out of her hands or to stand there for that matter. I walked over to my stool and sat down. She invited herself into my room.

"Fe, Jay really loves you." She volunteered her opinion.

"Girl, don't nobody feel like hearing all that." I wasn't in the mood.

"Okay, that's cool, but I'm going to need you to get dressed." She grabbed my Reeboks from under the bed and my uniform from off the bed rail.

"I don't feel like going anywhere." I pushed her hand away that held up my uniform.

"Falicia, please . . . don't do him like this. If you could have seen him, you would understand why I'm standing in your room begging you to hurry up and get dressed. I looked up at her. She had only been one of several who brought me a message or something from Jayden from time to time, and now she was standing in front of me about to cry. It touched me.

In less than fifteen minutes later, I was at the gym about to sit next to Jayden in church a few rows back from where she had been sitting with MeMe a couple of nights ago.

"Oh, Allah!" she exclaimed as she jumped up at the sight of my presence, wrapping her arms around me. Naturally, I tensed up. Hoping she would release me before I flipped. But instead of protesting, I just waited for her to release me, so I could sit down. "Baby, what the fuck?" I shot her a mean stare because she was cursing in church.

"I meant, what the heck?" She made an attempt to clean it up. I rolled my eyes and crossed my leg away from her. I thought maybe seeing her would fill me with compassion, and I would just forgive her, but I wanted to hit her instead. "So why you been in bed all weekend?" She made another attempt. I didn't even look her way. "Baby, I have been worried about you."

"Girl, please . . ." I looked at her and sucked my teeth. She stared at me for a few seconds.

"Are you . . . are you high?" A hint of disgust filled her tone. Instead of answering, I just plopped my elbow on the back of the empty chair next to me and rested my head on my hand. "I know good and fuckin' well my woman is not fuckin' high!" She was beginning to get a little louder and obnoxious.

"Jayden, stop disrespecting these people services," I spat back.

143

"Stop ignoring me!" She punched herself in the chest. "Why are you high?" She propped her elbows on her knees and stared at me.

"It's a long story, but why do you care? You all out here sneaking with MeMe. Don't worry about if I'm high or not!"

"Falicia! You don't pop pills."

"I am going to say it again. You were not concerned about how your actions would affect me before you did your lil' unnecessary, so don't worry about my state now."

I wish I could say that was the end of Jayden and me. Considering the emotional toll her actions took on me, it should have been, but just like most women in unhealthy relationships, she somehow managed to finesse her way back in. And like every reunion when we take a lover back, she was on her best behavior at first, and I could only think about why I loved her so much to begin with. But hurt people only hurt people, and a broken woman has no idea how to make you whole. The final straw didn't take long to present itself.

Our relationship was on the rocks because she had expressed how a black girl named Cornbread had tried to have sex with her, and they were still cool. My roommate had made some very strong sexual passes at me and all hell broke out, though I distanced myself afterward. Jayden felt I should have went to jail and got put in another room.

One evening I was doing Meat's hair as usual during four o'clock count. She would pay me to twist it up in some style every other week.

"Hmm, I can feel heat coming off of you," Meat commented as she sat at the desk and stool nailed into the wall behind our lockers. I stood behind her dressing her hair.

"Really? Because I'm not hot. It's kind of cool in here," I answered, oblivious to the direction the conversation was going.

"Uh hmm, I'm talking about the warmth coming from between your legs," she boldly corrected me.

What in the world? I questioned, not sure how to reply, or if I even should. One thing was for sure, I did not, under *any* circumstances find her attractive.

"Meat, it's not—"

"I just want to touch you," she cut me off.

"Girl, I got a girlfriend and so do you!" I was taken aback. I had been in the room with this broad for months, and I would have never suspected she looked at me like this. She had become kind of like an aunt or somebody to me.

"You and me both know that sorry piece of shit ain't being faithful to you, so why you worrying about her?" I was glad her back was to me because I couldn't believe what I was hearing. I didn't say anything else, I just tried to speed up and get done with her hair.

"Falicia, you don't have to put your mouth on me, just touch me. I have been thinking about what it would feel like if you would just touch me." Now maybe I was lame or scared as shit, but the thought of touching the almost three-hundred-pound, five foot woman made my hands shake. There was no way I was doing that.

"I'm good," was all I mustered up the courage to say. I had been in some dangerous situations before and talked my way out of them, but *this* left me speechless. She allotted me a few minutes of silence as I finished up her hair. "Touch me, come touch me," Meat cooed in a sensual voice as I washed my hands.

"Go 'head on, Meat," I stated, once I turned and noticed she was pulling her shorts off and lying back on her bed.

"You scared? Is that what this is about?" She looked me straight in the face. I couldn't believe she was serious!

"I just . . . I just don't . . ." I stumbled over my words. *Lord, please let count clear,* I prayed.

"Just what, Falicia? Nobody has to know." I walked toward the ladder so I could climb on my bed, but her round behind was quick and grabbed my leg before I could get on the first step.

"You scared . . ." She pulled me gently toward her.

"I'm not scared! I just don't want to." I was both scared and disgusted.

"You don't have to be afraid of me," she said, nearly above a whisper as she leaned back onto the bed. "Touch me like you like to be touched." I watched as she spread her extremely thick thighs.

"Come on," she encouraged.

I'm not doing that! I thought. She was a beautiful woman, but she wasn't my type, nor did I appreciate her trying to seduce me like this, and her girl stayed about six doors down from us.

"Nah, I want to see you touch it," I lied, trying not to show my true feelings on my face. In silent repulsion, I watched her spread her legs even further, reach past her stomach and pull the hood of her clit back and begin to play with herself.

"Now, you come do it," she instructed.

"No, let me see you make yourself cum." I sat on the desk and looked at her. She whined a bit, and then began playing with herself again. Seconds passed, and I heard the officer announce count was cleared. I got up without saying a word and walked out the room without looking back and locked the door behind me. God had answered my prayer and let me get the hell out of there! The subject never came up again, until I told Jayden and she made a scene on the walk after dinner shortly after the incident. She carried on and on until Carla, Meat's girlfriend, asked what the problem was! The perfect opportunity for Jayden.

"Your bitch trying to fuck my bitch!" she screamed.

"Excuse me?" Carla asked.

"Baby, she's not talking to us," Meat lied.

"Your nasty ass wife trying to fuck mine!" Jayden screamed again.

"Jayden, please!" I pleaded, grabbing her by her arm. "You're embarrassing me." I looked around at all the people whose attention Jay had averted. Meat had her arm intertwined with Carla, and they were walking toward the dorm.

"Fat, nasty bitch!" Jayden yelled.

"Really?" I shouted and snatched my hands from her arm. "I have to live with these folks. You do the stupidest things sometimes." With that, I stormed away to my dorm.

After that, Meat and I barely spoke, only notifying each other if it was count time so we could get up and stand by our door. No other words were exchanged.

This Caucasian woman, who appeared to be about twenty-five but was actually older, had the intellect of someone even younger. I'll call her Marilyn. She got out of lockdown and became Jayden's roommate. At this point, we had been trying to get Jayden moved into the dorm with me. She had made an agreement with the unit manager that if she stayed out of trouble for a certain amount of months, he would move her, but that time had come and gone. She was still housed in the behavior dorm. At first, Jayden seemed to be helping her roommate Marilyn. Keeping people from getting over on her when it came to two for one-ing, those that borrowed stuff from her, or simply making her spend her money more wisely. Now the first thing that raised an eyebrow for me was one morning Jayden was ranting and raving about the 'dumb bitch' who gave away all of her detergent!

"We take turns purchasing Clorox (for colors) and mix it with a box of Tide. It's cheaper that way." She further elaborated when I asked why they shared detergent.

"I know how you are about your *stuff*, so I still don't understand why you're sharing *your stuff* with this broad?" A clear explanation was never given, but months later it all came together when the rumor surfaced that Marilyn went to Protective Custody because Jayden had been whooping her with fan cords for being disrespectful. Of course, she denied it. Denied they had been having sex too, but people don't flip and get physical because someone won't listen to them! If they want to give all their money away, it's their money! Not yours, or is it? I just wanted her to leave me alone, and when she wouldn't, I threw my boots in a trash can by the gym on my way to church service one Saturday. So when Monday came, I couldn't report out to my detail because I didn't have the proper gear.

There was a Caucasian girl, about five feet, seven inches, stout with a diabetic shape. Big up top and small from the waist down named Diego who worked on sanitation with Jayden and me, plus she stayed in the dorm with me. Diego hadn't admitted she was digging me, but it had showed in her actions. Several times I had to talk her good mental-health behind out of fighting Jayden because she'd heard something disrespectful or she had upset me. At first we always hung out together and watched TV. She asked to go to chow with me whenever I wasn't waiting for Jayden. She called me boo, and too often I caught her staring when I was getting out the shower with that ol' perverted, 'I'll drink your bath water' expression! Disgusting! But she was funny and cool to be around. We had even eaten together plenty of times on the weekend, until I found out she was bulimic. For some reason the thought of her wasting my money, throwing up my food pissed me off. I had had several extensive conversations about the dangers of being bulimic, and no matter how hard I begged, she wouldn't go to medical and get help. She told me she would stop, and I was holding her to it.

"Hey, boo!" She didn't knock or wait for an invitation to come in. She pulled my door open and walked in, straight from work and leaned against the door frame.

"What's up?" I looked up from my word search, as I sat on the top bunk. I knew she had a message or an update for me.

"Girl, you should have seen that lame questioning the police about why you weren't there."

"Honey, I'm not studden that girl." I set my attention back on my puzzle.

"Well . . ." I could hear the reluctance in her voice. "She told me to tell you that you better bring your ass to work tomorrow." I didn't even have to look up at her to know her face was twisted up. She had taken the remark as a threat.

"I guess someone will be disappointed because I'm not going. Thank you for the message though." I turned over to my side and faced the wall. I was done discussing Jayden.

"Falicia, if that motherfuc—"

"Diego, chill with that," I cut her off. "She's not going to put her hands on me. Now, go take your shower, relax or something." She stood in the same position as she registered what I had said.

"See you later," she said after a few seconds of silence, but she didn't move. I turned to faced her.

"Girl, stop looking at me and get out of here!" I snapped. She just laughed and walked out. It was sad how well I knew her. She was weak for me, and I didn't find that appealing. I was attracted to a woman with some backbone. Someone who was a little rebellious.

I managed to remain out of work all week. I would get in the shower around the time she was getting off, just in case she came looking for me, I had a legit excuse why I couldn't come to the window, but I got plenty of letters that week. I didn't go to the store that week, so I didn't have a reason to run into Jayden. I wasn't surprised when I received a net bag full of food. I went to my room and got down on my knees and prayed.

"Lord, I need you open an avenue of financial blessings for me. I want to stop dealing with this girl, but it's times like this that I struggle with my decision to completely cut her off. Because in all honesty, I don't have to want for anything with her." I had been asking God for the strength to leave her alone, and I recognized this was one of the reason it was so hard to let go. The ultimate reason was because I loved her, despite what she did. I loved the young girl I had fallen for. Her issues didn't take away from that; though I deserved to hold her responsible for her actions because it affected me in a major way! And it was time for her to grow up. I couldn't just keep loving someone who couldn't appreciate the kind of love I had to offer. So I spent much time in prayer, asking for Jayden to have a change of heart, or to mature, or something . . . promising that if God got me out of this, I wouldn't go back.

CHAPTER 27

It was going on the third week since I had been off work, and half the compound had been telling me how Jayden had been showing out, upset because I wasn't being forced to come back to work. I knew it would only be a matter of time before I was called out, or was unable to avoid her.

That day was "chicken on the bone," as we called it. Simply oven fried chicken for dinner. Diego asked to go with me and I agreed. Thinking that if Jayden just so happened to run into me, she wouldn't show her butt too much with Diego's mental health behind lurking nearby. We not only ate in peace, I only had to see Jayden through the window, and she was being all dramatic, looking pitiful as if she missed me. I wasn't falling for it, but I would be lying if I said I wasn't disturbed. I just wanted to get to my room so I could pray. Diego took notice of the change in my disposition, and against my better judgment, I opened up to her about how it sadden me to see Jayden looking so sad.

"Fuck him! He should have thought about all the shit he was doing! Especially, when he had a good ass woman riding for him," she retorted, as we walked up to our dorm.

"Shh, Diego!" I snapped, looking around. "I don't want everybody in my business!" She just looked at me. Who was I fooling? Everybody already knew what Jayden had been doing. Most people were probably grateful to see I was finally starting to get some back bone.

"I'm just saying, some of us wish we had someone like you to give our heart to, and Jay out here playing games, doing the most." She finally spoke again once we were in the dorm sitting at a table alone. All I could do was sigh.

"I just hope God cuts our soul ties, or let her move on or something . . . Anything to make this easier for me." I knew by the longing in

Diego's eyes that she wasn't the best person to have this conversation with.

"Falicia, I need to ask you something." Her tone got really serious. I took a deep breath, trying to brace myself.

"What, Diego? What is it you want to ask me?" I tried not to look as if she was about to piss me off.

"Is there . . . I'll be right back!" Suddenly she jumped up.

"No, sit down." I grabbed her arm. "Say it now," I said, wondering why the sudden need to get up.

"I'll be right back. Just give me a second." She was adamant about it. Not realizing she had a genuine need to dismiss herself, I started horse playing with her. Trying to make her sit back down and spit out whatever it was she was trying to say. She flipped me off her back and rushed toward the steps. "For real, ma. I'll be right back." I stood there dumbfounded as I watched her race to her room. She attempted to sling her door shut behind her as she doubled over, vomiting in her toilet. She had been making herself vomit up her food for so long that it naturally came up on its own.

"This bitch!" I couldn't believe she was still doing that. My heart ached for her, but my anger flared exponentially. "And I believed this dumb broad!" I turned on my heels and went to my room and locked the door.

About ten minutes passed before I came out and headed to the shower. Diego was fast on my heels.

"So, we gonna finish talking?" She was her normal smiling self.

"Let me ask you something." I stopped mid-step and pointed my finger at her. "What did you do when you went upstairs?"

"Nothing, just brushed my teeth," she answered calmly.

"So, you just looked me in my face and lied!" She couldn't say anything; she just looked at me. "You been just wasting my money, looking me in my face every day acting like you have stopped, and the entire time, you still throwing up your food?" She opened her mouth to say something. "Save it! When you had the chance to keep it real with me, you wouldn't. Stay out my face! I'm not going to sit around and watch you kill yourself!" With that, I walked away and got in the shower. When I got out she was nowhere in sight, but there was a letter on my bed. I opened my door wide so she could see. I figured she was standing in her cell across the dorm, with the lights off watching me. I grabbed her note and held it over the stainless steel toilet and flushed it without reading it. Then I closed my door all the way.

The next morning they called me to work, but when I showed up and explained to my supervisors that I didn't have any boots, they allowed me to go back to the dorm. I was in and out before Jayden had a chance to know I was present.

That afternoon, Diego walked up to me as I was picking up my laundry from the shelf outside the laundry room.

"Hey, boo. How was your day?" She spoke to me like any other day. I walked past her. Not long after that, I got in the shower, and she came to the door to talk to me.

"Diego, what part of don't talk to me don't you understand?"

"So, you really ain't gonna talk to me?" she questioned as if I wasn't speaking English. I didn't respond. I can't really say why I was being so mean to her, other than the fact I was passionate about people not taking life for granted. I felt if she saw how serious I was about not dealing with her because she wouldn't get help, maybe it would encourage her to seek out help for herself.

About fifteen minutes later I was getting out, and she popped up from somewhere. "Listen, Fe . . ." Her eyes were dancing in her head.

"Damn, leave me the fuck alone! You think I'm playing witchu'? I don't want to have nothing to do with you!" I snapped and closed in the few feet that led to my cell. I went to pull my door shut, but she blocked it from closing.

"What!" I yelled, frustrated she wouldn't go away.

"Let me see your pussy," she requested, eyes wild and looking all crazy.

"What kind of shit is that?"

"I'll leave you alone if you just let me see it." Her eyes were still dancing as she looked into my eyes.

"You'll leave me alone?" I asked. Of course I knew better, but it sounded good.

"Yeah." She nodded swiftly.

"Leave me alone, like don't talk to me anymore?" She nodded swiftly again.

Bet! I thought as I stepped back and squatted gradually. I pulled my housecoat open, moved my towel, and pressed my index and bird fingers against my lips, pulling them slightly toward my abdominal area, revealing their plushness.

"Now leave me the fuck alone!" I stood upright and pushed her out my door, then slammed it in her face. She stood there speechless. I imagined she was amazed she actually saw it. But it didn't matter to me; she would never see it again. Then I had a more intriguing thought. *If something like this got back to Jayden, she would sho' nuff be done with me.* I just didn't realize how soon I would find that out.

"What the fuck!" I heard Jayden yell from across the warehouse.

I sat nonchalantly in the back of the building, hating that I had been called to work just to discover I had a brand new pair of boots waiting for me. Jayden stood near the officer's booth smiling like she was about to receive a birthday present. I didn't want to be there, and I made very little effort to hide it. I knew today wouldn't be a pleasant one for me. So, I wasn't surprised to see Jayden walking toward me like a bear approaching its prey.

"Lord, protect me," I prayed.

"Help me understand, Falicia?" She rested her hands on the portable desk I sat at, hovering over me as if I was prone to getting slap any second. Not being the kind to tell on myself, I played along.

"Help you understand what, Jay?" I sat back and folded my arms across my chest, hoping I would be able to block a hit, or get out of dodge if necessary.

"Why the fuck is everybody talking about how this white trash . . ."

She was so animated, waving her arms and taking her time with each word! "Nutting the fuck up on *my bitch* last night!"

"I'm not *your bitch*." I spoke barely over a whisper. I knew right now wasn't the time to correct her, but if I didn't speak up for myself, no one would.

"What! You are mine! Fuck you talking about? My wifey, my bitch, my woman, my girl, mine!" Her shoulders rose and fell with each breath. Though her eyes danced, it seemed she made every effort to pierce through me. I knew her well enough to know one false move, and she would attack. I looked around, and to my surprise no one seemed concerned about the scene Jayden was making, or they pretended to be oblivious because she had a way of making you want to slap the mess out of her. I didn't say a word; I just stood. She stepped in front of me.

"Falicia, do not play with me!" My heart pounded in my chest. *I could kick Diego in her rear for this!*

"If you want to talk to me, then you need to sit down and act civilized." I looked her straight in the eyes because she was the type that preyed on your weakness and fear too. "But I'm not going to talk to you, Jayden, if you're going to stand here acting like you're about to lose your temper." I sounded more confident than I felt. She didn't respond at first, just stood there glaring at me. A minute went by and she sat down at the desk. I took a deep breath as I thought about the possible outcome of this encounter. *Well . . . at least I know I loved this broad with all that I had to give.* I prepared myself for the worst. I just knew when she heard what I was about to tell her, everything would change, and I wasn't even prepared for her reaction.

I had gone outside to yard call and enjoyed the sun on what would have been my last day off. I had received a message from Jayden telling me she didn't understand how I was okay spending all this time away from her. I really didn't have much to say. She seemed to think it was okay to cheat on me, and just because she said it wasn't like that, I was supposed to be all right with it. By the time yard call was over, I was getting off, and I could see Diego's funny-shaped ass walking toward our dorm. I got up and went inside the building. After getting some fresh ice water, I stopped in front of the laundry room and was sorting through the net bags to retrieve my own.

"Hey, boo." Diego walked up next to me. Clearly, she missed the memo last night that I agreed to show her my privacy in exchange for her not speaking to me. I didn't utter a word. After I found my clothes, I sidestepped her and walked to my room, where I put my flap up to keep her from looking in. It was weird, but I felt relieved that I didn't have to concern myself with her and her mental health.

Sometime later I got in the shower. On the way there I spotted Diego sitting in the day area. By the time I was lathering my rag and scrubbing the dirt away, I heard a knock on the door. I looked beneath the door and I could tell by the legs it was Diego so I didn't answer. A few minutes passed and I felt a wind. I turned around only to discover the shower door was wide open, and Diego's dumb ass was standing there staring at me.

"Diego! Shut the damn door!" I yelled, trying to cover myself with my arms and hands as other people in the dorm realized what was going on and either stared at me or got someone else's attention so they could stare together.

"You don't want to talk to me!" she yelled, still holding the side door open.

"And you wonder why? Shut the door, with your mental-health ass!"

"Fuck you, Falicia! You don't want to talk to me . . . I'm going to jail!" She shot me a bird and stomped toward the benches beneath the TV. She plopped down in one of the seats and lit a cigarette. "Fuck you, Falicia! Fuck you and that lame ass kat you with. You'll forgive him, but you want forgive me! You won't talk to me, I'm getting the fuck out of this dorm!"

I wish I could have disappeared down the drain with the water that fell from my body! I could not believe she had just put me out there like that. I rushed to the front of the shower and pulled the door closed. My heart pounded fast and hard, and I suddenly felt as if I was suffocating!

If this got back to Jayden, it wouldn't be good for me. I tried to relax and finish up my shower, but when a herd of officers came in to escort her out, because she had a reputation of showing out, I knew this would be anything but swept under the rug.

"Stand up and put your hands behind your back!" I could hear one of the correctional officers yelling.

"You'll forgive buddy whack ass, but you hold some dumb shit against me!" Her voice triumphed over all the others.

"We can do this the easy way or the hard way!" I heard that same voice.

"Put that cigarette out!" another CO yelled. There was a brief silence. I assumed she was complying.

"You won't talk to me. I'm getting the fuck out this dorm!" It was the last words I heard. I cut the water off and stood still, anticipating hearing the door close behind the madness. I was done taking a shower. No amount of water could wash away how filthy I felt, or the reality that possibly half the dorm had seen my naked body! I just wanted to isolate myself in my room. A few seconds passed, and the door slammed. Finally! I sighed, not realizing I had been holding my breath. I wished just like that, it was over and done with, but the way my hands were shaking made me keep in touch with reality.

"Ain't this some shit?" Jayden's face openly displayed her disgust. She sat back crossing her arms across her chest, looking out in the distance as I concluded telling her what happened. Omitting the part about me actually showing her my vagina. "So this bitch got the whole dorm looking at *my* bitch, and you didn't deem this important enough to come tell me?"

"Jay, you really haven't given me a chance." I leaned closer and tried to make eye contact, hoping her vulnerability for me would smooth the situation over. "Plus, I'm embarrassed. It's hard thinking about how I must look."

"What the fuck ever, Falicia! You ain't been having a problem pulling me to the side when some shit need to be said. You had no intention of telling me about this shit, and from my standpoint, the bitch is in love with you!" Her voice was excelling, and she was becoming more animated. I knew where this was headed.

"Jayden, please," I called out to her in hopes she would lower her tone.

"Please what, motherfucker?" she retorted, snapping her head around to face me. I was so taken aback I couldn't reply. *She's just frustrated, that's why she's talking to me like that,* I thought as I tried to convince myself I wasn't being belittled. "Please what! You can't talk now?"

I looked around casually, concerned about if we appeared to be fussing. I made eye contact with a few remorseful eyes. *Must be the ones who saw fit to enlighten Jayden,* I thought, as my eyes slowly landed on Jayden. Her lip curled up on one side, less than an inch beneath her flared nostrils. Her jaw twitched, and the distance in her eyes made me feel defeated.

"I don't want to fight with you."

"You don't have to because I'm done. I'm not fucking with you no more." She stood to her feet.

Did my ears just serve me right? Did this nigga just break up with me? I asked myself. "What did you just say to me?" I was surprised at the level of hostility I heard in my voice.

"You heard me! It's over. I'm done with you!" she snapped. Instantly, a dagger pierced my heart, but I was too prideful to cry, or even let on of my pain. I started to plead my case, but for what purpose? If something this petty could result in her breaking up with me after all the mess I'd put up with, then let her carry on. She stood there looking at me, as if she was waiting on a reply.

CHAPTER 28

Have you ever dated someone, and he or she tells you it's over? They don't answer when you try to call, or act as if they don't want to speak when they see you in the street? So what do you do? Move on, right? Right! Jayden said we were done and since I had been praying, I ran with it. The only concern I had was about the condition of my locker, but God just started showing me favor! This lady named Jane walked up to me as I was ironing my clothes that Saturday morning.

"Oh, you do such a good job at that! Is it possible I can pay you weekly to iron my clothes?" The short woman looked Indian, with her deeply tanned skin and long, dark hair, but she was Caucasian. She stood out to me because of her physique and the way she wore the sleeves of her uniform cuffed with her white T-shirt. Her boobs set up better than mine, but I would never ask her were they real. She carried herself like she came from money and didn't mind speaking her mind.

"Well, I wouldn't mind doing that for you, but I have no idea what to charge you for that," I replied, finishing up my uniform shirt.

"How about a dollar a uniform? I normally get three uniforms ironed a week, except for when I go to visitation."

It sounded good to me. That would guarantee my Dove soap every other week, which was $1.85 and some Ramen bag soups that were $.40 each. It was a start on my own, plus Ken was still faithful with sending me thirty dollars a month. I would just have to learn how to get on my grind.

Other doors started opening for me, and this was all in a week's time. A younger white girl wanted to know if I would micro braid her hair.

"Name your price, Falicia, and I got you." I wasn't sure, but I said fifteen dollars. "Make your list. I want to do this once a month." I was convinced things had to get better. What Jayden wasn't doing, God was!

I went to church that weekend and was beginning to feel that peace I once felt in the county jail.

That Monday when I went to work I just stayed away from Jayden. I didn't eat with any of our friends, and I only cleaned upfront where the officers could see me at all times. I wasn't sleeping on Jayden, some of her ways had begun to remind me of Ike, and that meant I didn't know what she was capable of. My stress-level was so high from watching my surroundings all day that I just had this sporadic idea to go jog when I got off. I walked into the gym like I was supposed to be there and went out back to the track and just ran until the gym officer called for Wellness Walk. Wellness Walk was something that almost the entire compound had on our operating monthly schedules (OMS) at least once a week for the purpose of going outside behind the gym for an hour to walk in hopes of balancing our health through exercise. My day was on Fridays. Dorm orderlies were the only ones that went almost every week day.

As I walked back to the dorm, I realized I felt great! The burden of everything I was carrying was gone! I just felt light and free. God had ordered my steps without me even realizing His leading. I was actually smiling as I spoke to several people in passing. I made up my mind then that I would do this every day. I made it to the dorm in time to get in the shower. I was getting out and headed to my room when I noticed someone moving in. The cloth cart forcefully came bursting through the door.

"It's about time these motherfuckers moved me over here!" Jayden announced as she walked in behind the cart, smirking at me. If I was a superhero, I would have blasted that broad onto another continent! God or Jayden one, had a cruel sense of humor, and I wasn't finding this mess to be funny in the least! All that joy I had just obtained went out the door! Just when I was getting into my own routine without her, she moved in the dorm with me! I could not believe this was actually happening! I walked to my room as fast as I could without being obvious and locked myself in. In mere distress, I fell to my knees and cried out to God, which I had become accustomed to.

"Why would you do this? Why would you permit this to happen?" Those were the questions I needed answers to. Either one would do, if not both of them.

That night, for some strange reason my door wouldn't lock, not even with the key, and the on-call maintenance man wasn't coming, so my roommate and I weren't able to remain in the room. She wasn't so eager to leave, but I was more than willing to move, hoping that I would end up in another building. But I just landed across the dorm, beneath the stairs. A blind spot to the officer's view from the control booth aka Bubble. Something else that made me nervous with Jayden being in the dorm.

The next morning I got up early as usual and showered before getting dressed for work. My new roommate was a pretty, dark-skinned girl with natural long hair. She was from Savannah and looked like she could be kin to me. She waited for me to get situated, and then got ready. I headed toward the chow hall for breakfast in the beginning of the line. Jayden wasn't that far behind me, singing loud and being obnoxious. She was in one of her moods; I knew today would be a challenge. I just didn't realize how much so.

We had just been cleared from lining up for eleven-thirty count by dorms and were waiting for our pack outs, normally a peanut butter sandwich and a meat sandwich. An apple, orange, or a banana, cookies and a milk. I could feel Jayden staring, and after a few seconds of acting nonchalant, I looked in her direction. The dark image that looked back at me gave me chills. For the first time, I caught her gazing at me with nothing but pure hatred.

Lord, if you get me out of this, I promise you I'm done. A prayer I prayed several times when she had done something and I spent my night tasting tears, suddenly came back to my remembrance. *This is my scapegoat,* I reasoned as I felt a combination of relief and grief. Jayden had become my life, my every day routine and a purpose inside these walls, no matter how much of an emotional rollercoaster it had been. It felt good to be held, sought out, and showered with material stuff, but the pain felt unending when she betrayed my trust, or made me feel disrespected.

Falicia, you have to start thinking about yourself. I looked down at my thin thighs as I sat in the portable desk. I was stressed out and underweight. *Let her go. You can do bad by yourself.* Without saying a word, I stood to my feet and walked toward the opposite aisle. *Is my HIV-positive status the reason she really broke up with me? I gotta figure out what to do so I don't go hungry now.* I asked myself a burning question as I walked into an empty restroom stall so I could be alone for a few minutes. "This breakup is a good thing, right?"

CHAPTER 29

Jayden grabbed a thirty-eight ounce bottle of floor stripper; it's what we used to get the wax off the floors. She began to untwist the top off. "Bitch, you gone learn to stop—"

Before she could even finish speaking, I charged her and began wrestling with her to get that bottle out of her hand. I was not fighting her, though I could have had the advantage with her having something in her hand. Even though her actions clearly displayed she didn't love me, I loved her and did not seek to hurt her. I just wanted to free myself of the endangerment she put me in. Some of the liquid was spilling on my hand, and my only thought was to make sure she did not splash it in my face. I was trying to force her into a corner when she lost her balance along the way and dropped the bottle. I kicked the bottle out of her reach and stepped on it, forcing most of the contents to spill on the floor as I ran out. With purpose, I walked the seven or eight feet to the restroom to immediately wash the chemicals off my hands and arms. It was silently calm in the warehouse. It's crazy how one could be fighting for their life or being raped in another room, and life proceeds as usual for everyone else in the next room. At the sink, I moved with haste because I didn't know if Jayden was coming for me. I needed something, anything to protect myself. I spotted a broom and grabbed it and ran to hide in a stall. In silence I wept, sitting on the toilet in disbelief about what had just happened! My heart broke as Jayden's facial expression flashed in my mind. "I just can't believe this . . ." I whispered repeatedly, hoping God or somebody would take notice of me. I really wanted to go back to the dorm, but it was count time, and I didn't want to be seen talking to the police.

After I regained my composure and was certain there was no sign of her coming, I grabbed the broom and sped out of the restroom area. I could neither spot her, nor could I relax. And I most definitely was not about to go mop the shake down room. I dared not be alone like that. I wasn't sure where to go, but I knew I needed someone to talk to.

Leyla! She was *my* friend and not Jayden's, a safe place. I quickly made it across the room to her station.

"What's wrong?" she inquired before I could say a word. I sat down next to her and didn't speak right away, trying to maintain my composure. She repeated her question. I opened my mouth to speak, but words didn't come out. Instead, tears raced down my face.

"Falicia?" Leyla pulled me into her petite frame. She not only looked as if we could be some kin with her beautiful chocolate skin and brown eyes, our pasts coincided in many aspects. Back in the county, she felt more like a sister, genuine and very open, innocent in my eyes. Present day, it was apparent that some intimate relationship had robbed her of her free spiritedness, and for some reason she seemed slick, but in this moment, she was my refuge.

"It's it Jay?" she whispered in my ear and held me in her embrace. Not wanting anyone to see me cry, I nodded yes.

"Judging by your locks, y'all got into a fight." I hadn't even thought about that. I sat up slowly and felt my way through my locks. Several were no longer in my up do. I removed the few pins I had in it.

"Girl, she tried to ram my head into a nail and pour stripper on me!" I explained as I permitted my locks to hang.

"I hope you beat her ass!" Leyla snapped.

"Girl, no . . . She keep saying I deserve to die, but it's like she's trying to die. You remember that time she fell out?" I proceeded to tell her about the time Jayden was leaving the gym and just passed out on the sidewalk. She told me the doctor said she had a knot in her head, exactly where it is, I didn't know. But if she got hit in the head, she could die.

"I don't understand why she's trying to fight me, knowing she has that knot in her head." Leyla rolled her eyes.

"If she asking for her ass to get whooped, you need to whoop it!

What would have happened to you if she had succeeded in throwing that floor stripper on your face?" Her downturned mouth and sad eyes showed genuine sympathy. I was sitting there trying to tell her how I wasn't only scared that I might her hurt, but scared she possessed the will to hurt me. Suddenly someone was hovering over me from behind with her face resting against the side of my head, opposite Leyla. She was so close I could feel her breasts on my back. I didn't have to question who it was. I already knew!

"Keep these bitches out of our fucking business! Before I deal with this 'ho too! If you tell one more person, I'm going to kill your stupid ass!" she whispered into my ear, and just like she came she was gone. But when I looked up at her as she walked away, we made eye contact. As she was glancing back at me over her shoulder, Jayden had that same cold look Ike used to have when he threatened to break one of my limbs or suddenly jump on me. Chills crept down my spine.

"What did she say?" Leyla asked. I just nodded no.

"I love you. I will talk to you later." I didn't want to put her in harm's way.

"Falicia, you don't have to be afraid of her! We can jump that bitch. And she only acting like this because she jealous of you."

"I love you." I gave her a weak smile and walked back toward my work station. I didn't affirm Leyla's comment, but I couldn't understand how my ex-girlfriend was jealous of me.

Jayden stood in the aisle next to my previous work-station talking to someone, making it obvious she was watching me. Everything about her gave me chills.

How did I end up in this situation? But the more pressing question that taunted me was, *Would it cost me my life to get out of it?*

CHAPTER 30

When count cleared, I left work under the pretense of going to pill call. I went, but I didn't go back to work. I went to the dorm. The first person I went to go see was Miss Jane.

"Listen, Jayden did some foul mess today, and I don't know what's going to become of the rest of my night. I do know that I can't live like this." I walked into her room uninvited and was pacing the floor.

"Well . . . Did you at least beat her ass, bursting in here like you running from the police?" she asked, sitting at her desk just as calm as she sounded. I looked in her eyes. I wished it were just that simple. Leyla and she both made it sound so easy. *How do you just put your hands on someone you love?*

"No," I admitted, suddenly feeling defeated.

"Then, baby girl, what do you want me to do?" I took a long pause before I answered.

"Can you tell me what to do in order to go to Protective Custody?" A sad look came across her face, or was it disapproval?

"Come here, Fe." I felt like a child all over again, needing to learn how to walk as I came near. I leaned against the lockers, standing next to where she sat.

"Running is not going to fix the issue at hand." She held my hand in hers.

"No, it won't, but it will give me some time alone for God to deal with me and give me the space to get my mind right to face whatever this is I have yoked myself to." She looked at me for a moment. I knew she had it in her to convincingly argue her point, but I don't know if she saw the pain in my eyes or the fear. Fear, because it freaked me out just thinking about the possibility of taking another life trying to defend myself.

"Well, do you have plenty of food and personal hygiene products?" she finally asked. I didn't have much, but I would survive.

That night was overwhelming! I told my roommate what had happened and asked that she lock the door whenever she came into the room and when she left out. I was willing to get up and let her in whenever she was ready to come back. I even asked the officer not to pop my door for anyone.

Miss Jane watched my room while I took a shower. I was relieved to get out and see all my stuff still in its place. I expected Jayden to come steal everything I owned, or lay all of my clothes and shoes in the center of my bed and pour all my shampoo, lotion, sodas, Kool-Aid, and even bleach on top of it, like most ex-girlfriends did when seeking revenge in prison when their girlfriends moved on.

I skipped dinner and didn't leave my room for anything else. Sometime around eight, my roommate said she was going to call it a night. I lay down in hopes of getting some rest, but as soon as I fell asleep, Jayden came banging on my door, demanding I open it. I could hear her asking somebody to ask the officer to open my door. I jumped up and grabbed my door just in case it was opened I could shut it right back. My heart pounded as I prayed she would just go away.

"You just like me!" Jayden yelled as I stared at her through the glass window. I wasn't sure what she meant by that comment. "We've been through the same shit! Open this fuckin' door, Falicia!" I couldn't place the significance of her remark at a time like this, but I thought about what Leyla had said. Was it possible that Jayden envied me because we endured similar traumatic incidents, and I still had my sanity and had made peace with my past? Is that the reason I saw so much hate in her eyes? But that didn't explain why she felt I deserved to die.

"Why are you doing this?" I finally found the courage to ask. But ten minutes passed, and all she had done was yell for me to open my door and kicked it because I wouldn't, until somebody else in the dorm told her to just leave me alone. They then began to get into a tongue wrestling match.

"Don't tell me what to do when it comes to my bitch!" Jayden yelled toward someone across the day area.

"Apparently, that girl doesn't want your company! And some of us would like to go to bed." I couldn't recognize the female voice.

"Who gives a fuck what you would like? This prison, bitch! Deal with it!" Jayden retorted. Now I didn't like the idea of people getting involved in my business, if I hadn't invite them. But this time I was relieved. I could hear her voice getting further and further away from my door.

"I'm sorry, bunkie." I turned and looked at my cellmate sympathetically, who lay on the top bunk waiting for the chaos to stop so she could go to sleep. I felt awful about subjecting her to this.

With a heavy heart, I cut the lights off and fell to my knees. The agony of the entire day poured from the depths of me, like water from a cracked dam as I pleaded with God about my situation. In that moment as I kneeled, begging God to protect me and to do a work in Jayden's heart, the Holy Spirit revealed to me that this is the reason God warns us against sin. It's not about keeping us from enjoying ourselves, but desiring to spare us of the pain, danger, and aftermath of committing sin. God knew what lied ahead as a result of me dealing with this woman, and every other man I had been with in fornication, and He went to great extents to prevent us from such situations. What was it going to cost me in order to learn that just anybody didn't deserve me, despite my shortcomings and medical diagnosis?

Early the next morning I woke up on a mission. I jumped out of bed and made sure my door was secured. I noticed an envelope under the door. I picked it up. I had late mail.

1-26-05

Boo Boo,

Love you, Baby! But God loves you more, no matter how you feel. The pictures are coming soon. Here's some money.

Love you,

Letty and Man

Alongside the small envelope was a money receipt for two hundred dollars. I wanted to cry. Not simply because I had received the money, but because God had answered my prayer. I was concerned about how I would maintain while staying away from Jayden, and now I didn't have to worry about that. My granddad had also just sent me fifty dollars; things were falling in place. Now I just needed to get this yoke off my neck.

I decided to skip my morning shower to avoid uninvited drama. While my roommate was still fast asleep, I stuffed all my property into two net bags and secured them in my locker. I left my bed linen on my mat because I didn't want to give off the indication I was going somewhere.

"PI, laundry detail report out!" the officer yelled from her desk inside the dorm. It sat inches from the bubble that centered both A building and B building and consisted of the control panel and officers' restroom. It was about thirty minutes shy of six o'clock. The sun hadn't even thought about gracing us yet, so it was a dark trot up the walk. I walked at a decent pace and blended in with the crowd. I didn't want Jayden to catch me in a blind spot. She would most definitely try some BS. I skipped the breakfast line and found a friendly face toward the front of the line.

"Do you mind if I skip you? I have a medical appointment to go to," I politely said.

"No, not at all," the Caucasian woman replied and gestured with her hand for me to get in front of her. We ended up sitting together. As I sat down, I scanned the chow hall. The lieutenant wasn't present. *Good,* I thought. *No one will see me talking to him.*

"When are you going to do another praise dance?" she asked, catching me off guard. She then drank the last of her milk after eating all of her frosted flakes.

"Me?" I know I sounded stupid asking her that.

"Yes. Aren't you the girl that danced at the minister's service not too long ago? A lot of people at work were saying it was your first time."

"It was . . ." The thought made me smile a little. "I don't know, but hopefully it won't be too much longer before I get my mind right." As I was speaking, I spotted Jayden coming through the door. When she saw me, she started talking a little louder. The woman didn't say another word; she just stared at me as I placed my milk carton on the tray and laid down my spoon. As I began to rise, she reached out for my wrist.

"You are exactly where God predicted you would be. He isn't looking for perfect people, just the willing." She released me. "I'll be praying for you." I stared at her for a few seconds longer.

"Thank you," I said, barely over a whisper. The compassion in her eyes made me want to cry.

"Have a blessed day," she said as I walked away to put my tray in the dish room window. I busted a right to go to security, instead of the left we all normally take to go to the gate that leads to PI and Laundry. The first shift officers were just leaving Briefing when I pulled on the security door and stepped inside. A few people from my detail stood across the walk in front of Medical waiting for pill call to start.

"Blakely, what are you doing in here?" my dorm officer asked, as she was exiting the door I had just walked in.

"The lieutenant wants to see me." I made it sound like someone had called for me. When the coast was clear, I eased in front of the supervisor's door.

"Excuse me."

"What?" Lieutenant Bleckley answered, without looking up. The graying Caucasian man was gentle looking. The perfect resemblance of a grandfather. He was always even-toned, never displaying external signs of being upset. So his reply made my uncertain heart suddenly increase its pace, and my stomach began to do somersaults. I opened my mouth to speak, but nothing came out. For some reason, I was scared as hell!

"What is it that you want? You're not standing there for nothing, or are you?" He spoke again, but this time he looked up to acknowledge me. I searched his face to discern his mood, as my mind tried to process what I had practiced over and over. But instead of words, a sea of emotions reached its peak and forcibly made its way down my cheeks.

"Miss Blakely, what is the matter? Is someone mistreating you?" He rose to his feet and pulled on his belt as if he were a cowboy, standing no taller than five-ten. "Come on in here." He gestured for me to get out of the threshold and stand in the same cut I was in a few months ago, on the verge of going to lockdown. It's crazy how I prayed not to go that day, and now I was praying that he would just simply let me go.

"LT, I would like to go to . . . to Protective Custody," I whispered as I spat it out, before I lost the courage to say it as I tried to regain my composure. I wasn't sure if I just dreaded lockdown, or in my heart I knew I shouldn't run from the situation, but I couldn't deny the sinking feeling in my stomach that I should just turn around and walk back out the doors I had come in.

"Hold up a minute now . . . Why are you crying? Has someone caused you bodily harm?" He looked me over with great concern in his eyes.

"LT, please . . . I just want to go to PC." Tears flowed freely from my eyes.

"I can't just *put* you in Protective Custody. You have to feel threatened, and you have to write a statement on the person who is the result of this feeling." I stood there in silence, swiping at my tears. Knowing without a doubt there was no way I could tell on Jayden. Though she had broken my heart and openly displayed that she didn't give a damn about how I felt, I couldn't deny who I was and reacted as such.

"It's a lot going on at home, and I don't trust myself," I lied. "I work around a lot of sharp objects. The people in my dorm are so disrespectful at times, talking loud by my door while I'm trying to sleep . . . I just need some time alone to clear my head and sort through the reality of the life I have made for myself."

"Miss Blakely, are you saying that you are suicidal?" he quickly retorted.

"No, sir. I am simply saying that we all have limitations, and I strongly believe that I am reaching mine. I need some time alone to regroup and being in a cell with a cellmate is not permitting me the solitude I need. Please, do not give me a reason to make you put me in lockdown. It is not my intention to get in trouble this morning," I pleaded tearfully. He just stared at me. I could tell he was considering what I was asking of him.

"Let me ask you something, Miss Blakely."

"Feel free to." One might have believed that I was using my tears to manipulate the situation, but I was so full of sorrow from the condition of my life and heart, the tears came freely without my consent.

"Do you know the Lord?" I nodded yes. "Good! If I grant that you be permitted to go, you better do whatever it is you have to do, to get yourself together and you can start by lying down your will, your agenda, and picking up God's. Your peace alone is in Him, and you can still have peace no matter what is going on around you, no matter who comes into or walks out of your life. Do you understand what I'm saying?" Again I nodded yes. "You were not made to run away from an obstacle, you were created to overcome it! So get yourself together, and the next time I see you, I better see the best you! The strong, peaceful you that I believe God created you to be. Now go write me a statement."

"Yes, sir," I answered quietly, as he pointed to the wall behind me where a clipboard hung on the wall with several blank statement forms attached to it. And just like he busied himself with whatever paperwork he had in front of him when I first approached the door, he reset his focus back on it, as if I had never interrupted him.

I sat in silence as I wrote my made up excuse of why I was requesting PC. Fresh tears wet my face and at times my statement. But this time I cried because I felt a sense of hope. The lieutenant believed in me. He saw something in me that I didn't see in myself, and I was convinced I would discover it in lockdown.

CHAPTER 31

Willingly being alone in a cell for thirty days had done a wonder on my mental. It seemed like the remedy I needed to broaden my perspective on the purpose of doing time. Walking around broken hearted was not the quest I would desperately strive to survive anymore.

One day I was sitting on the bed eating some chips when part of a dust mop swept a letter beneath my door. It was folded tightly as small as it could go, with a piece of tape wrapped around it. I looked up and barely caught a glimpse of the orderly through the window, nodding her head as she proceeded past my door. I stared at it, contemplating its contents before I picked it up. It had barely been a week since I was gone, and the absence of my prison life felt pretty serene. Obviously, Jayden had managed to pay, or convince the orderly to bring me some mail.

Lord, guard my heart, I prayed before I began reading it. Jayden had a way of playing on my emotions, and I just didn't want to be neither vulnerable nor stupid for her anymore. I can't recall word for word, but it went something close to this nature:

Wifey,

I can't believe that you actually just left me like this. No goodbyes or nothing. But why would you, after the way I've been treating you? You probably don't believe me when I say that it seems harder to get through the day knowing you're not across the room or in the dorm when I return. I don't know if you have the things that you need, if you're eating or what up there. I found out what side you're on, and I have been going to the pill call line every day hoping you look out the window and wave at me. That smile is embedded in my mind.

Falicia Rose Blakely

Why Falicia? Why would you just leave me out here alone
like this? Do you believe that I still love you? Do you even care?
I love you until the end of time . . . One Love

After I put her letter down, I got on my knees, conflicted with being logical in matters of my heart. Many people in my life had claimed this great deal of love for me, but their actions displayed the total opposite. Jayden may have loved me, but fell short when it came to considering how her actions affected me, and I understood that she needed time to mature in that area, but that didn't give her or anyone else a pass to treat me like shit in the process. I needed to learn to establish and enforce boundaries in my life, and I would start with Jayden! The love and loyalty I naturally brought to any relationship deserved to be reciprocated, or at least attempted. That day I vowed to love myself more. I decided against writing her back and instead of lying around sympathizing with her lack, I celebrated my gain and my accomplishment of putting my needs first. Yes, sometimes I went and waved down at her from my top range window, as she stood about two hundred feet away from the gated building with her shoulders slumped, as if she was so broken. There wasn't a day that passed that she wasn't standing there on that corner, and even though I didn't write back, she still wrote me, but by the time an officer came knocking on my door with a move slip, instructing me to pack up because I was moving back on the compound, I wasn't the same passive, desperate, misled girl. I was a young lady, and I had different aspirations to live for.

To my disappointment, I went back to my same dorm, E8-B into a cell three doors down from where I was. The room was empty. Someone who held the door open as I pushed the cart in told me the person who formerly occupied that cell went home that morning. I was convinced God was allotting me some more time alone. I was closed off alone in my room wiping down the lockers, both bunks, the walls, steel toilet and sink, everything. Eventually, I would even get on my knees, using a sanitary napkin as a mop to clean the floor. It seemed cleaner than using the mop that the dorm had used.

Suddenly my door slid back, and as I turned back to see why, Jayden burst in like a bat out of hell and wrapped her arms around me. I stood frozen in my tracks. It felt good to be in her embrace, but feelings were so deceiving, just like your heart—it changed like the weather. I didn't allow myself to be moved. After a few seconds she released me. I turned and continued to clean.

"Did you receive my mail?"

"I did. Thank you for taking out the time to check on me." I stood upright, walked around her, draped the cleaning rag on the sink and washed my hands. She leaned against the threshold of the door, observing my every move. "Is there something I can help you with?" I wanted to go ahead and establish where I stood before I lost the courage to do so.

"What you mean?" She nudged herself upright, commanding the entire space where she stood. Her shoulders were broad like shoulder pads beneath a coat, her arms curved by her sides leading the path to her balled up fists. Her legs were evenly spread apart. Her stance was aggressive to say the least, but so was mine. Finally, I was willing to defend myself. I had discovered the strength to fight for me! I glanced into the cloudy mirror that was made of some type of metal. It had been drilled into the wall over the sink. A beautiful, black, courageous young woman looked back at me. I smiled, and she smiled back.

"I'm about to put my property up." I grabbed one of the net bags and set it in front of the locker. "If there is nothing you want in particular, I would appreciate it if you leave me to myself and put the door back how you found it."

"Fe, what the fuck?" Her brows kissed as her mouth twisted; she looked very confused.

"Jay, I love you, but I won't sit around and just pretend you haven't hurt me over and over again. You know just as much as I do that you are not ready to settle down and commit to me."

"Girl, you my wife! What the fuck you talking about. I love you!" She poked herself in the chest with every word to emphasize her point. "So now you don't know that I love you?"

Falicia Rose Blakely

"Of course I know. You love me so much you tried to pour stripper on me, in hopes of burning my skin. You remember?" I felt myself getting emotional, but now was not the time. "You want to be with me so bad, you yelled in front of our entire detail that I deserved to die, and then you tried to mush my head into a nail. How could I ever question what I mean to you?" Jayden just stood there speechless for many heart awakening seconds. I turned my attention from her and proceeded to put my stuff back in my locker.

"Fe, I'm . . . I'm sorry. When I get angry I say and do shit that I don't mean, but I'm in love with you, straight up." She approached me as she spoke.

"Well, if you love me so much, I need you to respect that I would like some time away from you." I never looked up. I didn't acknowledge her as she eventually eased back out of my room, or when she pulled my door back up. In fact, days turned into weeks that I didn't acknowledge her, and it was one of the most difficult things to do, but it was necessary to nurture the woman God was molding me into being.

A mental health evaluation was submitted as a result of my request to go to Protective Custody. It seemed like a gift from God because I signed up for a Day Treatment program. About fifteen of us that were on mental health caseloads and were not taking any psychiatric medication were required to take groups all day and scheduled to an hour of Wellness Walk Monday through Friday for three months. The groups ranged from Anger Management to Cognitive Thinking. I enjoyed every one of them. I no longer was bound to a detail, and it was refreshing to get up, clean my room, go for a jog, and then to group to challenge my mind. Plus, I learned that one of the girls in my class was in another program, The Children's Center. This program would turn out to be very beneficial to me. Every third Saturday of the month, it gave mothers the opportunity to bond with their children through personal interaction other than regular visitation. Which allowed the mother and child/ren to play games, work on school work, do each other's hair, eat together, watch movies, do arts and crafts and much more without a correctional officer standing over you, patrolling your every move. In some ways, the mother is given the privilege of feeling like she is contributing to her child/ren's development. And to make it that much more effective, a non-profit organization was willing to transport the children to and from the prison, that stayed in the Atlanta district for only fifty cents per child. I signed up immediately, but my entry was delayed a few months because I had to take a parenting class.

A month had passed, and Jayden began to take on the interest of someone else, but on the slick tip. I watched as she pretended to be going out to dinner but snuck into someone else's cell. As she sat around and played board games and ate food that other females cooked. It wasn't easy to deal with, but I made myself see it, and what tripped me out the most was that I wasn't talking to her. So why sneak! But being sneaky was a part of who she was.

I had been roommates with a young Caucasian girl who was a hot head, always on go mode. She would freely curse the officers out and was willing to fight, even though she really didn't have hands. One morning she woke up in a foul mood, and I wasn't surprise when I heard she had got into an argument in the chow hall, and it escalated into her tray being thrown across the room. Unfortunately, several people ended up with that gooey peanut butter mixed with syrup all over them! And she was hauled off to lockdown. It was some time after six, and I was sitting at the desk in my room reading my Bible and eating a meatball and rice wrap. My room was pretty much my safe haven. I didn't care to see Jayden in action, nor did I agree with the way she would be posted up on one of the television benches with one of her side pieces watching my room, or every step I took when I came out of my room. My door slid open from the control panel, then I heard the front door shut. I didn't get up, just continued to eat my wrap.

"Hey, I'm your new—" I looked up, and a brown-skinned stud with a birthmark on the left side of her face above her eye stopped in her tracks as we made eye contact.

Really, God? I thought as I realized she was the girl my co-defendant was dating in the county jail. Shane had even showed up a few times to our court hearings in colorful baggy shorts and oversized long shirts sporting corn rows, appearing to be the very image our lawyers sought to liberate us from (being a thug).

"Well, hello. I'm Falicia." I went ahead and introduced myself like I would to anyone, especially being that we had never officially met. I ignored her wide-eyed stare, as if she was taken aback or caught off guard.

"I'm Shane," she replied, and finally walked into the room.

"I've already wiped out your lockers and your bunk, but there is some bleach, tile cleaner, and cleaning rags behind the trash can if you desire to clean your area yourself. Feel free to use whatever you need." I pointed against the wall, right next to the door. "I'll give you some time to yourself." I considered putting on a pair of bigger shorts, but decided against it, in a haste to give her some space. I looked decent in my white T-shirt and gray shorts; they were just a little smaller, so I normally only wore them in the room. I grabbed my food and excused myself. She just stood in the middle of the floor with her property at her feet. Her expression was blank. I couldn't read her. It seemed she either wasn't expecting me to be polite, or she wasn't sure how to take me. I walked out into the day room smiling on the inside. I had grown to enjoy making people eat their words and opinions about me. This was going to be an interesting living situation.

CHAPTER 32

The Day Treatment program was ending, and I didn't want to be put back in PI, so when my quarterly session came with my General Population counselor, I asked her to request through Classification that I be made an in-house laundry orderly. I felt this would be to my advantage in many aspects. Being that I was growing in my relationship with God, it was important to me that I humble myself and be of service to others, instead of always asking people to do something for me. I could do this by not only washing and drying my dorm's clothes, but folding them as well. Taking the liberty to make sure everyone got back all of their things. Secondly, it would provide me plenty of time to read my Bible, pray, and worship. Likewise, I wouldn't have to be on the compound as much. Which meant I would see less of Jayden in action. My store day could change, and I wouldn't be subjected to being in her presence or hearing her mockery for almost an hour, every week I did make store. It seemed like a win-win situation to me! By the grace of God I got the position!

My faith was beginning to flourish again because I was activating it. I heard about an audition for Minister's Gray's choir. I wasn't that familiar with her, or any of the current members, but I did recall going to a couple of her church services and a lot of people looked up to her. I wasn't yet in a place where I prayed about my every decision before I acted, so I didn't ask God if this was His will, but the day they called for auditions, I went.

"What's up, cuz?" Minister Gray greeted me at the door as she pulled me in for half of an embrace.

"Huh? . . . Hello." I smiled, not sure how to respond to her unusual greeting.

"You look familiar." She stood about five feet six inches like my mother. Her black-cherry colored hair danced on her shoulders, and she had a set of the whitest teeth I had seen since I had been incarcerated.

"I danced at your service once," I clarified, nervously. She fussed at our section in church because Jayden was being extra. Jayden believes Christianity is the white man's religion and they used it to put fear in our ancestors, and we are ignorant for believing that our salvation comes through believing in Christ, so she doesn't respect the services. And clearly, she didn't respect that this was my form of worship. So it does make me wonder why she was even there to begin with.

"Oh, I think I remember. Anyways, come on in. I'm glad you're here." And just like that, she was tending to the next person. Something about her compelled me to watch her. I know my encounter with her was short, but I felt I loved this lady.

By the end of the night, my nervous behind managed to sing a hallelujah hymn with all the sopranos, laughed until my stomach hurt, and realized this gathering felt like family. Like something I wanted to be a part of. It was sad that the night was coming to an end because outside of that room was the oppressed life that we lived. Back to being talked at and not talked to. Treated as if you are unworthy of simple things that human beings give and receive: respect, freedom of speech, and opinion. Constantly being denied the power to choose what to eat, wear, or when to wake up, the liberty to express yourself in the uniqueness of your own personality through the styling of your hair, the application of your makeup, or the way your clothes fit. Denied decent medical assistance, the suppression of our erotic power, and being provoked just to prove that we are what they believe about an inmate, which is: you are an animal who is incapable of cognitive thinking and reasoning.

"Form a circle, everyone. Everyone hold someone's hand. I hate to say that we have to call this evening a night." Minister Gray looked around the room. I don't know about anyone else, but the thought of what I was going back to at the dorm suddenly made me weary. "God is not restricted by walls and bars. The same God that was present in this room, is the same God that shall go back with you to your dorms and throughout your week. He'll come if you invite Him. Everybody bow your heads." I wanted to comply, but I was so fascinated by the peace that was settling on my heart as this woman spoke, I just stared at her.

"All minds and hearts on Christ Jesus," she gently instructed, and then looked at me as if she could read my thoughts. She smiled and so did I as I dropped my head. I can't tell you word for word what she said, but I do know that she spoke life into us, into my very existence!

"I declare unto you that God has purpose for your life. You are not here by chance! You didn't just trip over death and are still alive by luck. No, it was God who carried you through the valley of the shadow of death. And it is God who is declaring now, you belong to Me! I have loved you with an *everlasting* love. I laid down my life that you may have life, a life free of bondage, abuse, and defeat. I want to raise you up for My glory! When others see what I have done for you, they will know that I am God, mighty to deliver, mighty to save, and greater than all other names! Live my child and not die. Come out from the ways of this world and live!"

I left understanding that there was a purpose for my pain, purpose in my current situation, but most of all, purpose for my life. God wouldn't let me die because my purpose had yet to live. Yes, I had made my own decisions, and every action I took led me in a direction that positioned me to be in a place where a grown man could prey on my naive mind, and that condition positioned me to commit such a horrendous act, and my freedom was the least they could take for such devastation. In the midst of this misfortune, however, God was at work in my life, in my spirit, and He alone could manifest something that brought Him praise. Somehow He would be glorified.

A week passed before the results from the audition came out. I didn't need to see the paper to know God had given me a position on that choir. I obtained too much for it to have solely been just a one one-night experience.

We had choir rehearsal every Tuesday around six until about eight,

eight-thirty. It was more of a worship service than rehearsal because the presence of God was always present and so tangible, many of us often ended up on our faces crying out to God. A longing to know God in His fullness was giving birth in me. The desire to be like minded and have a heart after His precepts was beginning to be priority in me. There's a story in the Bible about Moses petitioning God for His presence to go with him and the Israelites as they headed toward the promise land and for a better understanding of God's ways. As God expressed that he had found favor with Him and would do that which he asked for, Moses said to God, "Show me Your glory, I pray."

God said, "I will make all my goodness pass before you, and will proclaim before you the name Adonai, and I will be gracious to whom I will be gracious, and will show mercy on whom I will show mercy. But," He said, "You cannot see my face, for no one shall see me and live." (Exodus 33:18-20.)

This passage became my motto, the motive behind every sacrifice I was beginning to make and would make in the future. No man can live and see God. I had to die to myself, die to justifications of operating using people to secure my means of having, die to my self-centeredness. Stop making demands of my friends to do every little thing for me, like they were my whores and not gifts from God. I had to die to my need to prove my love and loyalty to another human being. I had to die to my insecurities. The way I was operating wouldn't permit me to go where I desired to be. I had to die in order to see God's glory!

Darvis Gray, Minister Gray's son explained in one of his sermons that when you're in an airplane, the higher you get in the sky, the smaller the things on earth appear. Likewise, the closer you get to God, the smaller and minute the things on earth mean to you. Life had a new spin on it, and I was no longer buying the nonsense from anyone. I had been hearing many things about Jayden that I wasn't fond of. She walked around with a pocket full of pills and was taking fifteen to twenty pills a day. She went to lockdown for making a dummy, so she could spend the night with her new girlfriend, who also always popped pills. She got into fights and was asked to leave church because she was being disruptive. Finally, Jayden was telling people to tell me she felt like she was losing her mind. Unfortunately, when I saw her in church after some months, her facial features had changed a bit and twitched a lot. Something about the way she kept literally pushing her locks out of her face and bucking her eyes told me that all that medicine she was taking that wasn't prescribed to her was causing a chemical imbalance. The Jayden that had stolen my heart was gone, but to some degrees so was I.

CHAPTER 33

Though things were beginning to look up from a spiritual perspective, I was struggling in the physical realm. I was accustomed to calling my grandmother every Sunday, and for the past two months every time I called, the recording said there was a block on the phone! Grandma Olivia was my voice of reasoning and my plug to my mother and son. Letty didn't write, nor did she have a landline phone and at this time (2005), you couldn't set up an account with a cell phone. So, my grandmother did three-way calls and kept me posted. I had been doing my best to keep my sanity, but my resistance was wearing thin after I was called to the mail room for legal documents. I received a letter from the Georgia Department of Human Resources Child Support Enforcement telling me that I was scheduled for a court date to fulfill my obligation to pay child support. Now tell me how in the hell was I going to pay child support and I'm in prison? If I was free, my mother would have never applied for government assistance to begin with. I wish I could just hear my grandma's voice, something to reassure me that things would work themselves out. But since I couldn't, I just went in, drew a cross over the letter with my finger, and prayed to God. That night I received some mail. I couldn't deny God was mindful of me. He had used this very same woman to help me forgive myself back in the county jail, when I first got saved.

My Dear Sweet Angel,

Darling, I don't have any paper so I found some in a booklet, I wanted to just tell you hello, and how much I love you. God is very present in the midst of your hardships. He has the power to hide you in His mighty hands. I miss talking to you. I have called the phone company four times, they keep telling me there is no block on the phone. Today is Monday, April 5, 2005. I am going to call again to have the phone checked one more time. I miss hearing your voice on the phone. I dialed the house number, so I can hear your voice on the voicemail recording message, but it is not the same.

 I hope to come to Atlanta soon. Then I can come see you.
Love you!
Love you! ALL my love,
Grandma

One day we were locked in our room waiting for eleven-thirty count to clear. It was the weekend, so we didn't have to be inspection ready, though some of the old school officers would demand that we put on some clothes instead of us walking around in our pajamas after noon. Shane lay on her bunk above me.

"Bunkie, can I ask you something?" Shane and I had long ago aired the dirty laundry out. As to be expected, Pumpkin had given her an impression of me that wasn't true, and after she read the *Creative Loafing* article, she realized there was a lot that she was left in the blind about. One of the things she said she respected about me was, I wasn't trying to run from the truth. I took ownership of my actions and my condition, regardless of the outcome.

"What, Shane?" I jokingly answered, as if she was getting on my nerves.

"Are you going to the store this week?"

"What? Why are you asking me that?"

"Because if you're not, I'm going to make sure you're straight. And I want you to know my locker is always open to you."

Something else that I had to come to terms with was, when dealing with any type of virus, sickness, cancer, diabetes, even a common cold, your attitude and level of stress plays a major part. I had been conquering HIV for about two years, and by the grace of God, it had been undetectable for at least eighteen months. However, the circumstance I placed myself in as a result of being lonely, was taking a toll on my immune system. During the course of the previous six months, I felt I needed to get back on my medicine.

At one time the HIV specialist felt I was doing so well he was willing to take me off my meds, but after a dose of Jayden, my immune system wasn't performing at its best, and HIV was multiplying in my body. That was my revelation. I chose the word revelation because I realized that sometimes just being affiliated with certain people can be toxic and have negative effects on you. You just so happen to be placed in certain situations you wouldn't normally be in, and you're faced with making decisions that may have long term effects on you.

On May 14, 2004, I had my first appointment with the HIV Specialist. I had not been in Diagnostics for about a month. The following is my viral load, which is how many HIV cells that were producing in my blood and my CD4 count, which is the T-cell count that fights against infections in the blood.

My viral load was <50, which means less than fifty, not enough to detect a number, therefore, referred to as 'non detectable.' That term is not the same as non-active. Some people in prison like to play on people's intelligence and tell them that they are not HIV-positive because they're 'non detectable.' My CD4 count was 550.

On August 30, 2004, I was still in Diagnostics. My viral load was <50 and my CD4 count was 694.

In September 2004, I was now in General Population, and I would see the Chronic Care doctor every three months. This was my first time. My viral load was <50 and my CD4 count was 694. I started dating Jayden in October.

In January 2005, my viral load was 8,370 and my CD4 count was 570. I requested to get back on my medicine. In March 2005, my viral load was 426 and my CD4 count was 492. This is the month we broke up. In May 2005, my viral load was <50 and my CD4 count was 782. In August 2005, my viral load was <50 and my CD4 count was 947. I was within the top 33% range of the average healthy person's immune system.

As far as I was concerned, the proof is in the pudding and it was obvious to me that being in that relationship was unhealthy. Do you have any unhealthy relationships that you need to set aside for the sake of your physical or mental health?

CHAPTER 34

August 6, 2005

My Dear Sweet Angel,

I know you have given up on me. Please forgive me for not writing sooner, but I didn't have any paper. Every time your uncle went to the store he would forget the writing tablet. I wanted a smaller tablet, but I am not going to complain. I am just glad he finally remembered.

I miss you so much, but I have not been back to Georgia since January 2004. I hope you are still praying for me. Are you still going to church? I hope so. I have not been going to Kingdom Hall. There isn't any particular reason. I know and love God, just don't feel like going out.

I do not have any idea what the problem is with the phone. MCI keeps telling me there is no block. I am going to start early Monday morning, and if it takes all day, somebody is going to give me some answers.

Your lil man asked me three different times last week to have his mama call him. You will not believe how grown he is on the phone! Your mother showed him the speed dial button to call me. Well the first day he called like nine times, not all at once but he was busy letting me know what was on Cartoon Network. He also had to call me back because I forgot to kiss him goodbye. The last two days he fell in love with you saying on the voicemail, 'Have a blessed day.' He calls me and tells me not to answer the phone because he is going to leave me a message. Yesterday, I had four messages. Smile.

Your mother probably already told you, but she just got out of the hospital. She told me you are going to school. Write me back and let me know what subjects you are taking.

As soon as I get to Georgia I will come see you. I cannot travel by bus anymore, if I could I would have been there before now.

I love you so very much. I miss you. Please keep yourself safe. I am walking with a walker, and I am on oxygen, but I feel pretty good.

Your uncle will begin sending you money soon.

Love forever,

Granny

The misunderstanding that we face with our family during incarceration is the perception that most of our family feels it's best to not tell us when tragedy strikes, or misfortune settles in our home. My mother didn't tell me she was scheduled for a procedure at the hospital. Let me tell you how I found out.

It was in July on a Sunday morning when I was called out to visitation. To my surprise, my mother and son sat waiting for me until Man spotted me coming, in which he jumped up and ran into my arms. It has always been the best part of the visit. After I checked in, we greeted my mother. She smiled weakly, and then sat back down.

"Hey, Momma! You all right?" I couldn't help but notice she wasn't absolutely herself.

"Yeah, I'm fine." She made an attempt to perk up.

"Mommy, Mommy!" Man stole my attention. "Let's eat some hot wings!" He smiled big, as if he was about to get away with something he normally couldn't do.

About one o'clock, my mother announced that they had to leave early.

"Ma, do you really have to go?" I looked back at the clock. I was used to them staying until three.

"Yes, Boo Boo. I'm sorry. I really need a cigarette. I've been trying to deal with it for about an hour now." I just stared at her for a couple seconds. Was she serious? Was my mother really ending our visit early for a cigarette? After she had driven about four hours to come see me? I didn't say a word.

"Come on, Man." I helped him out of my lap and held his hand. He extended his other one to my mother and grabbed her opposite hand. Then we all bowed our heads, and I prayed for their travelling mercy, shield of protection, and that God would continue to provide. Once we said amen, I looked at my mother. She winced as if the hard backed chair was hurting her butt, or the cold room was making her bones ache. Her eyes were slightly shut, and she barely smiled.

"Ma, why you look like you're in pain?"

"My head just hurts. That's why I need a cigarette," was her reply.

"I love y'all!" I said. I didn't mention it, but something wasn't right. My spirit was left disturbed. All week in ABE as I tested to get in GED level, I struggled thinking about my mother. I paid someone to do a three-way to my mother, and for three days straight she did not answer. Finally, I called her goddaughter.

"Hey, Rosa. How are you doing?"

"I'm fine, just enjoying your son."

"My son?" My heart began to pound.

"Yeah, you want to speak to him?"

"Please . . ." *Stay calm, Falicia,* I tried to coach myself. Just because my insides were confirming something wasn't right didn't give me the right to upset my child.

"Hello."

"Hey, baby!" I sang into the receiver.

"Hey, Mama! What you doing?"

"Nothing. What my baby doing?"

"Playing games. We eating dinner in a little while."

"Who? You, Aunt Rosa, Anthony, and Nana?"

"No, Nana at the hospital."

"Hospital!" My stomach sunk, immediately I knew I had to have a bowel movement.

"Yes, ma'am. Nana had to see the doctor about her woman parts, and I'm staying with Aunt Rosa until she come back. She should be here tomorrow. We are going to durse her back to heath." I smiled at the sound of him trying to say 'nurse her back to health.'

"Well, if she has you, then I know she's going to be all right!"

"Mm hmm! You don't have to worry, Momma."

It was three days later before I was able to address her over the phone about having a hysterectomy, and when I asked why didn't she tell me what was going on, she replied, "I just didn't want you to worry."

"Ma, I wouldn't if I knew what was going on, because I can pray. But when I don't know and something is troubling me—*that* is when I worry because I haven't the slightest idea what is taking place." Unfortunately, this would be a repetitious experience for me and most offenders as the years proceeded, because our family was convinced it's better that we don't know.

Just like no one told me my grandma's condition was declining to the point she relied on oxygen and had to walk with a walker. But Grandma Olivia, just being herself, would tell me what was going on, assuming I most likely already knew.

One morning Shane went to breakfast, and when she came back she flew into the laundry room, where I had begun my daily routine.

"Jay got transferred this morning." She studied my face as if she sought out a reaction. But I didn't have one. I wasn't sure how to feel. I hadn't spoken to her in months, as a result of her level of disrespect in church and her need to always be high. I stood there in silence for a minute, and then I sighed. I didn't want to admit it, but it was a sigh of relief. I had passed my test concerning her. Even though she broke my heart, I loved her. She played a major part in the woman I was becoming. Because of her, I finally decided to take a stand worth something. I wished her well on her journey and hoped she found the help she needed to reposition herself for the world.

It probably sounds worse than it is, but since Jayden had left, I took back up the habit of going back outside to the pavilion. I didn't have to concern myself with any outbursts or observation as Jay practically fell over her own feet, or spilled handfuls of pills from her pocket. I didn't have to sit around and wonder what happened that made her just start wilding out.

This particular Friday, I went outside with my cellmate because she and her girlfriend, Diamond were beefing. She asked me to go because she wanted to just laugh for a change, so she sat on the picnic table as my choir sisters and I cracked a few jokes on how Minister Gray would chastise us. We had been out about ten minutes, and Diamond just appeared. She was a very striking young Egyptian woman, but her attitude oftentimes classified her as less becoming. She marched up to where we were all sitting and placed her hand on her hip. Her face, full of heavy makeup, wrinkled as if she tasted something sour.

"Shane, let's go. Right now!" she demanded as she approached.

"Hello, Diamond. How are you doing today? How was Jumah?" I asked, not trying to be sarcastic, but hoping she would take a second to reflect on her attitude.

"Hey, Falicia and everyone else." She shifted her weight from one leg to the opposite one.

"Hello. Would you like to join us?" one of my sisters welcomed her.

"No thank you." She closed in the space between her and Shane. "I'm going to knock the shit out of you, if you don't get up right now." I suppose I could hear her because I sat so close to Shane. I looked her over, both she and Shane were no taller than five feet six inches. Together they probably weighed 210 pounds, but Shane, being dominate, could have handled her easily. But I believe she just didn't want to put her hands on her.

"Let's go!" Diamond yanked on her shirt, pulling her slightly off the table. Shane started laughing.

"Diamond, stop barking up this tree, nah. I'm not up for your drama," Shane addressed her as she rose and began walking in the direction Diamond was headed. "Catch up with y'all later," Shane told us, looking at me and throwing up some deuces.

We proceeded in our conversation. In my heart I took a moment to thank God I wasn't still caught up in an unhealthy relationship. About ten minutes passed, and someone started calling my name to get my attention. I looked behind me, and to my disappointment Diamond was swinging on my cellmate. Shane was laughing as she dodged several blows, but there were a few that connected, and one of them busted her lip and blood began to flow. Shane was still laughing as the realization entered her mind that she was bleeding. She touched her mouth and looked at her hand. In a matter of seconds she had Diamond in a headlock punching her in the stomach. COs came running from inside the gym. Shane just stopped punching her and shoved her to the ground, then turned around to cuff up. We made eye contact.

"I tried, bunkie. I tried," she said aloud as her mouth poured blood. It was a sad situation because I knew she didn't want to fight Diamond nor go to jail. I received a revelation in that moment. Sometimes in life when you are trying to move ahead, there may be people in your life that don't want to see you change and purposely set out to do you harm. Therefore, we have to examine those whom we call friends ahead of time, and only affiliate with those who want something out of life and have just as much to lose as we do. When you're down and out, do your friends or spouse take out the time to remind you why you can overcome, or do they encourage you to stay where you are and be like everyone else?

CHAPTER 35

I finally made it to GED level, and I set a personal goal to obtain it within a year. By all means necessary! What I didn't know was my new cellmate would be a living hell! Everything you could possibly imagine that would make you dislike staying with someone, this forty-eight-year old Caucasian woman did. Just being the person that I am, we started off on a bad note. I noticed she had some complications going on with her feet, so I told her she could wear a pair of my shoes, since the boots were so uncomfortable. In three days my white Nike's were covered in red mud. She made no attempt to wipe them off, ever, and could not explain how they got so filthy. I just gave her the shoes. There was no way I was going to walk around with them on.

It took her almost two weeks to take her first shower from the day she moved in. I tried to be grown about it and explained that I had HIV and the importance of her maintaining a sanitary environment for us both, but that didn't matter. She didn't bathe for another week. To make matters worse, she caked foundation on her face for visitation, but she never washed it off. She ate food in her bed, spilling crumbs and cups of Kool-Aid everywhere. Sleeping all day long. If the officer assigned her to clean the showers, I would wake her up. She would go clean them, and then get back in bed. If I asked her about taking a shower, she would promise to take one in the morning. When the morning came, she'd rolled over. I forgot to mention I never saw her brush her teeth, and the state thought it was okay to house us in a room together.

One of the most frustrating things I've experienced is being forced to share your space with strangers. You try to push beyond your own personal preference for sharing a toilet. You set aside your judgments for the sake of making the best of the arrangement. But the most understanding person is challenged when you can't find rest or privacy in the confinement of your own room, well—the cell you're assigned to. Nothing here belongs to you. Not even the panties you possess. The moment a correctional officer discovers you have more than five, he or she may take the extra ones. And you don't get to choose which ones you keep. That's with any of your property. I have had someone take all my shirts from home and leave me the state-issued ones! Like why in the heck would I want the state shirts over the new ones my mother sent me?

Back to my point. It's hard to keep your head on straight when you feel disrespected, or a lack of consideration in the *one place* you seek serenity. To constantly be awakened out of your sleep by a nosy, rude bunkmate and you have to go to work the next morning, can make you start thinking about laying hands, and I'm not talking about at the altar! I had been talking about this lady so bad, I felt compelled by the Holy Spirit to go and apologize for not telling her how I felt, instead of my friends. Unfortunately, even after we talked, nothing changed. She continued to make us live in filth, and our cell smelled awful. It didn't matter that I washed her bed linen, wiped our space down with bleach daily, and even had the officer spray air freshener. She carried an odor, and that damn odor hindered my ability to be polite. I would walk in my room and instantly get an attitude!

I heard that next door (E8-A) didn't have a dorm wash orderly, and I immediately stepped to the counselor for the position. The next day I was throwing up the deuces to Satan's advocate and moving into the room with Rocky, a short, red, slim stud who was smart as hell and most of all CLEAN! The room was immaculate! And she just so happened to be a teacher's aide for GED! Now what's the possibility of that? My own live-in tutor! This arrangement proved to be God ordained! Gladly, she assisted me with my schoolwork, and many nights we fell asleep discussing the Bible.

Rocky's birthday was coming up, and I was responsible for the food aspect of the party. Not the desserts though. Karie would be making a cake molded into the shape of boxing gloves. About fifty dollars' worth of brownies, strawberry rolls, and honey buns with a little bit of Kool-Aid and water, with an ID card, that cake would be the highlight of the meal.

Rocky was a picky eater, so I had to think outside the luxury of just our commissary. I bought two loaves of bread from the kitchen, some turkey and cheese, which I'd cut up in fours. Along with some chips and dip would serve as appetizers. I'd take cheese and salsa to make one dip. Mayonnaise, creamer, pickle juice, black pepper and chicken seasoning to make a ranch dressing. Then I'd take the hot dogs I purchased and a cooking pouch, which is a ready-to-eat pack (meatballs, beef stew, etc.), a pack that had something else in it that we washed and recycled. Put some hot water in it, clamp the flat iron around it, cover the water with a paper towel or saran wrap and boil the hot dogs. Separately, take some beans, squeeze cheese, chili seasoning and salsa with onions, put it all in a tortilla wrap with the hot dogs, then wrap in a tissue wrapper and toast on the flat iron. Thus, making a chili cheese dog. Slice some pickles for the sake of color. Can't forget the Bombay. As many flavored Kool-Aids as possible, a Sprite, and coffee lid full of coffee. Mix it up with sugar and hot water. All that would be lacking is the presents for the birthday girl. Everything was well-planned out, so when Friday came I was excited to see all our planning come to fruition. I had heard that Rocky would even have some dancers who had made outfits in PI. But at about one o'clock, Administration came down the hill with buggies and all available staff. Somebody must have tipped them off.

"The pigs are coming down the hill!" someone screamed, and everyone took off like roaches, running to their rooms to flush contraband that could send you to lockdown.

"They cut the water off!" someone else yelled, sounding as if they were panicking. Rocky and I pressed the toilet button just to see. Nothing.

"Oh shit! What are we going to do with all this bread and stuff?" Rocky asked me. I had no idea. I was going to ask her!

"Maybe we should just put it in the trash, then it won't be that they personally found it on us."

"That's a great idea!" Rocky yelled at me as she fetched all the meat from under the bed, on ice in our trash bin. But before she could get it all rounded up, our dorm officer walked through the door.

"Everyone stop what you're doing and go to your rooms and lock the door!" she yelled from the middle of the floor. "If I catch anyone doing anything other than going to your rooms, you will be locked down!" Rocky stopped mid-stride and looked at me.

"Finish getting it all together. I'm going to see if I can just make the door look shut." I grabbed a book, held it by the latch, and pulled the steel door shut, hoping it wouldn't catch. It didn't. "It worked!" I said, excited. "Now, if she doesn't check the doors, I should have enough time to run to the trash." I watched her every move as if I was willing her to leave, but it didn't work. In seconds, everyone that would be assisting in the shakedown walked through the door.

"If your door is not secure, you secure it now, or you going to jail!" The black, at least six feet tall, thick boned, raised-on-collard-greens-and-cornbread-eating woman on the CERT Team began to direct the show.

"Just lock the door." Rocky sounded defeated. I complied. "What are we going to do?"

"I think we should pray." It sort of felt awkward asking God to protect us under such circumstances, but I am His child, and he does know what I am trying to accomplish. "Rocky, what else is there to lose?"

Rocky pushed all the food back under the bed and joined hands with me in the middle of the floor.

"Father God, who are in heaven, we present ourselves to you. Lord, if you don't do something, this is going to end badly for the both of us. It's Rocky's birthday. Lord, I know You know we are just trying to make the best of a bad situation. Please keep in mind that I am in the Children's Center and cannot afford a DR, much less go to lockdown. In conclusion, I'm asking that you increase her faith. Show Rocky that ultimately You are in control, in Jesus' name we pray. Amen."

For the next five minutes, we just stood by the narrow triangle that was carved out and filled with hard plastic called a window, awaiting our fate, trying to see how the shakedown was being conducted. It was about six rooms being tagged at once. The officer or Deputy Warden would approach the room they were searching. The officer in the Bubble control panel would pop the door, and then the offenders were instructed to come out and stand by the door, where they were pat searched, and then ordered to sit on the floor with their backs to the door as their living space was invaded. Some officers were extremely thorough, and others just threw some stuff around for the sake of it appearing they had went through the offenders things. If something was found that was questionable, the offender would get called back in the room to explain. The top locker went with the top bunk and the bottom locker with the bottom bunk, so the officer would generally ask, "Who stays on the top bunk?" Or vice versa. Upon completion, we were instructed to go back into our cells, and we were either good or instructed to pack up our property because that individual was going to lockdown.

About ten minutes had passed, and security was making their way around the U-shape bottom range. We would be hit up shortly.

"I got an idea!" Rocky lit up like a Christmas tree. "Take all your stuff out the locker and throw it on your bed like we already been shook down!"

"You think it will work?" I asked as I started scattering my belongings on the top bunk.

"It's worth a try. The idea just popped in my head!" We made the room look like a hurricane had swept through, and then we sat back and waited. A few minutes later, a CERT member looked in the window. "Y'all already been shook down?" she asked.

"Yes." We nodded. She passed on to the next room. A few seconds passed and the Deputy Warden looked in, saw our clothes and kept going. Rocky and I turned to each other and jumped up and down on the floor like two kids.

"It worked!" she sang. I couldn't believe it, but I dared not confess it aloud. "It really worked!" We ran back to the window and watched what we could see from our angle. I began to be so overwhelmed with gratitude that I got on my knees to pray. It was important to God that my roommate enjoyed her birthday, or so that was my thought process.

"Thank you Lord!" was all that I could say! And despite the curve ball, we still had a nice turnout.

CHAPTER 36

February 12, 2006 (Sunday)

I longed for the week to pass so I could speak to my grandma on Sundays. And today was no exception to the rule.

"Hey, Ma! I miss you!" I didn't hide my excitement to hear her voice.

"Hey, my angel! I miss you even more." She sounded tired.

"What's wrong, Ma?" I pressed my index finger against my ear to block out all the noise around me.

"Oh, baby. Nothing . . . just a little shortage of breath. But it's nothing to be concerned about. How are you doing?" Just like her to downplay how she feels and switch the attention on me.

"I'm blessed, Ma. God has given me a peace that I didn't know existed. I wake up feeling as if He has smiled over me all night long. How's your knee feeling?" About a month ago she was going to the doctor's office and for some reason lost the feeling in her legs. She told me that she had lifted her foot to step up on the curb, but instead she tripped over it and fell. Some of the staff at the doctor's office rushed out to assist her. She hurt her knee and elbow.

"It's healing I imagine, just a little sore at times when I'm running to the bathroom."

"We all about you running to the bathroom," I responded.

This woman would come racing past me, peeing on the way to the bathroom, but I was too young to understand the effects of a weak bladder (incontinence). She giggled a bit, and then took a deep breath. It was taking a lot out of her to simply laugh, possibly to have this conversation.

"So let me tell you about the choir." I decided to start talking so she could catch her breath and just listen. This woman would rather tough it out, rather than tell me it was too much.

"You have one minute left," the prerecorded operator announced.

"Well, Ma! I love you so much."

"I love you too, darling. Never forget that." I could hear her wheezing. Suddenly, this sinking feeling landed in my stomach.

"Ma, I'm sorry for all the times I disrespected you and had you worried about me. I apologize I didn't make the most of all the potential I possess."

"Angel, hush that fuss. You are exactly where you need to be. God is about to use you right where you are. I love you, and I forgave you before you even did those things. . . Remember that. I love you with all my heart."

"I love you too."

"Thank you for using MCI. Good-bye." The phone disconnected.

I just stood there with the phone stuck to my ear. In my spirit I had this little nagging feeling that, that was it. That would be the last time I spoke with her. My heart raced and my thoughts wandered.

No, it can't be. I got to be trippin'! I refuse to accept that. I didn't realize I was still holding the phone until it started buzzing in my ear. I hung it up and walked back to my cell. "Girl, you trippin'." I dismissed the thought.

February 18, 2006 (Saturday)

I was braiding someone's hair and my grandma was heavy on my mind. I kept thinking I needed to call her, but would dismiss the idea, considering I normally called home on Sunday. Sometime around one o'clock, I could not shake the feeling. "Hey, do you mind if we move over to the phone?" I asked the girl whose hair I was almost finished braiding.

"Not at all." She stood up, grabbed her chair, and set it down next to the phone. The phones were aligned on the post that stabilized the steps, so it gave off the resemblance of an actual pay phone.

I could dial my grandmother's number with my eyes shut, so within seconds I stood anticipating she'd answer, but not until the phone had rung almost to the point of the answering machine. Grandma believed the phone should ring long enough for the caller ID to pick up. She hated that I would take off after the phone, trying to answer before it rang twice, religiously!

"Hel . . . Hello?" My uncle's voice cracked on the opposite end of the receiver.

"What's wrong, Unc?" I felt my chest sink.

"Umm . . . Umm."

"Unc, stop stalling and tell me why you sound like that." I would have slapped him if I could reach him through the phone.

Silence.

"Where is Grandma?" I knew something was up when he answered the phone.

"Well . . . I hate to be the bearer of bad news but . . ." It seemed it was taking ten minutes for him to merely say what's up.

"Spit it out for heavens' sake!" I released the girl's hair and placed both hands on the post. I felt sick! I remembered feeling like God had spoken into my spirit last week, but I refused to believe it. *Was God trying to prepare me?* "Unc, please . . . just tell me what's going on."

"Are you okay, Falicia?" the girl whose hair I was doing asked. I ignored her.

"Momma is in ICU." *Am I dreaming?* The room was spinning. But ICU sounded better than dead. "Everyone is here, your mother and son, aunt and cousin from up north. They all are over Tasha's house."

"Why aren't you over there? Can you call over there on three-way for me?"

"They don't want to talk to me." He sounded as if his voice drifted, almost as if he removed it from his mouth and put me on speaker phone, but Grandma didn't have a speaker phone. He smoked crack, and I wondered how high he was trying to get in order to cope with what was going on.

"Well, just call Aunt Tasha's house then. Call them for me."

Silence!

"Unc, what the heck are you doing?"

Silence!

"Where you at? Where are you in the house?"

"In Momma's room," he finally said. "Where I been since the ambulance came and took her." I knew then he had been sitting there trying to numb the pain.

"Call Aunt Tasha's house, please." He did. I heard when he clicked back over.

"I didn't get an answer."

"Okay. Listen, Unc. I need you to pay attention to what I'm saying because I need you to tell my mother and them that this is Grandma's fight. It's between her and God. If she is tired, then He will honor her request to depart from this earth. You all need to be praying for her will to live and nothing else. Don't feel bad for her, pray for her desire to live. Did you hear—"

"Thanks for choosing MCI. Good-bye." The phone hung up. I didn't even hear the one-minute warning. But I wasn't going to panic. God was in control, and he would make sure they received what I felt He pressed upon my heart to say.

I finished her last couple braids and went to my cell. In silence I sat on my bed. Almost at the point of shock. This woman had served as everything I needed since I could remember!

"Lord, I asked you to see my grandmother one more time before you took her away from me. That has been all that I asked since her health has begun to decline," I prayed aloud as I swung one leg at a time on my bunk. They felt like anchors were weighing them down. My head flopped down on my pillow like someone had shoved my head into it, sounding off the loud metal bunk that lied beneath the flimsy mat the state distributed as a mattress.

"Lord, I know this isn't about me, but please don't take my momma away before I get to hold her again. You know what that woman means to me." For some reason I couldn't bring myself to ask for anything more, because I already knew if Grandma Olivia's prayer wasn't the same as mine, mine was pointless when it came to this. I closed my eyes to stop the tears that flowed. The weight of reality pressed me deeper into the mattress. *I could be right there next to my grandmother had I not been so dumb and gotten myself into this trouble!*

Time seemed to move at its own pace. I opened my eyes and there she was. I lay next to her, on her right side. The room was empty, except just the two of us. A significant amount of her white hair lay matted to her head. An oxygen mask covered her mouth and nose, tubes were in her throat, and IVs were in both her arms. She lay still on her back as if she was paralyzed, her eyes frantically searching the room.

"I love you, Momma," I whispered in her ear as I intertwined my fingers with hers. "Do you hear me?" I kissed her cheek. She squeezed my hand.

"I'm sorry, Momma. I'm sorry. I should have listened to you." I raised my head to look into her eyes. All I saw was love and sympathy. "I love you!" I couldn't tell her enough. She squeezed my hand again. "Is this it, Momma?" I buried my face in her neck, just wanting to smell her, feel the softness of her skin against mine. I wanted to be able to remember her touch. I extended my arm across her stomach and thought about all the nights we slept in bed together. The nights I cried for my mother, and she came to comfort me. The nights my tummy ached from eating every ice cream the store sold. I thought about how this woman never made me feel I wasn't enough, and I was someone she was always proud of. I looked up and stared into her eyes again.

"Momma, please . . ." was all I mustered the courage to say. She squeezed my hand. I laid my head on her shoulder and closed my eyes. When I opened them, I was lying on my side with a face full of tears, back on my bunk.

"What in the world?" I asked no one in particular as I sat up in disbelief. "Did that really just happen or was that a figment of my imagination?" I got off that bunk and fell on my knees to pray. Tears freely flowed from my eyes as I began to worship God. Like . . . I could really smell her. I wasn't tripping. As I worshipped, I thought of the Apostle Paul in the Bible, when he spoke about receiving revelations from God (2 Corinthians 12), whether he was in the body or out, he didn't know. He just understood that the encounters he had were a result of the hand of God, and to this day I am convinced that, that encounter was my answered prayer. To see my grandmother again before the Lord called her back to Himself.

I had been unable to get my uncle on the phone any of that weekend, but that following Monday I managed to reach him and got my aunt's number from him. Then I paid someone to make a three-way for me.

"Hello?" Finally, I would get some answers.

"Hey, Auntie! How are you all doing?"

"As well as can be expected." She sounded like the strong woman I had always known.

"I asked Unc to give y'all a message. Did you get it?"

"Actually, we did. It was on my answering machine. So when we all finally made it in from the hospital we all listened to it." *To God be the glory*! Who would have ever thought it was recorded. "And what you said put a lot of stuff into perspective for everyone."

"I credit it to God. It was Him not me."

"Hold on. Somebody wants to talk to you." Aunt Tasha probably would never know how much her strength encouraged me in my life.

"Hello," a familiar male voice boomed through the phone.

"Yo, cuz! What's up?" I was excited to speak with my cousin Travis.

"Just trying to keep my mom lifted right now, you know what I'm saying?" He sounded sad.

"Yeah, I feel you. Is it that bad?"

"It was just sad to see my grandmother that way, you know? She got tubes in her and an oxygen mask on and a bunch of IVs."

"Really?" I thought aloud, thinking about my encounter.

"Yeah, it's heartbreaking to see her like that, but what's worse was we were all standing around the room, and she kept trying to saying something, but since the tube is in her throat she can't talk. She kept trying to say something, and all you could see was her drooling out her mouth and stuff. Aunt Tasha kept telling her to relax, but she wouldn't. Finally, it became obvious she was asking for something to write with. She wrote down some stuff asking them to go get out the house before Uncle Tony stole it."

I wasn't even there, but it made me feel indifferent. *This woman is in ICU, and all she can think about is her possessions.* It pissed me off because I could recall a few times we conversed over the phone, and she would tell me how she started leaving money on the floor to keep Unc from going all under her pillow looking for money while she was asleep, or being woke up in the middle of the night with half the mattress in the air because he was under there looking for her rent money!

"So to make matters worse, Aunt Tasha and my mother went over there to get the stuff Nana wrote down, and when they walked in the house, Uncle Tony was sitting in Nana's room smoking dope. Aunt Tasha lost it!

"*'Nigga, you tried to kill my momma!' Aunt Tasha said and kept yelling as she charged him! She felt strongly that he had been smoking in Nana's room and that's what led up to her coming to the hospital.*"

"What exactly is wrong?" I inquired. I knew she was forced to stop smoking cigarettes, and she had quit drinking, but no one had told me.

"Her lungs collapsed, and she has fluid on them. Her sugar dropped too low, and her blood pressure is—was too high."

"It's a miracle she's still alive." I was in awe of God.

"I know. We know she's a fighter!" I talked to him a few more seconds, then I spoke with my son and finally my mother, who informed me that they were waiting to get her blood pressure stabilized, and then perform an operation that would leave her with a tracheotomy (trach) in her throat so she could talk. I may not have been the only person who felt like they truly knew my grandma, but I knew that she would not want a trach in her throat, like she was some freak. The thought left me in tears.

The next day I called my uncle and decided to encourage him. Yes, he had been a dope head my entire life and had stolen from the family, including me, but I would hate to hear they found him dead as a result of an overdose. Olivia was his mother too, and I don't believe he sat in her room and smoked while she was home. I think he was sitting in there trying to wrap his mind around the fact she may not come home and started smoking to cope. After we talked, he was willing to make my three-ways, so I spoke to my family almost every day. Finally, my grandmother had the operation done, and she pulled through just fine.

"Boo Boo, she looks so good! She been sitting up in bed all day talking and laughing. I wish you could see her!" my mother exclaimed when I spoke with her. "She's moving in with your aunt Tasha. You won't have to worry about anything. I'm going to see if I can arrange for you to speak with her sometime this week before I head back home."

My heart was relieved to hear my Olivia was still with us! I had hope once again that I would see that smile and kiss them fat, Cherokee Indian high cheekbones once more. I went to sleep that night worshipful.

March 6, 2006 (Monday)

I had just gone in my room for eleven-thirty count. The officer in the Bubble popped my door. I peeped my head out. She signaled for me to come here. I slipped into my neutral color suede slip-ins.

"What do you think she wants?" Rocky asked. I grabbed my khaki uniform button down shirt as I ran to the window to hear what she wanted. The look in her eyes confirmed the feeling I had in my gut.

"Counselor Brown is requesting for you," the officer said politely, and popped me out my dorm and into the sally port, and then into the door for next door, E8-B where her office was. Everyone was locked down for count, so it was a deafening quiet. The short distance became dreadful with every step. Once I got in front of her door, I didn't even have to tap because she was looking for me.

"Come in," she said from the opposite side. I complied. "Have a seat." She gestured, her hospitality always at its peak. "Do you know why I sent for you?" she asked. Counselor Brown was an attractive, brown-skinned woman that resembled my favorite aunt. She pierced me with her eyes.

"Not exactly, but I know my grandmother is in the hospital, so I figured it has something to do with that." My heart raced a little, but the Holy Spirit would not allow me to panic.

"Yes, your mother asked that you call home. Give me a second." I watched as she picked up the phone and looked at a sticky note where she had jotted down my mother's contact number.

"Lord God, please give me the strength. You are all the family I got in this place. Please give me the strength," I prayed as she waited for my mother to answer.

"Mrs. Ford. Yes . . . just a second." Mrs. Brown handed me the phone.

"Hey, Ma."

"Hey, baby . . ." I knew by her tone what this call was about.

"Momma died?" She didn't respond. "Ma, she's gone, ain't she? Just tell me. My grandma passed?" My tears clung to my eyelids waiting for my mother's answer to release them.

"Yes, Boo Boo. She passed last night. We were so surprised! She was doing so good! The nurse called Tasha shortly after midnight and told her if she wanted to feel Momma while she was still warm, she needed to hurry up because her heart had already stopped."

"Well, Ma. I told y'all it was her decision."

"One of the nurses said that most of them be very energetic, upbeat, and alert the day before they pass. Like the glory of God has settled on them. It must be some truth to it because Momma looked so good, Boo Boo. We were making all these plans, and now she's gone." I heard her crying. I sat with the phone to my ear, slumped over in silence as my tears poured down my face. I didn't want my mother to know how hurt I was. She didn't need to be worried about me as well.

"Ma, we just going to have to hold on to the fact she isn't hurting anymore, and one day we will all meet up for eternity."

"You're right," my mother eventually said. "It just hurts because she had become my best friend." We talked a few more minutes. Counselor Brown was very generous. Her home going service was that Thursday, the ninth, and I knew they wouldn't permit me to attend because not only did I not have the possibility of parole, the service was in another state. No sheriff's department was willing to even be paid enough money to be responsible for me all the way across state lines.

The next few days just felt surreal. I was grateful for my time alone in the wash room all day; it provided me with an opportunity to be in silence. When I shut the door, I could not hear one iota of the noise in the dorm, and the hour I had on wellness daily gave me a chance to minister to others and forget about what I was going through. So if you are persevering in a complicated situation, the best thing for you to do is take the time to uplift someone else. God will minister to your heart like no other when you set your burden aside in hopes of helping someone else survive their storm or misfortune. So if you're in a dark place, unmotivated, or hurting, look around. Who looks like the way you feel? Ask God to give you the words and make an attempt to tell them that you understand how they feel and they will get through it. You will never grow unless you attempt things that you cannot do. Take on challenges that seem impossible and stretch your faith to accommodate your desire.

I read somewhere:

> *Too often we underestimate the power of a touch, a smile, a kind word, a listening ear, an honest accomplishment, or the smallest act of caring, all of which have the potential to turn a life around.*

—Leo Buscaglia

CHAPTER 37

One afternoon I was braiding Rocky's hair, and the officer called me to her desk to tell me to go pack up my property. I was moving to E6, to the Faith and Character dorm. I stood there in shock for a few minutes. It had been *months* since I put in to go to that dorm! I had totally forgotten about it! I walked back to the bench where my roommate was sitting.

"Bunkie, come here for a minute, please," I asked, and then walked straight back to our room. I waited for her to walk in the door. "I'm moving," I just blurted out. There was no other way to say it.

"What you mean? Where are you going?" She instantly looked pitiful, with her shoulders slumped. I felt for her; we really had grown to be a family. We read books together, prepared and ate meals together, sometimes prayed together. She helped me study, and I kept her hair fly. We even broke bread together.

"I signed up for the Faith and Character dorm months ago when I was trying to get out of that room with that nightmare and forgot about it. I never heard anything, so I didn't think about it."

"Can't you refuse or something?" She looked so desperate. "Who's going to do my hair? And who's going to help you with your homework? And who am I going to get as a roommate?" Her thin, high-yellow face reddened.

"I'm not going to refuse the move. I feel like maybe this is God's will for me. I have become a different woman since we have been roommates, and maybe God has something over there in mind for me." She just looked at me for a few seconds.

"You're right. You are evolving, and this environment may be hindering you." Without saying another word we embraced, and then in silence she began to help me pack. In an hour, I was kissing my other

213

choir sisters good-bye and wiping away tears from seeing my roommate so emotional about my departure.

However, the second I walked in the door to my new living quarters, I *knew* this was God's will. I felt like I was at another prison! I moved on D-hall, and I only had twenty-two other women to deal with, outside of my roommate. Instead of ninety plus. Our beds were beside one another, instead of stacked on top of another. The sink was separated from the toilet! In fact, a small wall divided the toilet from the rest of the cell. I would now be having a little privacy! And I wouldn't have to cringe in the middle of the night from having to sit on a freezing cold stainless steel toilet. No, both the toilet and sink were ceramic. My steel wall locker was at the foot of my bunk, on my side of the room, and my additional foot locker was beneath my bunk. I didn't have to wait until my roommate finished plundering in her locker before I could get in my own, being that the lockers were stacked on top of each other as well. Life already looked hopeful.

My new roommate, Su'anne was a quiet white girl that got locked up as a pregnant teen. Got cased up riding with her boyfriend, and now she was tucked away in prison for murder. She would give the system over twenty years of her life before they granted the seven-year lifer parole, she'd also be a survivor of breast cancer and a troubled son by the time freedom rang.

I unpacked and headed to the showers. I was ready to call it a night. I can't explain why moving was so draining. I guess it's more mental than physical, though physically it did require a lot. I walked out my room and across the hall to the door that led to the shower area. My Lord! When I pulled the door open, behind another door was a tub that lay in the back of the 'tub area' surrounded by pretty pink tile all over the entire room, including the floor. Three showers stood open, inviting me to get in either one. But the best part about them were, I could adjust the temperature. I no longer had to press the metal button that sprayed water out, demanding that you press it every minute or so, in order to take a decent shower. Nor the water that was always the same temperature. Nice and hot first thing in the morning. Luke warm before the sun set and barely warm at night, when most people took a shower. I smiled because I knew those days were over!

Once I completed the task of getting freshened up, I was ready to eat something and call it a night. As soon as I stepped off the hallway, immediately to my left was a TV room with several chairs in it. I didn't go in, but I admired the fact it was behind closed doors. It was going to be wonderful to watch something and actually hear it! The entire setting was peaceful, but I naturally felt out of place. There were some people I recognized from work. Kareena, a girl who got locked up at fifteen, along with another broad and a couple dudes. Accused of tormenting a young girl that led to her death. She was someone I would eventually get very close to and dismayed by the fact she would be over forty years old by the time Pardon and Paroles granted her parole and sent her to the Transitional Center, leaving behind her co-defendant. Another white girl name Dania was a facilitator who would conduct my first phase course on Religious Diversity. She too was in for murder and chose to marry a man she met on a write a prisoner website and be straight her entire sentence. After being denied parole twice, she would finally get the chance to enjoy the life of a married woman. There was a Jamaican woman, Jalynn who was doing life for trying to keep from losing her life. She, too would lose both her breasts to cancer, but would be the first female the state paid to give implants and serve almost twenty years on a seven-year life sentence before she was restored to her family. Angel, a young black lesbian, took me by surprise when she confessed what landed her in prison as I braided her hair one night.

"It had been a struggle for months," she explained as her shoulders slumped. "I would get him ready for school, make sure he got his bath at night, and cook his food. But one day when we were alone, I got him out the tub and as I was drying him off, the urge would not go away. I couldn't fight it anymore. So I touched him, and I touched him some more. He said, 'Auntie, I don't like you doing that. Please stop.' I said, 'I'm sorry. Please forgive me. I'm sorry.' Then he ran out the bathroom.

When my mother got home, tearfully I explained what happened. I explained how it had been done to me, and everyone just acted like they didn't know what was happening right beneath their nose. When my sister found out, she pressed charges and here I am."

Am I hearing correct? I questioned in my mind. Nothing could have prepared me for this confession. I could only pray. There was nothing I could say because I wasn't God, and I knew how I would have felt if it was my child. So I just prayed for her.

"Falicia, I really do want to get help. I really didn't want to abuse my nephew. I really love him." She dropped her head and began to cry. She would end up serving all seven of her years and endure some physical aggression from some of the women during her sentence. I got to know plenty of women with various reasons for the crimes they committed, and each one of them gave me something that made me a better woman. Even if it was to witness the power of loving someone. The joy of not being judgmental. I eventually discovered the liberty of being me, even if I stood alone. I could sit down at a table full of strangers and not feel out of place. I could go to church alone and sit next to people I really didn't know and not be uncomfortable. And it was all because I had begun to understand my worth and part of that meant it's not your past that defines you but your present. What you do today, what you do in the face of misfortune, what you do when someone else is hurting or starving or being bullied—that defines you! What you do when no one else is looking is really who you are! This is my understanding of being comfortable in my own skin, and this truth set me free to the point that God began to set others free through my life!

CHAPTER 38

Minister Gray got it approved for her choir to put together a Mother's Day program for the institution. We would give them a mini concert; her son Darvis and his band would be our live band, and he always gave a few words of encouragement as he sang a few songs. Once the entertainment was finished, Minister Gray would give the entire compound some refreshments. All in the name of love and wanting to encourage the mothers as we persevered in the reality of being separated from our own. Losing my grandma weighed heavier on my heart than not seeing my mother and son at the time, so I made every effort to be in the presence of God. I refused to be overtaken by depression or pity.

It was a Friday morning when we all gathered into the gym waiting to unload the truck Minister Gray arrived in that transported the goodies. I believe it was roughly seventy-five choir members. When Minister Gray pulled up, we all began to cheer aloud and rejoice out of excitement for the day. It was bound to be encouraging. It didn't take long to get everything off the truck and situated.

"Hey!" Minister Gray said aloud and got my attention.

"Ma'am?" I wasn't offended that she couldn't recall my name right away.

"Lee-Lee?" It was the name she gave me; the compound called me Fe.

"Yes, ma'am. That's correct." My heart began to swell that she remembered.

"I need you to dance today. Do you have a song in mind?" I just stood there staring at her. It was less than two hours before the program began, and she wanted *me* to dance! "As long as you got a song, God will handle the rest. I was praying about this program last night, and the

217

Lord showed me you dancing. Go get with the sound system crew and pick out a song." With that, she patted my shoulder and carried on with her mission. I imagined my face must have looked shocked, as if I had seen a ghost because several people asked was I all right. But one woman in particular, Miss Arlina, Minister Gray's secretary, always managed to say whatever I needed to hear, or show up at the right time. The caramel-complexioned woman stood about five feet, six inches. Her hair hung past her shoulders, and her accent made it apparent she was from New York, even though she had already spent twenty years in prison for taking the life of an abusive lover who tried to take hers. She would give the system five more years of her life before she was able to go home and hold her first grandbaby. After finally getting to go home, she was confronted with all type of health issues pertaining to her legs and joints. I imagine walking on concrete every day, sitting on metal to eat, watch TV, or write a letter, as well as sleeping on metal would eventually have some effects on the female body.

She spotted me walking across the gym floor and called after me. "Fe, you look like God is surprised."

"Ma'am?" I was trying to get out of my head and listen to what she said.

"This day has been ordained by God, all you need to do is show up. Whatever song you have been listening to, that ministers to you, dance to that song. If it moves you, it will move us." And just like Minister Gray, she walked away on to her next mission.

I took a deep breath and pursued my mission. I claimed to love God, to trust Him with my life, to want to be used by Him. Now was the time to prove it. I walked up to the table where Stephanie was hooking up speakers and working her magic.

"I hate to bother you, but I need to look through your music selection," I said. Stephanie didn't give me the impression that I was disturbing her, but she didn't smile or even say a word. *Maybe she isn't too fond of being interrupted,* I thought.

"I have to dance . . . no—*minister* today. I was wondering if you had

Marvin Sapp's, "Never Would Have Made It?" I asked. She stopped what she was doing and grabbed her bag full of CDs.

The ladies from the dorms on the big side of the compound started coming in and filling up every chair in each row and eventually all the bleachers. I felt honored to be able to serve them, but was afraid the dance wouldn't be good enough because I didn't have any time to practice. But instead of sharing my feelings with anyone, I prayed. Minister Gray brought the choir out by sections, and I stood in the second row of the sopranos. I stood tall, attentive, waiting for her cue to start rocking or singing. She opened up in prayer, acknowledging God first for making the day possible, and then she asked Him to have His way in the place. After we all said Amen, she introduced her son, his band, and her award-winning choir.

"We about to get started, so I ask that you put your hands together for your sister, Lee!" Everyone began clapping, and my bowels rushed to my butt hole! Nobody told me I was dancing first. But I didn't have time to stall or procrastinate with Minister Gray; she would embarrass me. She was serious about you witnessing for God. I stepped out of the line and walked up on the man-made stage and closed my eyes. "Lord, anoint my limbs, use my body as Your vessel to usher Your people into Your presence. Holy Spirit, guide me into every move I make, every gesture. May it all bring You glory! Amen." I was finishing my prayer when I heard Marvin Sapp's voice boom through the sound system. "Never would have made it." I took a deep breath. I was going to catch the next chord.

♪ *Never could have made it without You!* ♪

I crossed my arms in front of me, as if signaling something to be cut off and stopped, then stumbled as if I barely made it to a destination and emphasized the You by pointing up toward heaven. The audience began to clap, the tension in my body was leaving.

♪ *But now I see how you were there for me and I can say, never would have made it!* ♪

My grandma's face flashed before my eyes. All the people in the gym began to disappear, and all I could see was what resembled a throne, but the light that surrounded it was so bright it was hard to look at. I had an audience of one, God alone, and I wanted Him to understand that I realized I would have lost my mind in the midst of all that Ike put me through, being diagnosed with HIV, facing the death penalty, waking up every day not knowing if my son would forget me, or hate me for leaving him, if he would feel I loved the life I was living more than I loved him. Realizing that I had actually taken precious lives away, being haunted by the fact I may never touch turf again. Coming to the realization that my so-called friends would never ride for me, and the unnecessary situations I placed myself in with Jayden, and now accepting that I would never be able to pick up the phone and hear my grandmother's voice again, see her smile, brush her hair, or hold her hand. Which is the very thing I forced three families to endure in my own naivety.

As I danced I understood their grief, their heartache, their misfortune, and I worshipped the God that I hoped carried them, just as He had carried me! By the time the song was ending, I had a face full of tears, and as I looked out at the audience I first began to dance for, many of them were crying as well. Many freely extended their arms toward heaven, and I couldn't withhold the urge I had to yell the name of the Lord! I threw my head back and screamed Jesus! Many hallelujahs followed as well as tears! It just felt like a purging was transpiring. A burden that I couldn't lift dismounted my shoulders and back. I was receiving a breakthrough! I didn't have to carry the weight of my past anymore. God was giving me the grace to forgive myself and forgive those who had hurt me.

For weeks I had been fasting, which is setting aside a specific time to seek the Lord through reading His word, prayer, and the sacrificing of something significant, such as food, beverages, television, music, sexual gratification, etc. Depending on the individual's lack of self-control in whatever area of their life. The goal is to discipline the carnal nature into submission of the spiritual nature. Thus, positioning you to be sensitive to the spiritual realm and the nature of God. So in my case

I was sacrificing any food from the time the sun rose to the sun set, in hopes of breaking any soul ties from my past. I prayed regularly in hopes of hearing God's voice, or His leading about the issues that weighed on my heart. I wanted to be sure that I had forgiven Ike and those that violated me in my youth. It was important because I felt to some degree I was bound by my past and didn't want to someday discover that bitterness or distrust lay dormant within. Crippling me to embrace people wholeheartedly. The Lord revealed to me that my heart was like a piece of rug, nice and soft on the top, but if you dug past the superficial surface there was this thick, rough texture that couldn't be ripped with natural hands or torn. It had to be cut in order to penetrate the fabric. If you're getting a tattoo, the first time the needle penetrates you, you may be caught off guard. So the next time the needle sticks you, you are a little tense trying to prepare yourself for the needle to drive into your skin. Fifteen minutes into the masterpiece, you cannot relax. Your entire body is tense, and you are doing everything mentally and physically to brace yourself for the pain that is sure to come.

My heart was tense, trying to brace itself for the pain, disappointment, and separation that was sure to come. I let people in superficially, because new friends were bound to leave me behind in prison and someday fall off. No relationships I had seen ever lasted. People changed like the weather. As long as I met their expectations I was wonderful, anointed, a blessing, sent by God, but the second I climbed off their pedestal, I was full of hypocrisy, arrogant, and selfish. It was easy to love people, but I wasn't comfortable with them loving me, if that makes sense. I can make sure you're straight and give you whatever out of my commissary bag, but wouldn't ask a soul if I needed something. Stop whatever I'm doing to pray with you, but dare not utter a word about what I needed prayer for. I lived expecting to be let down, and as a result, I couldn't recognize the people God was sending into my life because everyone just about wore the same face.

One day while I was in the shower, the Holy Spirit spoke to me. *Forgive him,* I heard. I didn't need to ask who, I already *knew*! "I thought

I have," I spoke aloud as if He was in the shower next to me.

"Forgive him." I heard it again. I started to get frustrated, but then I thought that would be premature of me, so in my mind I started trying to think of ways I could forgive, ways I still may need to let it go. Then the story of Samuel when he was a boy came to mind. Samuel was lying down in the temple of the Lord, where the ark of God was. And he heard his name being called.

"Here I am." He jumped and ran to where Eli the priest was lying, thinking he was calling him. Eli said I didn't call for you, go lie back down. This happened twice, but by the third time it happened, Eli realized what was going on and told Samuel, "Go lay back down and if it happens again say, 'speak Lord, for your servant is listening."

Samuel went and lay back down, and the Lord called him again and he answered accordingly and God began to speak to him. (1 Samuel 3) I stood there with the water running trying to figure out the significance of that story and my situation.

"Okay. Lord, I am listening. Speak," I said aloud and shut my eyes, anticipating an audible voice to give me some instructions or direction. Something.

Silence!

"Here I am, Lord, with an open heart, listening." I figured I needed to be more humble in my approach so I reworded it.

Silence!

"Well, what's the point?" I asked aloud, getting irritated and started bathing again. Just as I was finishing, the thought came to my mind like a light bulb blinking above an animated character's head: *Just confess it out loud.*

Why hadn't I thought of that? I thought.

"Ike, I forgive you for everything that you put me through. I forgive you for physically abusing me, every time you left me feeling like I wasn't enough. I forgive you for preying on my love for you and manipulating it to your advantage. I forgive you for robbing me of my life with my son and every heartache this will cause for him. I forgive you for being so broken and misguided. For being so entangled in deceit that you couldn't be real with yourself, much less me and anyone else. Ike, I forgive you! I release your power to further hinder or affect my life in any negative aspect! In Jesus' name.

"And I forgive everyone who has sought to do me harm, spoke curses over my life, over my existence and purposely set me up to fail. I forgive you and release you to live and stop preying on others from this point forward. In Jesus' name." By the time I said amen, I was doubled over with my hands on my knees and the water pouring up my back, saturating my hair and dripping from my face as it mixed with my tears. I knew I was being made whole. The power I felt in every fiber of my body convinced me that every word I had just spoken was activating itself in heaven and forcing earth to get in alignment with it.

In that moment I realized God is simple. We make things so complicated. He gave us His word, His Spirit, His Anointing and His Son. What do we do with it? Sit back in bondage, *acting* as if we are some defeated foes. *Acting* as if God is suddenly unable to deliver. *Acting* as if we have gotten so far away from God that He can't reach you where you are. *Acting* as if we somehow have come to hate our Maker, when even in the worst situation we can see how we are being kept, even if it's just the fact that we are still in our right mind. Let's stop *acting* as if one day we'll receive a Grammy for our performance and start living. I operate best when I'm myself. Please allow me to be myself as I invite you to be the real you, and not what everyone wants you to be, or who you have convinced yourself you are. Come forth, true woman of God! Woman of Empowerment, woman of Strength! Nurturer, Healer, and Forgiver! Come forth, man of God! Man of Integrity. Provider, Protector, and Overcomer!

Live!

CHAPTER 39

I was notified that it was time to start the qualifying test for those who were planning to test for their GED not long before I found out my grandmother's health was failing. I had at least two more months of work left in Math before I could even mention being ready to test. This disturbed me because I set a personal goal to obtain my GED in a year, and prior to coming to prison, the only goals I set and adhered to was making my daily quota and not getting my head rocked. I kept praying, *Lord, You know what this means to me!*

One day that same week my teacher called me to her desk. "Ms. Blakely, why have you been looking so stressed all week?" I'll never forget it. God had allowed her to take notice of my countenance and pave the way as an opportunity for me to say what I didn't think to simply address on my own. Told you God is simple.

"Well, honestly, Ms. Roberson, I was hoping that I would have been ready to do the qualifying test. I wanted to be out of here in a year."

"What subjects do you still need to complete?" Her chubby face and mocha skin put me in mind of a Cabbage Patch Kid. I knew she was grown, but she didn't look a day over twenty.

I sighed. "Just math." I sounded just as defeated as I felt.

"That's it?" Her eyes widened and her neck slightly jerked back. "If you feel you are ready to take the qualifying test, you can. I'll sign you up."

"You will?" I popped up from the chair she had sitting next to her desk as if something hot was underneath me. This had to be a God thing! Favor really isn't fair. Most times we receive mercy we don't deserve. And as I looked around the class at all the people I had just disrupted, I felt remorseful for my outburst, but I couldn't deny the urge to praise God. So for a few seconds I did a foot work, praising God. A dance that you might see one of the mothers in a Pentecostal church doing.

The next two weeks, Ms. Roberson had me on my grind. She assigned one of the teacher's aides to me, and she made me work out one geometry problem after the other. By the end of the two weeks, I was discouraged. Whenever I studied alone, I would somehow figure out how to get the answer, but when my aide asked me to demonstrate, I could not carry out the formula correctly, though my answer was correct! Ms. Roberson worked with me and let me go ahead and pretest on the other subjects. By the end of the third week, science and math were the only ones I had left. I decided to just do it; it was a sink or swim situation. To my surprise, I scored above average on math, but my science was a train wreck. Ms. Roberson stopped me as I was packing up my material to go back to the dorm.

"Ms. Blakely, this is garbage!" She walked up to me with an exam form shredded in several pieces. "I don't know if you were stressed about the math exam or not, but this"—She held up the shredded form— "Is not going to cut it. This one subject can keep you from taking the actual exam. Now take this book and blank bubble-in form and go sit your behind in that empty room and past this test!" I could only stare at the usually soft-spoken woman. She had never been stern with anyone, let alone make any demands. "You said you wanted to be out of here in a year, then act like it!" I was left speechless. I just did as I was told, and when I sat down at a desk in the empty class next door to Ms. Roberson, I dropped my head.

"Lord, please take the test with me!" Needless to say by the end of February I was taking my exam, and on March 15, 2006, I was called to the Education building to receive my Certificate and $500 voucher because I had successfully obtained my GED! One month and eight days over my one-year goal! For the first time in a long time I felt I possessed what was needed to accomplish anything I desired. I was ready to further my education, and it would begin with Cosmetology school.

At this point, I was entering my second phase of the Faith and Character program, Confronting Self I and II. Twenty-four of us reported out to the Program's building every Thursday night from six to eight, to pile up in a classroom and form a circle with long tables in between us. The cramped room forced us to accept that it wasn't intended for this type of arrangement, but we made it work. Along with the chaplain and a volunteer, we openly discussed and reasoned how we ended up in our current state and what cognitive thinking we could exercise to overcome the previous way of thinking and replace it with effective responses.

This program began to show me the importance of team work. There were many committees set in motion on each of the four halls to accomplish the greater purpose. The Birthday Committee was responsible for keeping up with all twenty-four residents' birthdays on their hall. Making sure that the card was made and signed by everyone, except the birthday girl. Along with providing them something sweet, usually a honey bun with chocolate swirled on top. The Sanitation Committee was responsible for making sure our hall received our allotted chemicals to clean and disinfect our living quarters. They also were the ones you address if the dorm orderlies failed or neglected to clean their assigned areas. The Hygiene Committee had to be someone who had a great personality and could hold a conversation with anyone because they had to be the person to tell someone if their hygiene wasn't up to par and try to direct the individual in the direction of how to make it better. It's hard telling a grown woman that her behind is smelling. If the individual didn't have the required personal products to accomplish the task at hand, the committee would provide that individual with some, as a result of a generous donation from the Chaplaincy Department. Then there was the Welcoming Committee. They were responsible for making a welcome card and having all the dorm sign it so that when new residents moved in, they can have an inviting welcome. It made it easier to get settled in. This particular committee started after I moved into the dorm.

Confronting "self" required me to do a family tree. With this assignment I had to pin point my family members who had a high school and college education. Which strongholds repeated itself throughout the generations. I needed the assistance of my mother to complete this assignment. What I discovered was most troubling to me. Domestic violence was something the women in my family suffered more so than any drug or alcohol addictions. This saddened me because when I was being abused, I was ashamed to tell anyone what was happening to me. It caused me to question how I would have reacted to the situation had I known this type of thing wasn't foreign to my family.

During this time I began my quest to get into Cosmetology school. I kept getting the run around about getting an application to apply, so when I saw the cosmetology instructor leaving the mail box picking up request forms, I stopped her on the walk.

"Excuse me, Miss." I walked up to her, but gave enough space between us so she wouldn't feel threatened. The woman stopped and looked at me. Her expression had a resting bitch face. Her big, wet and wavy hair flared out from her head like sun rays and danced on her shoulders, resembling Chaka Khan, but her attire put me in the mind of a nurse because she was wearing scrubs. "I'm not trying to hold you up; it's just that I have been trying to apply for your class, but I have been unsuccessful."

"Well, the first thing that I see wrong is the fact you are breaking institutional rules with your hair," the African American woman stated, matter-of-factly. I had to chuckle just a bit to maintain my composure and not say anything that incriminated myself. *Did she really just go there?*

"Breaking institutional rules? I don't understand why you feel that way." I felt myself getting heated! I had never had a conversation with this woman, and this was our introduction.

"Y'all are not permitted to have locks." She frowned, and I promise I saw her chest rising and falling. She looked at me like she was about to arrest me.

"No one has ever told me that we were not permitted to have them."

"I'm not about to stand here and tongue wrestle with you!" She shifted her weight and stuck her neck out as if she was accepting a challenge. I burst out laughing. This encounter had just went all left, and I still hadn't fulfilled my purpose of stopping her.

"I feel you. If you don't mind, could I pick up an application, or can you send me one through in-house mail?" I checked my tone and asked as humbly as my body would permit.

"When you're ready, come see me." She looked me in the eyes as she stated her benediction, but it felt more like she sized me up, and then walked away. I donned a smile, but internally I was a wreck. I just knew after I had a chance to speak to her I would secure a position, or at least be added to the waiting list, but I felt anything but that. In fact, I wasn't trying to make it a race thing, but it was beginning to feel like all my sporadic issues were with my own kind. I couldn't wait to get back to the dorm so I could lay before Him. As far as I was concerned, my encounter with her was a spiritual attack, and the only way to battle spiritual warfare is in the spiritual realm. Prayer was a key weapon, and I used it gladly. Every time I walked past Cosmetology, I placed my hand against the window and made a confession of faith:

"I declare in the name of Jesus, I will be working here soon."
"I declare that is my booth right there." I would point one out.
"I declare room is being made for me, right now, in Jesus' name."

Once a quarter, every three months we had what was called a Community Meeting. The entire dorm gathered in the day area to address our concerns, issues, and requests that related to those who were in the program. Our new warden, Mr. Tim Chipman, Deputy Warden of Care and Treatment, the Chaplain, along with our GP Counselor were also present. We put together a program to display what we were learning and expressed our spirituality in creative ways. During this particular meeting I was asked to do a praise dance. I felt this was a major opportunity to make a different impression on Administration. I danced to Yolanda Adams', "A Prayer Away." Several residents were crying, and I affiliated their tears with God ministering to them, but the warden seemed uncomfortable with the fact some were emotional.

"How come when you touch that inmate's hands she began to cry?" he asked, after he called me over to him once the meeting was over.

"Honestly, sir, the only explanation I can give you is that something about the meaning behind the song and the Spirit of God moving on the hearts of His people as He does at church, is the reason they cry."

"Hmm . . ." he murmured and leaned back into the chair. "They don't do this dancing stuff at my church." He looked me straight in the eyes. There wasn't a frown or a smirk anywhere present in his expression. I wasn't sure how to take him. *Lord God, you know the intentions of my heart. I need you to give me the words to say.*

"I don't know if I want you to continue dancing at these meetings." I just looked at him.

"Warden Chipman, with all due respect . . ." I kneeled next to him, so it wouldn't appear I was hovering over him. "A lot of denominations choose to exclude praise dancing because they don't understand the power behind it. It is a ministry within itself. Some people find themselves able to identify with the worship dancer as they demonstrate the emotions and words of the song. Dance is a form of worship.

"King David danced before the Lord with all his might as the Ark of God was being brought back from the household of Obededom to the city of David. Don't be like David's wife, Michal, the daughter of Saul who despised his worship in her heart and was without children to the day of her death. This is a form of worship for me and many others. Try and understand, God is not always the god we have in the box of our minds. He's greater than the human mind can comprehend and wiser than the most intelligent person we know that exists."

"I don't know, Ms. Blakely." He shuffled in his seat.

"That's fine, Warden Chipman. God understands your inability to receive what I'm saying. With time you'll see where I'm coming from." He gave me a weak smile, but I, on the hand, was showing gums and all. I felt privileged to have such a conversation with one in such high authority. God had just arranged a divine encounter, and what I said to him could possibly lead him away from traditional church and into a

Spirit-filled worship setting. Were God's words present and manifesting His glory? Some churches are so adamant on following their program every service, the entire congregation quotes certain scriptures, sing certain hymns and the pastor preaches, never permitting God the chance to intervene and move by His Spirit.

I was about to walk away when I thought about my pressing concern. "Oh, if you don't mind, Warden Chipman. May I ask you something that isn't related to this program?" He nodded yes, still sitting there looking uncomfortable. "I'm trying to get into Cosmetology school and—"

"Talk to Deputy Warden Flowers. That's her department, Care and Treatment." He cut me off. I looked in his eyes to see if he was being malicious, since he interrupted me before I could finish. His expression looked gentle. "It's the chain of command. I allow my deputies to handle their department, and if they don't, then I get involved. Remember that." He finally smiled genuinely and set his attention on the other activity going on in the room.

I went and stood in the short line to speak with Deputy Warden Flowers. It wouldn't be long before someone would keep Warden Tim Chipman occupied again. As I stood there, my heart celebrated the fact I was even having this chance. Nowhere else on the compound did Administration take out this kind of time to listen to inmates.

My chance finally arrived after standing in line ten minutes. I saw Mrs. Flowers look down at her watch. I knew to make it brief because they would be ready to leave soon.

"DW Flowers, if you have the time I would like to bring something to your attention that doesn't relate to the dorm."

"What is it?" She looked me directly in the eyes as she gestured for me to sit down in the chair next to her. Her aura felt very loving, like one of a grandparent. The longer version of the auburn pixie cut she donned seemed suitable by the way she out dressed her colleagues.

"I'm trying to get into Cosmology, but all my attempts have been unsuccessful," I stated with caution. Not knowing if she led with a velvet glove or a hammer.

"Talk to Mrs. Prease," she answered with ease, as if the problem was solved just like that.

"I have, and the only thing she wanted to discuss was my hair." With suspicious eyes, she looked up at my hair.

"What's the issue with your hair?" She looked confused.

"That's exactly what I want to know!" I was beginning to feel as if this was going in my favor, so I let my guard down.

"What are those in your hair? Plaits?"

"No ma'am, these are locks," I confessed. Her face twisted into a slight frown.

"Locks, as in *dread* locks!" She leaned away from me as if the wind would blow something foul on her any second.

"Not necessarily dread locks, ma'am, but my hair is locked," I replied respectfully. Trying to overlook the fact that she suddenly was acting as if I was diseased. "Ma'am, my hair is not nasty. I shampoo my hair every other week and maintain all my new growth. You have never seen my hair look a mess."

"Those things are disgusting! And you will not ever work in my Cosmetology as long as you have them," she retorted. I was taken aback, confused by how this sweet woman had just flipped on me.

"This is a part of my culture, and I would appreciate it if you got enlightened before you walk around calling people's hair nasty." I stood up and walked away.

I heard her say, "I didn't say you were nasty, but your hair . . ." I didn't even reply. If someone's head is disgusting, how could the individual not be as well? If a part of someone carries an odor, that person stinks as a whole. If someone doesn't brush their teeth, that individual is viewed as sorry and/or lacks the ability to maintain their hygiene, period. I went to my room infuriated. First my dance and then my hair! No doubt I made the outcome of this experience a reflection on the color of my skin.

One of the things I was beginning to realize in my Christian walk was that God would often put people in your life to assist you in your walk with God. My first close encounter with a prophetess came in the form of a young black woman name Alisa. She moved into the FCBP dorm about two months after I had. The first conversation we ever had was her correcting me in the Lord.

"Miss Blakely, I'm not comfortable telling you this, but the Lord is not pleased with your prayer life." I looked at this woman like: *How do you know?*

"I can hear you thinking, 'How do I know,' and I do because God told me so. He is calling for you to be consistent. Pick a time and meet him there daily."

I wasn't sure how I felt being around someone who knew me, knew me—like—could see through me, but she made it easy to be around her. My walk began to progress drastically by me simply taking the time out after count. I would get two loads started, and then go in my cell and put on my headphones and worship. *Gospel Wow 2007* was the first album that assisted me in reverencing God. At first I didn't understand what was happening. I would just be singing along with the artist and the words got personal. Next thing I knew I was crying, and before long I was on my face, prostrate before God. You never realize what you need until you get it, and then nothing goes right without it. My entire attitude was beginning to be a whole lot sweeter and humbler as I met God Monday through Friday in the middle of that floor. Whenever Alisa and I would join hands in prayer, I saw something in the spiritual realm I hadn't seen alone.

One day in choir rehearsal, Minister Gray had heard that there was hostility and backbiting going on in the dorm between two choir members. So she called them to the circle, so they could openly discuss their issue, and in decency, agree on a way to get past the offense. At some point, one of the sisters was very defensive and unwilling to be corrected about her attitude. Minister Gray told all of us to pray. I don't know if she instructed us to pray so that we wouldn't have time to sit in judgment if we were talking to the Lord, or she felt a demonic spiritual force oppressing the sister. Whatever the reason, I grabbed Alisa's hand on my left and another sister was on my right and began to pray in my spiritual language. Alisa did the same, but hers was more forceful, as if God was revealing something to her. Suddenly, I saw the sister's (the one who had been hostile) features change. Her ears became pointy, her eyes shifted, and her entire countenance darkened. Alisa's language changed, and I blinked several times, assuming I was tripping. Later that night Alisa asked if God allowed me to see in the spirit behind the face. This was the beginning of things that God would show me, though not always in this form.

I connected with another young lady who was almost the same age as me from the day she moved across the hall. Her name is Kimee. She's a beautiful, short, chocolate thing with glasses.

"Hey, I'm Falicia! Welcome to our hall. Would you like a hug?" It was the first thing I said to her. She stopped in her tracks and looked at me with a puzzled expression. I knew I was being over the top, but as she carried her property down the hall to her new assigned room, panic and uncertainty screamed out from her face like a genuine smile declares you're in a good mood! "You can give me a hug, we family over here." She gave me a weak smile, but extended her arms to receive my embrace. From that day forward, we were two peas in a pod. She was a really good cook, and I specialized in eating so we spent a lot of time talking over meals! The relationship we developed was special to me. I felt as if I had found my long lost sister. Whenever we discussed my past and the things I had been subjected to, she would often cry. I felt the burden she bore because her mother died while she was young, and she naturally felt like her two younger sisters were her responsibility. Then at the prime of her youth, she discovered that the man who had been raising her and was the father of her two sisters, was not her biological father. When she met her real dad, he made a pass at her, openly displaying his sexual attraction to her. I cried with her. It was hard enough coming to accept the man you love and adore isn't rightfully yours, and then your very own makes an attempt to have sex with you! What kind of sick games were being played?

CHAPTER 40

As the weeks passed, God began to deal with me. *If it's My will for you to take your locks out, would you?* This question came up often, and in the beginning I was dead set on the fact I shouldn't have to. I felt like a rebel at heart. But as time progressed and wisdom began to guide me, I came to terms with the fact that in this world we live in, some people will never know how to embrace people in their individuality. Most people fear what they do not understand, but because of the beauty of which God made me to be, I can still stand tall no matter the label tagged to me: stripper, murderer, manipulator, sick, lifer, black, uneducated, poor, selfish, stupid, etc. . . . I have been misunderstood from the beginning, and just because I make a few adjustments in my life to ease your discomfort, so you can stand in the same room with me and not feel inferior, doesn't make me weak. It makes me humble because I recognize being black, beautiful, and strong isn't about proving anything to anyone. It's about rising above the judgments of someone else's mind and still shine.

Fifteen minutes per lock. Seven and a half days total. Six days alone of gradually ripping a part of myself away as I combed out one lock at a time. It's sad, but I still can't explain how a piece of me died. On the seventh day, my roommate Mrs. Black assisted me in completing the task of removing all my locks. After the fact, to many, my hair was so beautiful. To others it was long. To me it was just a stepping stone, doing what I needed to do so that I could conquer my next ambition in life as I secretly held on to the fact that through my ignorance, I had willingly chosen this life for myself where people, even those of the same skin color, found purpose in oppressing us. Without hesitation, they believed it was okay to prepare meals in a kitchen that rats dominated, to scoop our servings from pans that cockroaches crawled across or lay dead in, or flies freely landed on. Make no mistake, in this place we are not human. We do not deserve to be respected. We are inmates and inmates are animals. "If you don't like how you are being treated, you should not have come here," many correctional officers often said.

Another thing I realized about prison is that you are categorized by social status, based on the amount of money you spend weekly at the store, or accumulate weekly through various means of hustling or gambling on the card table. In other words, the amount of food you produce weekly and your ability to make moves.

High Class spends sixty dollars every week or has some form of plug and can produce some form of contraband in a way that others can't. They always have commissary and are never in a position to ask someone else for anything. Most likely, these are people who pay other people to wash their clothes, shoes, bed linen, and do their hair. Middle Class goes to the store regularly or hustles in order to survive. If they lack something, they normally make some form of trade-off. Sell you something from the kitchen or off their detail to prevent being in debt to anyone. They are the 'go to' when you need something because their detail is a means of survival for them, so they are willing to take risks to make sure they have. For example, chemical detail workers will sell a bottle of pure bleach for two dollars. You don't mind paying for it because the bleach you get in the dorm is so diluted it's not even yellow.

Kitchen detail workers are always selling something for a dollar. On days when the compound's breakfast menu is oatmeal, eggs, chicken sausage, and muffins, someone who is a cook may make ten to twenty eggs, cheese, and toast sandwiches all for a dollar. And it's a system in which residents work together. The cook will trade off something for bread and cheese with the person who makes pack outs (two sandwiches, a piece of fruit, and a snack (cookies on a good day)) in order to make the sandwiches. Someone who works in the bakery may trade off a couple gloves of sugar for a bag of oatmeal that can go from anywhere from one to three dollars. Everyone benefits when they work together. Or on a day when the menu is chicken and rice for dinner, chocolate cake with powdered sugar on top, instead of icing. The cook is supposed to boil all the chicken, then break it up and mix it with the rice, but instead she will set a pan of at least thirty pieces of chicken aside. Remove the skin, season and batter it and drop it down in some grease for a few minutes and make fried chicken skins, which are sold a dollar per bowlful. Take the chicken and either repeat the same process to make fried chicken, which is a big deal because the prison only serves oven fried chicken or makes toasted pulled chicken sandwiches, minus the BBQ sauce for a dollar. Some cooks, depending on how much leeway one may have, make onion rings as well. Some bakers make apple or peach turnovers or donuts or even brownies, depending on how experienced of a cook they are (knowing what to make with what they have to work with). And those who just clean up or work on line always just brings back extra food to the dorm so they can make a few dollars by selling three meat patties for a dollar or four or five bananas for a dollar. Inside maintenance gets paid to transport stuff or fix things like the frame of your glasses, your fan, or watch. Medical orderlies most likely are the ones putting the hand sanitizer out on the compound. Which is unfortunate because some people used to drink it.

Low Class are those who are indigent and never make store. Most lifers, those who have been sentenced to life, fall under this category. Poverty is the number one reason for murder in our communities, so most lifers come from poverty-stricken homes, and their families are unable to support them. They may have shamed their families to the point of having no moral support, or their family has died over the years and they are left alone. Thus, resulting in a group of people who solely rely on what the state provides.

And those who are indigent most likely have an account that is hundreds of dollars if not thousands of dollars in debt to the state for utilizing the systems that are set in motion for them. Requesting envelopes, paper, writing utensils or carbon paper, sending out mail weekly through indigent mail and being charged for it. Eventually it adds up, just like all the five-dollar copay trips to Medical and the dentist, along with the five-dollar-fee for every prescription you leave with. This class of people stands out like sore thumbs. Their clothes are dingy, as a result of sending them to the institution laundry, which claims to wash our clothes, but they always come back brownish looking. More than likely, their clothes were washed with too many other clothes and barely got enough soap or was burnt from the heat of the dryers, you guess which one.

Their shoes are worn because they probably received them as 'hand me downs' from someone who didn't want them anymore for whatever reason, or even took them out of the trash. I have seen a few incidents where someone bought an indigent person a brand new pair of shoes, but after six years, a pair of white sneakers will look yellow and may even be bursting at the seams. Their teeth are yellow, from only having state toothpaste to brush their teeth and most drink black coffee because that's what the chow hall serves, and it's cheaper to obtain as opposed to asking someone for coffee, creamer, and sugar every day. Though these individuals usually try to survive by washing other people clothes, only a few make enough money to live comfortably, and those who do, often suffer from blisters on their hands from repeatedly being exposed to pure bleach and scrubbing dirty clothes clean.

As society enforces certain standards without ever personally discussing your take on the matter, so it goes with these categories that are also set in motion and acted upon without anyone ever saying a word. People naturally treat you with respect and seek to befriend you if you are financially stable. Everyone wants to be in good graces with the 'go to person' because you want that person to always keep you in mind when they come up. But when it comes to those who go without, the only people that take heed to them are those who have compassion on others, or can relate to what it's like to be in their shoes.

CHAPTER 41

On March 30, 2007, we had a formal graduation. My mother and my son showed up. I had my hair in a straw set. Man seemed to be the most excited about being able to run his hands through my hair.

By April 6, 2007, they moved every single one of us (except one person) who went to the Honor Dorm moved into E9-A. Under the pretense that the purpose of the program was to create leaders who could go out and shift the atmosphere and perception of others who lacked the skills we had obtained. Therefore, by moving us together in our new living quarters, we had a better chance of demonstrating to other inmates the skills we had just learned to actively walk in, and our first challenge would be to bring the sanitation of our dorm up. Get the other women motivated to clean and take their neighbor into consideration, encourage teamwork, and build some form of unity, which would be our toughest challenges.

A new program, Career Center, was being developed as my time was coming to an end. I spoke with my counselor in hopes of remaining in the dorm, but it wasn't my time. Nothing I said or demonstrated was enough to secure me a position to remain in the dorm, and I had to accept that. If it was God's will, it would happen.

As we all walked in the dorm with multiple pushing carts full of our property, the entire dorm came to a standstill and watched to see who was moving in, and those who had empty bunks listened for who would become their new roommate. It was a process that could be a little uncomfortable, knowing that all eyes were on you, sizing you up and checking you out to see how much food you possessed. In my mind, the majority were scoping the scene out to see what they can come ask you for later, and if you told them you didn't have any of what they asked you for, some people would tell you, "Yes you do. I saw it in your bag."

In this instance, I just tried overlooking the foolishness. And I would do so by excusing myself, or looking past that person without a reply as I searched the room for familiar faces.

"Niecy Fe!" a very familiar voice called out to me. I looked in the direction of the voice and locked eyes with one of the most beautiful women I had come to know. My heart felt as if it leaped for joy. Aunt Carol stood by the laundry room smiling at me. This woman had taken me under her wing in the county jail and helped me understand what God was doing in me and through me. Many days she dried my tears and stood in her faith when I had none, until I was strong enough to stand alone. She even came to visit me after she was released! This was my God-given aunt, and without any shadow of a doubt, she loved me. Her family had grown to love me as a result of her love for me.

Unfortunately, I didn't even know this woman was here, let alone in this dorm. We embraced, and I immediately felt the heaviness of her heart. I knew her well enough to know she was beating herself up for coming to prison. It was clarified in that moment that God had sent me over here.

"I want you to meet someone," she told me, unable to restrain her excitement as she extended her arm to welcome the presence of an older, heavyset woman with graying hair. "This is Mom Dukes." I wrapped my arms around her, and she too was heavy.

"Oh Lord, please strengthen this woman," I prayed, barely above a whisper. When we released one another, Mom Dukes' eyes were misty, but she smiled brightly.

"You the girl that does those praise dances, aren't you?" She looked so excited. I nodded yes. "Oh, God sent you over here for me!" she exclaimed. "My son got killed Sunday, and tomorrow is his funeral. I have seen you dance. You are anointed, and God put you over here with me." I watched as she went and sat back down at a table. She wouldn't stop smiling, and it blessed me that—one: she had the will to still be smiling, and two: a woman who had just lost her son to violence could be so encouraged to see me, the very person who'd left several mothers to bear the same burden she was now carrying. I was convinced God was shifting me in the spiritual realm, and the purpose for me being here wasn't just to help others, but for me to recognize what lay within me as well!

I had moved into a cell with Tammy, a Caucasian woman who once stayed across the hall from me in the Faith and Character Dorm. It was kind of comforting knowing I was in the room with someone who could relate to what I felt about the transition and the mission that Administration expected us to accomplish.

The next day I went next door to Mom Dukes, but she was already gone to her son's funeral by the time I got there. Being that it was such short notice, I didn't have time to make her a banner, so I just went through my pictures and picked her out some flowers and signed the back declaring God's word on her. Ken loved to take pictures of nature, so I had all types of lilies, sunflowers, morning glories, etc. Auntie Carol had a card that she let me sign and put my pictures inside. She and I spent the afternoon catching up. Mom Dukes was legendary in her small town. She had been pushing dope for years, and her son was set up by his friend whom she took into her home when they were lads. All because her son wanted to get out of the dope game and show his own son another way. His god-brother, who they know was present at the apartment had gone into hiding. The family believed he had something to do with it, but Mom Dukes was convinced her godson knew what happened but didn't want it to cost his head as well.

Aunt Carol had gotten caught up with them credit cards, and it landed her in prison this time. She was a quiet woman that didn't say much, unless it was necessary to speak. So as I sat across from her listening to her express how it concerned her that her mother's HIV medicine wasn't counteracting with her Hepatitis medicine, I knew her fear was that something might happen to her mother while she was in prison, and she wouldn't forgive herself.

Most women in prison carried this type of guilt. It's a common reaction to think, "If I wasn't in prison I could have . . ." But in my opinion, had it not been for prison, eighty-five percent of us would have been worse off had the law not interceded in our lives. For me, I would have been dead. I'm convinced Ike would have ordered my life be taken by now, or the streets would have claimed me behind his foolishness. So instead of thinking what I could have done if I was present; I openly apologized to my family for not being there and thought of ways to help the situation they were facing.

One day while I was upstairs in my cell listening to music trying to prepare a dance for the upcoming church service, this woman asked to speak to me.

"Of course," I replied as I took my headphones off and set them on the bed. "You can sit on the stool," I instructed her as I sat on the toilet. I began to pray because I didn't ever want to say something that I thought someone needed to hear. I wanted God to speak *through* me. So once she was settled, I told her I was listening.

"Well . . ." she said, then paused. Apparently, a little hesitant. I stilled my thoughts so I didn't assume I knew why her body language was uncomfortable. "Falicia, I know you don't know me, but I work for the City of Cochran detail." It was a small county that contracted with the prison for its inmates to clean the sides of the roads, the gutters, and perform grounds keeping duties. "This dude has been trying to talk to us for about a month from Dodge. Well today, he had an opportunity, and he asked if anyone knew his wife, Falicia Blakely."

"He asked for me specifically?" I was caught off guard.

"Yes. A tall, dark, brown-skinned dude, medium built." She extended her arm to describe a six foot tall man. "Low haircut. Does he sound familiar?" I didn't reply right away, but my gut already confirmed who this was.

"Let me ask you something. Did you or anyone get close enough to see in his mouth?"

"Actually, I did. When I told him you were in my dorm, he smiled. He has a gap or a chipped tooth or something in the front. No offense. He isn't cute, but he's sexy." I felt as if I could have shrunk and disappeared into one of the cranks in the floor. It had been five years with no signs of Ike, not a single word. And now suddenly he was locked up on this detail inquiring about me. Ken was the first person I wrote to get him to look Ike up.

"Thank you for taking out the time to come tell me." I stood to my feet and gave the woman a hug.

"Well, do you want me to tell him anything if I get to speak with him again?" She seemed genuinely helpful.

"No, ma'am. You can say whatever you want, but I don't have anything I desire for you to carry back." After she left my cell, I sat down at my desk on the stool and just kind of zoned out. I was unsure how I was supposed to feel. This man had altered my life and was still walking around calling me his wife! Hate wasn't the feeling I experienced, and that caused conflict within me because I believed I should have felt something of that nature. Anything opposite of love. Nothing. I got down on my knees and I cried to God. I cried because somehow Ike still had the power to disrupt my life, to affect me. I cried, relieved that if he was incarcerated he wasn't free to corrupt another young girl's or woman's life for that matter. I cried because maybe, just maybe, God had answered my prayers. Maybe Ike had come to understand his ways were evil, and he was willing to surrender his life and will to the Lord.

I wrote Ken a letter with the latest info, knowing if there was any truth to it he would find out about it. Afterward, I put my headphones back on and got in the middle of the floor and danced to Yolanda Adams', "Step Aside." With a face full of tears, I mimicked the words of this song with my body. Thirty minutes ago this song was powerful. But now it was relevant! I needed to step aside, get out of God's way, and let Him do what only he can do. This would definitely be the song I danced to at church that Friday night. I believed in my heart it had to minister to me first before it would touch anyone else.

Minister Gray's Friday night service came, and the power of God was so strong she didn't even have to say a word. People just cried out to God and worshipped in their unique ways. For me, I had my mind made up that I would not leave out the way I came in. The weight of the unknown would not rob me of the joy Christ bled for. It didn't matter if anyone was looking at me, I was determine to get my breakthrough. Before the service even began, I got in the corner and completely opened my heart during praise and worship service. I wanted to be in alignment when God extended the invitation to the Holy of Holies. I did not completely understand how I was being affected by Ike, but I knew enough about God to know He understood me through and through, so I was taking the model back to the Manufacturer, and I would come out brand new. By the time I ministered through dance, I had a vengeance with the devil. He had been trying to play on my emotions, and I was determined that every soul that was able to witness me dance would leave that gym determined within themselves to step aside as well!

The next morning I was awakened to my roommate getting off the top bunk in a hurry to go outside for yard call. I let her finish rushing around while she was making a cup of coffee to take out with her before I got up.

"That woman didn't even brush her teeth," I complained as I reflected on her poor hygienic habits. Like clockwork I used the toilet, washed my hands, brushed my teeth and poured bleach on everything that needed to be disinfected. Then I made my bed. Afterward, I wiped down and swept the floor. I noticed some mail for me lying on the desk. It must have come in late mail, where the officer slid it under the door.

April 2007, I received my second subscription of *Sister 2 Sister* magazine and a money receipt. One day someone gave me a bunch of *Sister 2 Sister* magazines because I had been whining about not being able to sleep. This one article about DMX moved me because it was a raw interview in which he revealed his personal struggles. I was so moved that I wrote the magazine commenting on the article and had Ken get me a subscription.

After I finished cleaning, I took a shower and then fixed me some oatmeal and a cup of coffee with a little bit of creamer in it. Satisfied with the fresh, clean smell of my cell and tidiness of it, I lay back on my wedge, crossed my ankles and opened my magazine. Skimming through to see what would catch my attention. Then I flipped back to the *Peaches and Firecrackers* section where the readers commented on the articles. I almost spilled coffee on myself when I spotted my name misspelled and the prison I was being housed at. I wasn't expecting my remarks to be printed.

Beloved Jamie Foster Brown,

I'm sitting in this cell and (in) the previous two days I've read DMX and Tashera's article, along with Trina's, and Monique Wayne's. I commend! Your genuineness radiates and embraces so many as an aunt, mother, or grandmother's love should. I have absolute respect and love for you. I declare in Jesus' name that God will enlarge your territory.

I'm writing because so much of me lives with the Simmons (family). My spirit cries out for DMX because he's human and trapped in bondage by a force greater than himself, like so many. No one fully understands the pain of his struggles— wanting to overcome, battling to let go of the past, the hurt and the rage, but still falling short.

It's obvious so many are seeking his shortcomings, plotting his fall, trying to destroy whatever hope he's trying hard to achieve. Even Monique, had she been interested in Earl and not DMX, she would have taken the time to acknowledge he's bruised, confused, and yet abused. Then she would have been a benefit to his life, instead of a hindrance. I look Tashera in the eyes and I see myself—one who swallows her fears and lets go of pride. And depending on the circumstances, steps up to be whatever is necessary. When you love someone, it's not about the money or the reputation; it's all about doing what is needed in order to nurture your man into living out his destiny and his full potential.

My prayer for this family is that God will take control. I trust in the Lord that they will get through it all. God has chosen him for a greater purpose than just being DMX and all the trouble and pain is to line him up with his calling. May God's grace keep you all from making the most regrettable mistakes as I did, which landed me here.

God has more people praying for you all than you know.
Love,
Your sister in Christ

Less than a month had passed when I started receiving letters from random dudes in prison. Being that I wasn't looking for a pen pal, I kind of disregarded all the mail. A few weeks passed and Shelton, one of the dudes that was from a North Carolina prison wrote me again.

You may not believe the irony of this . . . But I never read Sister 2 Sister Magazine. My homeboy just handed me these couple magazines like, 'Here, read these.' And enclosed was your reply to an article you read, and I feel like you were speaking to me. You sound like a good woman.

He continued to emphasize his point for two more pages. A week passed, and I received another letter without me replying.

"I believe that God has a way of revealing things, and I don't know if you know this or not, but you will make a good wife." He threw the remark out there like casual conversation, but to me it sort of felt like the role he hoped I would fulfill in his life.

Here's the thing: I believe that I am a spectacular woman. Author and Life Coach, Andréa Dykstra once said, "In order to love who you are, you cannot hate the experiences that shape you." All of my experiences, good and bad, have molded me into the woman I am today. If I ever had the opportunity again, I would be a heck of a spouse, especially since I discovered the love of God and what it is like to live as a woman of worth. But I have come to terms that I am incarcerated, possibly for the rest of my life, if man has the final say. The only intimate relationship I was interested in was the one I applied myself to establish and maintain with the Lord, every single day. I wasn't interested in being someone's wife, so all of Shelton's attempts to enlighten me resonated as distasteful.

In the meantime, Ken had sent me confirmation about Ike being locked up and his address. So I wrote him a letter.

A few weeks passed, and I received another letter from Shelton, seeming genuinely excited that I had written back. He was incarcerated for street violence that resulted in the loss of someone's life, and he was unwilling to reveal who was responsible for the crime, so he ended up with a very lengthy sentence, and the address he wrote me from was his mother's. He perceived that the fact we were both in the same situation was a sign from God of destiny. I, on the other hand, wasn't that easily convinced. Alongside that letter was a letter from Ike as well. I waited until I was alone and on my bed, about two hours after I received it at mail call. I just wasn't sure if I was prepared to read it!

"Lord Jesus, I ask that You guard my heart and mind as I read this letter." I prayed before I even opened it.

"My Love," was scripted in a broader penmanship than the rest of the letter. For some reason, I wasn't surprised to hear the things that Ike was saying.

> *Just to hear from you is a true inspiration. If you only knew how many people I've asked to get online and find you for me, and now they say please don't write you back.*

I didn't take it personal that someone would tell him not to reach out to me, because technically, he had gotten away with murder, so one should be skeptical about interacting with the person who holds your truth. Plus, it was no secret I had done an interview with *Creative Loafing*, giving a detailed account about how my crime came about. And whether he wanted to admit it to himself or anyone else, he knew I told the truth and that's the reason I believe five years later I sat on my bed reading a letter from him.

But fuck them because not one of them mean what you do to me, and I know off top my Sunshine thinks that's some game, but you told me to be real, so here we go.

Sunshine is what he started calling me when we first moved in together. It was a joy to wake up next to him, and I was often impressed with the way he conducted his business, so I smiled freely, and he expressed that it was the sun rays on any day. Since then, Lyfe Jennings had come out with a song "Must Be Nice" that described who we once were to a fault; everything that Ike said made me his Sunshine, the reason he *claimed* he chose me was in that song. I often wondered if he had heard the song, and now I would have that chance to ask. Too bad he didn't have the sense to value me in higher regard and never let me go, instead of feeding me to the wolves, but I had long ago let that go. I was becoming a new kind of Sunshine to all I came in contact with. Whether I knew you or not. A simple smile was all some people needed or looked forward to.

He went into great detail about all that he encountered after I got arrested, bringing me up to date, not wanting to leave anything out.

I never stopped loving you. I will never stop loving you. Fuck the world. I understand that you had to make peace with God and yourself about a lot of things, and when you needed your nigga the most, I couldn't do shit for you. When it all went down, I was so helpless, and I've never been that way before. You were taken from me so fast. No hug, no kiss. When you were calling me telling me how them detectives did you in that room and I couldn't be there for you, just walking around in circles in that apartment by myself like a fuckin lab rat. I had gotten so used to anytime you got locked up I could free you, bring you home, nothing could hold us. My baby was such a good leader. When you left me I couldn't believe how hard it was to function in everyday life. I became a hermit in that apartment that whole first year. You know I couldn't wash clothes, barely wanted to wash myself. That shit was crazy. I had to touch myself, feed myself. Sometimes I just would sleep for two days, clothes everywhere . . .

I love you, Sunshine. Fuck everybody else. Your letter truly brightened my day. You will always be my only wife, the love of my life! I'll never forget you or my son. Believe that.

And I'm waiting for your next letter with a picture and I want a picture of my boy!

I love you Momma
Ike AKA Daddy

By the time I finished reading his letter, I was a little disheveled because this man sounded like he was in love with me. As if my incarceration depressed him and not merely from a financial perspective, but from a distraught spouse who had to figure out how to function and not just exist because the love of his life was suddenly gone. But I had a problem with that, now that I'm a woman who fully understands that love is action and not mere words, and *real love* won't ask you to compromise your morals, your self-worth, and it damn sure doesn't ask you to put your own life in danger. Night after night, you remain alone while your lover lays around probably getting his dick sucked by another 'ho that will eat off the food you supply.

Even in the streets, if that's the life you live, your dude should at least be by your side (on some Bonnie and Clyde), making sure the nigga *he* asked you to set up doesn't put a cap in you. What kind of man sends the woman he wants to spend the rest of his life with out to do his dirty work? The same kind of man that will drop you off at work, so he can joy ride all day in 'your car' and not be there on time to pick you up when your shift has ended! The same kind of man that doesn't mind eating up all your groceries, running up your electric bill, and sleeping in your bed, but never offering to help pay a single bill. That's what kind of man!

I didn't understand this at seventeen, but now at almost twenty-three, my eyes had the ability to see. Although I forgave him, for some reason

I needed him to explain how this could be. Because to me, it wasn't love that he possessed for me, and since he believed differently, I wanted—maybe needed—to peer into his mind and see how this was so. Was it possible that despite all he had done and subjected me to, could he still have the ability to love me in some sick and twisted way? Was he really that caught up in the street life that he justified his actions and yet believed in his heart that we would be happily ever after? Or was it the fear of telling my nigga who had started whipping my ass, 'I'm scared to go rob dude,' the justification he needed to believe that I wanted to carry out his orders, and thus gave him a pass because he never heard me say no? Did that validate his actions? If he was so convinced I wanted to live that life just as much as he did, why was I set on fire for not taking someone's life?

Ike and Shelton both managed to reply to my letters within two weeks. It became apparent that Shelton was a God-fearing man, and I found that very attractive. By the time we had been corresponding for two months, he had become sensitive to my spiritual man, always speaking on the things I was currently studying, the struggles I was facing, or simply knowing how to make me smile.

Freely, Ike expressed that he was the same man, if not worst, at the core of himself. Survival was his greatest instinct, and based off a conversation he recapped with someone about not changing and being the same person as he was in the streets, I questioned the depth of his dealings with other men.

"You have a nigga that makes your bed, another one that irons your clothes, and fixes your meals," the dude he was talking to had pointed out. "This one over here rolls your cigarettes and even lights them. You aren't changing, you are getting worse."

Ike defended himself by saying, "I pay people well for what they do for me," and he couldn't deny that.

Now, I don't know exactly how it is in men's prisons, but where I am, the only ones doing all that is either, your check (a sponsor, one who doesn't mind paying for a little attention and possibly some sex), a girlfriend, a cut buddy, a broad that is pulling out all the tricks in hopes of being the next one to be chosen, or someone who is indigent who irons, washes clothes, and cleans shoes for a hustle, and doesn't mind preparing a meal for someone else because they will get to eat too. But as a woman, it takes a lot to set my pride aside and be someone's 'do girl' just to eat; how much less a grown man, but hey, I don't know everything. Maybe dudes are willing to make the next man's bed for a lil' change. However, as I was still coming to terms about the things Ike was sharing with me in this particular letter, it hit me unexpectedly, and it seemed that all the answers that he couldn't or wasn't trying to give me, lay before me in this letter! All the things that left me wondering, *What did I do to him to be treated like this?* came to the light!

Between the Fulton County Deputy I caught [a CO he claimed to have on his team] *before I left, my second child's mother, Money, who is just out the hospital again and is doing fine, and Moniece, who is the person that we are about to talk about in a minute. My books stay over a thousand dollars most of the time, plus this is income tax season.*

I met Moniece when I was in Fulton after I got out of the hole and came back to the third floor. I was in her presence for ten minutes because she had a boyfriend in my dorm. After she got out, she wrote to her man and a couple friends she made in the dorm before she left, and sent everyone a little money. The dude she was kicking it with was already talking about how he was going to play her until he got out because he had a wife, which put his ass in there in the first place, but that's another story.

Anyway, a week later I got a letter from her that stated that she was interested in me. She told me she was from Texas, smoked weed, made her money from dating white men on the internet. I wrote back, kept it real, and ever since, she has stayed down. She is also HIV-positive, so I told her about NY and how easy it was to get an apartment and cash flow, so she moved up

251

there, followed my instructions, and it all worked out. She is no longer selling her body.

She was already very spiritual and now stays in church. They even want her to become a minister. She is about to go to college and receive those grants and loans like I was about to do. She is a very beautiful person on the inside and out. One problem: she is a transsexual. That's right, that body is hers, but a lot of it was bought by white men. She even got her name legally changed at twenty-four. Here are some pictures of her. Tell the truth before you read the letter. Did you think that could've been a boy at one time? The other pictures are of Money high on that shit. She went and got my name tattooed on her neck, which brings up another question. Do you regret my name being on yours? Would you mind if I put yours on me?

And to answer your question, yes baby, I accept my Sunshine for who she is, and the fact of the matter is, a nigga was not mature enough to realize what I had in you until you were no longer by my side. There is nobody on this Earth that can replace you, Mrs. Berry, and that's real. And that is also why I would ask you right now to be my wife? Fuck the world and everyone else in it because love conquers all. Or are you telling me you no longer love me in that way? Keep it real on the next letter . . .

I could not believe my eyes! For the first time since I'd known this man, he was expressing genuine empathy for someone else! Expressing pure concern for the direction of where this human life was headed, and it took another *man* to inspire it. It made perfect sense! He used to surround himself with women to try to prove to himself that he was a man. This explains why he regularly abandoned my vagina for anal sex. He was offended about the next man doing to her what he had done to every woman he came in contact with! Someone he had only been around for ten minutes, but yet he strived daily to destroy our lives! He told Moniece to move to New York in order to have a better life.

Educated her on how to obtain grants to go to college, but he introduced me to tricking off, hitting licks, and a life of crime, all while keeping me too busy to focus on finishing school. It wasn't about what I did or didn't do; he was just consumed with the life he wanted for himself, under the pretenses I would be by his side in the end! However, it all just felt like he didn't give a damn about my life.

Clearly, Ike only had compassion for men and/or transsexuals. And if that is what makes him happy, fine. But he didn't have to destroy the lives of women who sincerely took an interest in him, or made us suffer for things that transpired in his childhood. So naturally in the awakening of this profound truth, I lit into his behind. I had a lot to say and some of it was out of my character, but I wanted him to feel the depth of me and recognize that his prior homophobic attitude all made sense now. I could continue to talk about him and his letters, but you can find all his letters in a book: *The Falicia Blakely Letters, from her Pimp* by Sereniti Hall.

In the meantime, I had to accept that just because I once loved this dude, didn't mean that we were meant to be together. And I did not have to get answers to all of my questions to find closure. I found peace with the fact I had given him the best of me, even when I didn't understand 'me.' No, things did not plan out as I had hoped they would, but the woman I have become as a result of what I experienced with and through him has placed me in a caliber of my own, and if I so choose to give myself to another human being, their life will never be the same. They will never love another woman like me, and I can only say this because of the way Adonai (God) took all my pain, all my wrongdoing, all my guilt, shame, and disgrace and molded a woman who isn't afraid to admit when I'm afraid, wrong, or embarrassed. A woman who seeks to be forgiven, therefore is merciful. A woman who isn't ashamed of her past, but rather recognizes that her past is what makes her present worth living. And unfortunately for Ike, he couldn't rise to the occasion and be a part of my present. To some I probably shouldn't have cared either way, but I did and therefore, it was time when Auntie and Mom Dukes both made me get out of bed and eat. The two of them served as pillars for me when I wasn't willing to express to anyone how it affected me cutting ties with Ike. So instead of just sitting around hurting, lost in my thoughts, concerned about how he would perceive my actions, I prayed for him, his soul, his existence and his influence on people, especially women. And just like everything else, in time the heart heals and in some cases you don't even think about the pain. He would soon become like many others that I loved, just someone who I held in memories alone.

CHAPTER 42

I was fine living in E9-A, until Mom Dukes went home and Auntie had finally gotten her TPM (temporary parole month) and wasn't long behind her. I signed up for the Honor Dorm and before I could get Auntie's okay with the idea I was moving, I was told to pack up. E2, D-Hall room 145 was my new living quarters with a woman in her late forties name Aimee. She wasn't even five feet, but had a huge personality! She stayed to herself and loved to read suspense books. We grew pretty close and developed a mother/daughter relationship. In women's facilities most relationships that formed were mirrored like family. Someone was Momma, a stud or dominant lesbian was Daddy, and everyone else fell in, daughters or sons, sisters and brothers.

Aimee looked out for me. Fed me on weekends if I didn't go to the store, voiced her opinion about people who tried to befriend me, commented on how I spent my time, and even fussed if she felt I wasn't getting enough rest. She had become a source of strength for me, and I practically filled a void that she had being away from her two children, who suddenly decided to walk in her shoes and get in trouble with the law. Aimee was old school; she sold dope the entire time her children were young and youthful and never got caught up, until now. She had been adopted from birth by a couple who was medically classified as not being able to bear children of their own. When Aimee was about five years old, her mother ended up pregnant with her brother! Her godly mother just viewed it as a sign from God that they were supposed to have Aimee and wouldn't have if it would have been possible to have children of their own. Aimee got married young and left home, becoming a teen wife and mother, who ended up getting introduced to methamphetamines (meth), in which she began manufacturing and selling it. She got arrested one time for assault and met the woman she would leave her husband for. The woman she had been with for the past two years.

Shelton and I had slowly gotten pretty serious. I still really wasn't trying to commit to anything, however, the brother was gunning for me hard. Sending cards weekly, pictures of his handsome milk-chocolate-self posted in a chair, with his locks dancing on his shoulders, posted up on walls, his hands and arms appearing strong, eyes intense. He often spoke on things I was facing, things as simple as me getting a paper cut. And when he did, I had one! The fact that he was that in tuned to me was sexy to say the least. He had me contemplating trying the relationship thing, and his ability to impress me wasn't all he had going for him. Aimee was his number one fan! Constantly in my ear.

"That's a good man! You need to give him a chance. God put people in your life for a reason, Falicia!"

Around this time, one afternoon I was called out to the mailroom to pick up a package, and on the way back, Mrs. Ellen stopped me.

"Miss Blakely." The short, high-yellow woman who put me in mind of the actress Jasmine Guy (except with coarse hair), stopped in front of me. Her bitch face made it hard not to burst out laughing. It floored me how people went home every day, ate what they wanted, dressed how they preferred, and received a check for the job they chose, but still managed to be more unhappy than those of us who had lost the right to make any of those decisions! I stopped walking, and we locked eyes.

"Yes, Mrs. Ellen. How are you doing today?" I smiled, genuinely being polite as she mugged me. The last time I had even spoken to her was like three years prior when Jayden and I were in the library perpetrating, and she told us to get out. Jayden did what she did best and replied by saying something fly. I hadn't stepped foot in there since. At first, I stopped going because I was offended. How was it, that out of all the offenders present, she picked us. But as time passed, I just didn't have a reason to go.

"You're not in PI anymore, are you? What is your detail?" She ignored my greeting.

"No, ma'am," I replied in haste, trying to figure out why she was asking me this. "I'm a dorm wash orderly."

"Hmmm." She looked off in the distance, briefly. "Are you the only one?"

"No, ma'am." The tension left her face and was replaced with gentleness.

"Would you like to come work for me in the Library? In the General Library section?" I stood speechless.

"You want me to come work for you?" I managed to say. Hell, just five seconds ago I thought the woman couldn't stand me.

"Yes, if you are willing. I have noticed the changes you have made. You stay to yourself and seem to even encourage some of the other ladies here. If you are interested, I am offering you a job."

"Of course I would!" I was so excited! All I could think of was God's favor. You never really know who is watching you. I hadn't laid eyes on this woman in years, but apparently she had seen me.

"I won't be able to get it put on your schedule until next week, but I'm going to call you out in the morning, first track. So be ready."

"Yes, ma'am! Thank you for the opportunity! You will not be disappointed!" I practically skipped during the walk back to my dorm. I could not wait to tell my roommate.

There were three of us that stood at the checkout area, a long wooden counter top, sort of like an island that often sat in the middle of kitchen. With three wooden card holders that categorized three separate lines by your last name, A-J, K-R, S-Z. I was responsible for the first line. Two others, Ms. Arlina who was also Minister Gray's secretary and Kayla, the Mexican that Jayden used to date, worked in the Law Library. Working in the library ended up being a platform for me to be a witness for Christ. As I searched my card organizer for someone's last name, or made a new card for first timers, I used that time to encourage the souls that were before me.

"Why you look so sad?" I often asked. "Do you know that Christ bled and died in hopes of you being able to have a peace of mind? I'm not saying that life will be easy and that you won't go through anything, but God said:

> *Come to me, all you that are weary and carry heavy burdens, and I will give you rest. Take My yoke upon you and learn from Me; for I am gentle and humble in heart: and you will find rest for your souls. For My yoke easy and My burden is light.*
> (Matthew 11:28-30)

In other words, it's not God's will for you to walk around burdened.

At the time, I didn't completely understand the magnitude of the impact I was making. I just wanted others to walk in the joy God was blessing me with, so whatever it took, I was willing to extend myself to get it. My supervisor was okay with allowing me to pray with others, so I offered prayer to anyone who was struggling in any way, or expressed something they didn't have the faith to trust God for. Once a sister had something going on and wanted to fast about it, no questions asked, I fasted in agreement with her. I would meet the person at church if that's what it took to bring them in the presence of God, or I'd write down scriptures that related to their situation, whatever I could, all to the glory of God. Slowly, I was beginning to understand that just as God had anointed me to minister through dance, He had placed me in the library for ministry as well. But just when things seemed perfect, Mrs. Ellen informed us she was leaving in pursuit of a higher-paying job. At that moment all I could see was that someone who treated us like humans was leaving. I didn't know God had a plan.

Minister Gray wasn't just the choir director, she was a volunteer who had been coming to the prison about ten years at this point, and administration asked her to volunteer and run the Media Center aka the Library until they could fill the position. She gladly agreed, and my spiritual journey took a leap for the better. Everything began to make sense. Life was a constant spiritual battle between the kingdom of darkness (Satan's domain) and the Kingdom of Light (God's domain). Every decision we made affected one of these realms. We either brought glory to God and strengthened His Kingdom, or glorified Satan and gave him the right to rule in our lives. Minister Gray had the mindset: "For God I live and for God I die."

She was our walking example of what the life of a child of God should be like. I witnessed the love of God pour forth in abundance for everyone she came in contact with. She prayed with anyone who needed prayer; she made an attempt to encourage everyone. She was always giving someone a compliment; she would sacrifice her lunch for any staff member if they said they were hungry, even the ones that didn't care for her. Every week she had the choir fast that Tuesday morning. She fasted and prayed extensively for others and for God to touch the heart of our warden to permit him to allow her to feed her choir and the compound. Likewise to open the doors for her choir to travel and minister. But the most impactful to me was witnessing what it was like to still be a woman, get in your feelings, battle with desires and even emotions, but allow your love for God and the need to please Him to outweigh everything else. I saw the sacrificial life and as a result, I put my entire heart into becoming a woman after God's own heart. It was my desire that everyone who came into contact with me left my presence knowing that God was alive and able to deliver. For the next five years I shunned entertaining a woman because even if it wasn't wrong to be with another woman, it was a sin to fornicate and have sex outside of wedlock, so I cried out to God when I felt lonely, and He comforted me. I withheld from masturbating, not wanting to stimulate the desire to be sexually satisfied. I prayed He would remove the desire whenever the feeling came, and in time it was merely a passing thought.

Shelton and I had been officially going on three years before we encountered any kind of storm. I had testified in church how God had sent me a godly man who knew my spirit, a man that loved God more than he loved me. I had found peace in loving him until one day I was reading a letter, and he said he was about five feet, six inches tall. Now why it took three years before the topic of his height ever came up, I don't know. Other than it was so much more to him, and I wasn't interested in being in a relationship with him so I didn't inquire. You would have thought this man revealed that he wasn't the dude in the pictures the way this discovery about his height bothered me. I'm five nine. My momma is five six, and she is way shorter than me! This man said about five feet six inches, which meant he was possibly shorter than my mother. That was a problem.

About a year prior, God placed a girl named Nakeya in my life. She had first heard about me when Ken spoke to her Criminal Justice class about capital murder cases, and he used my case to explain how the system can sometimes fail us when it comes to completely getting justice, being that the mastermind of my case was still free. She looked me up some years later, and we just clicked. I got her put on my visitation list, and she swiftly became a part of my mother and son's life as well. I feel she is God sent, so I call her my god-sister. She told me that I was being superficial by making such a big deal about his height, but I was only keeping it real with myself. I had already struggled with the reality that we both had to deal with society frowning down on us for serving time for the loss of precious life (in my case 'lives'), which may result in us struggling for a time period. However, I knew by faith God would see us through, and we would make it together. But I didn't know if I could accept my man being small enough for me to rest my arm on his head. This truth gradually picked away at the future that once seemed so promising with him. "God, I'm trying, but I just can't see us together," I often prayed. I wasn't sure what would become of Shelton and me.

Some time had passed and some things changed. I took one final look at my makeup and hair in the mirror. "You are so beautiful," I told myself one last time before heading out the door. I had become accustomed to complimenting myself, that way whether anyone told me or not, I was already aware of the fact.

So far my morning started off pleasant. I had spent a little time in prayer, got everything cleaned and organized and now I was headed to work. It felt like it was a perfect June morning. The sun was shining on my deep mahogany skin, and the wind slightly danced through my hair. As I rounded the corner, I tried to suppress the anticipation in the bottom of my stomach, which started the previous day upon hearing Kayla, my co-worker and newfound sister, speak of someone named AD.

"Do you remember AD? Was she still here when you first got here?" the beautiful Mexican female asked.

"No, she was already gone, but why do you ask?" I responded as she continued to file papers.

"Because she's back. I saw her on the pavilion. I was surprised that she remembered me by name." I tried to ignore the flipping in my stomach, even the fact I instantly began to recall letters Jayden had asked me to read from her.

"What's wrong with you, Falicia Rose?"

"Nothing." I tried to check myself, struggling to refrain from smiling.

"She's always been nice to me. She looks good too." Kayla summed up the subject as she stepped back into the general library area. I had only heard part of what she said because I had drifted off to the land of the forbidden.

"That's good," I replied, hoping Kayla hadn't noticed that I wasn't listening. When she walked back in our office area, I brought the subject back up. I had some inquiries of my own. "I saw a picture of her years ago. Looked as if she had just started her locks and was about average weight."

"Must have been a long time ago, 'cause her hair is long now and she is slim." Kayla said, taking a bite of my bait.

"Oh, maybe it was." I had obtained exactly what I wanted to know.

I laughed at myself when I realized there was an extra bounce in my step. I wanted to be on point, just in case I ran into AD. First impressions last a lifetime. I wasn't looking for her, but something in me just knew it wouldn't be long. As usual, I cheerfully greeted everyone that I bypassed. The birds sung their praise, flirting with me. To me, when the birds began to whistle as I walked by, it was my Heavenly Father's way of expressing how good I looked. It was a little joke I believe I shared with God. Though I know the idea is far-fetched.

Only feet away from the long stretch of pavement that led to my work place, I spotted a stud that was every bit of five feet nine inches tall, with an even brown complexion. Locks that hung well past her shoulders were pulled back out of her face. Tactfully, and with her head high as confidence dominated every step she took, AD demanded the attention of all who was present. Her posture, her swag, seemed to scream "I'm that nigga!" She stood out in a class of her own, like a diamond among pearls, like me. *She's far from the common and ideal for me,* I thought.

Stay away from her! I immediately heard the Holy Spirit speak to me. *She will be trouble for you.* Now I know the Lord does speak to us through the Holy Spirit. Usually, it was just a knowingness inside of me, but this was more like an external voice. I heard the warning and desired to take heed, but it was something about her that made me want to do the opposite. *Let me take my behind to work,* I concluded, a little spooked by what I had just encountered.

And now this, I knew what I was and wasn't attracted to and I didn't want to be faced with the temptation of being sexually attracted to another man other than my husband. I decided it was best to just tell Shelton what I was feeling before he picked up on the conflict in my spirit, and it left him feeling indifferent or insecure. One of the things that I loved about him was he was willing to go to the highest of heights in an attempt to make me happy.

"If my height bothers you, I will just wear those shoes that make me taller, but as you know, I love my women to be taller than me," he had replied nonchalantly.

I didn't mention it again, but I began to obsess over the matter. Looking through magazines, I suddenly noticed all the men that posed sitting down because the model or their girlfriend was taller. I took notice of the medical shoes that added height, absolutely unable to see my man walking around in them! I kept trying to envision him coming up behind me while I was cooking, but instead of him resting his head on my shoulder, he'd peek from in between my arm and my side by my armpit. I was devastated! I read how some of the major church ministers weren't attracted to their spouse at first because one was spontaneous and loved to fly and the other didn't. Or it just wasn't the usual physical qualities they preferred. I really began to seek God, pleading to know if this was the man He had chosen for me. I would have many discussions with the older woman who had been in the faith longer than me. What I finally came up with was, as a daughter of the King, it was my choice to decide if I wanted to marry his prince or not. The Bible said, "Blessed is he that finds a wife." So now that I knew, I should have had some peace, right? Well, I didn't. I was still in turmoil that the man who was just everything to me, outside of God being what no human could ever imagine to be, was suddenly not measuring up. I was indecisive, and I started slacking in my letters. I wasn't replying back as fast as I had been during the past three years, nor was I addressing everything he mentioned in previous letters. My home front was on shaky ground for the first time, and all I knew to do was pray for direction. A part of me wanted to be with him, and a part of me felt I had gotten ahead of myself in believing this was who God ordained for me before the foundations of the world.

CHAPTER 43

On a Tuesday afternoon in June, it was Intake's day to utilize the library, and unfortunately for me, my understanding of myself was about to change. As to be expected, a group of women I had never seen came through the door.

"Good afternoon, welcome to the library! If any of you plan on checking out any books, please leave your IDs on the counter, so that I can make you a checkout card." It was my normal announcement whenever someone new came in. One female in particular was light skinned and was strikingly pretty. She approached the counter.

"Hey, do you all have any urban books?" she asked, staring directly in my eyes.

"The only ones we have will be in that section." I pointed toward an area that had very few choices.

"Thank you," she replied, sounding disappointed.

I glanced down at her ID. "Tameka, if you need any other assistance, my name is Falicia, just call me." She nodded and walked away. I admired her slim hour-glass physique. A few seconds passed before she approached me again.

"Does the store sell PowerAde here?" I chuckled at her off the wall question, but I was willing to answer.

"Yes, it does." She smiled and walked away. There was something about her that struck me as familiar, but I wasn't going to give it too much thought.

A minute or two passed, and someone walked past the counter to open the door. I had to do a double take because the stud looked very similar to this stud that Jayden once viewed as her best friend. Jayden had shown me a picture of the stud, and I thought she was very attractive, but I immediately dismissed the thought. Sometimes I would reply to comments she would make to Jayden about me, just being courteous. They had started out their sentence together inseparable, doing what most studs do in prison, dealing with females for gain, whether it's inmates or staff. But as the years passed, they fell apart and the friendship went down the drain. Inmate.com said AD and Jayden had a falling out, not long after she got transferred to Washington, after we broke up.

The only thing that made me question if this was her was—this girl was way slimmer than the one in the picture, and she didn't have glasses on. I gave my same speech about leaving IDs to get a check-out card, and then proceeded to busy myself with categorizing the return books on the check-in cart. When I finished, her ID lay on the counter. I looked at her name. It was the same name! Oh my goodness! What was the probability that I would get to personally meet her.

After I wrote her name, along with the others on the check-out cards, I walked over to where she stood talking to Tameka. Normally, I would have waited until they came back to the counter with their books to return their ID, but I wanted to know how she would react to my presence and to see just how tall she was standing next to me. "Excuse me."' I spoke barely over a whisper as I approached them from behind.

"What's up?" AD turned and gave me her undivided attention.

"I just wanted to return these." I handed her both of their IDs, indicating I knew they were together. She kind of smirked, and looked at me through her intense hazel eyes. Or was it curiosity? Whatever it was let me know that she didn't mind me invading her space. And for some strange reason, I didn't mind being in it.

"I know you!" Tameka exclaimed, looking from me to AD.

"Girl, you swear you know everybody." AD shook her head as if she was embarrassed.

"I do know her. I have been trying to place her face since I walked in the door. You were in Fulton County with me back in 2002. We were in a holding cell together, and you shared with us how you had got caught up with a nigga and was facing murder charges. Your son was like two years old. Do you remember? I was bonding out, but I can never forget what you said! You even said how you had such peace that God was in control of your life. Do you remember?" As she spoke, it all came back to me.

"I do remember, but it wasn't 2002, it was 2003," I replied.

"No, it was 2002," she stated, as if I'd asked a question.

"Meka, I think she knows when she committed her crime," AD chimed in.

"I know when I got in trouble . . . ." Tameka said.

The more she talked, the more I recalled thinking how she was so pretty, but acted very similar to a blonde that was out of touch with common sense.

"It's all good, but I know I didn't go Fulton until 2003. And yes, I remember you. You look good, but I hate to see you under these circumstances. I'll leave you two alone." Without another word, I turned on my heels and went to pass out the rest of the IDs. I didn't look back to see if she was watching me walk away.

A few minutes passed, and AD walked over to the counter and asked to use the restroom that was located directly in front of the checkout line where I was occupied with checkouts, but for some reason when I heard the restroom door opening, I looked up in that direction and ended up locking eyes with AD. She immediately looked away.

Oh, my goodness, she's fine! Jesus help me for real. Did I just catch her looking at me? Did she see me staring at her? Several questions of this nature crossed my mind. *I got to get myself together.* I didn't know just how desperately I needed to act upon that remark.

Approximately five minutes later, they fell in line to check out their books. I checked out the two people in front of them, and then they approached the counter. AD stood tall and quiet, staring as I wrote down the calculus book she was renting. She had to be five-eight because she was slightly shorter than me. Her skin was clear, except a few tiny moles that were adorable. I looked down for as long as I could because the way she was focused on me was making me nervous. *That's what your behind get, playing with fire,* I told myself as I tried to maintain my composure.

"Fe!" AD blurted out. I looked up at her. "Fe . . . Jayden's Fe?" she stated more like a question.

"Yes, I'm Falicia."

"You used to talk to Jay, right?"

"Yeah. That's me." Not so sure I actually liked answering to that.

"Damn, it's crazy to finally meet you!" She smiled so big it made me smile. She was beautiful.

"You have a beautiful smile," she complimented. I felt slightly uncomfortable with her girlfriend standing there.

"She has a beautiful spirit too, baby," Tameka joined in.

"Thank y'all." I stamped their books, slid them across the counter, and focused on the return books.

"I'll see you around," AD stated as they walked out the door.

"Lord God, I need your help," I confessed. "It is something about that girl that does something to me." I was confused.

I briefly glanced at them leaving, and for some reason compared myself to her girlfriend. She was light, and I was dark. The girl was thicker than me, and her hair was slightly longer, but after listening to her vocabulary and the way she conversed, I knew she was typical and that gave me an advantage. If I could ever get beyond those beautiful hazel eyes, I would give her what most females neglected to do. Grace her with the presence of a woman. Lost in my thoughts, I felt the Holy Spirit convict me. *She is a soul who needs to be introduced to the Savior and just like so many, you may be the only example of Jesus Christ that they'll see.*

For that reason alone I was grateful AD had folks. I respected myself enough to not pursue someone else's partner, especially when I had my own. Shelton seemed to be wholeheartedly devoted to our relationship. That same day I began to pray for AD. I also prayed she would see God in me in hopes of desiring to obtain her own relationship with God. Praying for her wasn't hard because she somehow stayed on my mind.

Years had passed, and I wasn't even attracted to another woman, but suddenly I was checking for this lady and feeling sexy. I didn't understand, and the thought made me heavy. I was disappointed in myself.

I tried to wake up a little earlier in the mornings, so I could pray and put on the armor of God because clearly I didn't know what I was capable of. About two weeks went by without any surprises, and I was beginning to feel better and not like some hypocrite, though I really hadn't done anything.

One Sunday night I was at one of my favorite church services. I didn't go with anyone in particular, so I figured I would sit next to someone God intended for me to meet. I managed to get an end seat and praised God throughout the service. The word was powerful, and I even had the chance to pray with someone who felt compelled to come ask me for prayer. The service ended and I reached up under my chair to retrieve my Bible. When I sat upright, AD and Tameka stood in the aisle next to where I was sitting, smiling. For one, I didn't even know they were in the services. And two, why were they standing in front of me grinning? I imagined my expression must have told what I was thinking.

"We were just sitting over there." AD turned and pointed to a row of seats that was about five rows behind me, to my right. "And decided to come say hello."

"Yeah, I enjoyed seeing you worship. I could feel it." Tameka smiled the hardest. She reached out and pulled me into her embrace. When she let me go, AD extended her arms and leaned in for an embrace. I gave her a holy hug, the one where you lean forward and the top of your upper body barely touches. There was no way I was going to allow this woman to wrap me in her arms. After we hugged, I could see that intense look in her eyes. I looked over at Tameka, and she was still smiling. I couldn't be trippin'; this lady was checking me out.

"Okay well, I'm going to get going. Try to get cleaned up before count. Y'all have a good night." I politely dismissed myself, not wanting to dwell on what I believed I was seeing. That night, I finally opened up to Aimee about her and the things I felt.

"Are you talking about this new stud all these girls are going crazy over, Falicia? AD, AK, or something?" I nodded yes. "They say she used to be here and got shipped for personal dealings. Sounds like you need to stay away from her. Y'all lead two different lives and that life she is living is one you have left behind." Everything she said made sense, and I had every intention of walking in that reality, until I found myself face to face with her. Something drew me to her, and it felt harmless to simply hold a conversation.

One Friday afternoon I went outside to the pavilion. We had church later that night, and I decided to just go outside. I told myself I was going to see if I could invite someone new to service that night, but in being honest with myself, I really didn't like being outside in the heat, so what was my new inspiration? At first, I did just what I said I would do. I found various groups of people sitting around.

"Hey y'all!" I waved and smiled at the group of females sitting on the bench, with plenty of various shades of eye shadow on and their white T-shirts sewed up to fit tighter than its original fit. "Y'all coming to church tonight?" I asked as I sat amongst them.

"Are you dancing?" was the usual reply.

"Maybe, you'll just have to come and see."

"Is Minister Gray preaching, or she got a special guest coming?" Instead of answering, I just slightly tilted my head and looked at them. We all burst out laughing!

"Okay, we have to come and see!" one of the girls mocked me. Gradually, I made my way within eyesight of where AD was posted up. I wanted to see if she would acknowledge me, or pretend to not see me. Though I was already convinced she was just as drawn to me as I was to her.

"Lee Lee!" someone called out to me as I walked past the bleachers that sat directly next to the basketball court.

"Hey boo!" I waved and blew them a kiss. "You coming to church tonight?" I stood only a few feet away from AD. I didn't look up under the pavilion because I felt her staring.

"Yes, ma'am."

"I love you!" I told the young lady I was speaking with and proceeded to walk away so I could get off the grass.

"Fe!" someone called out. I kept walking as if I didn't hear. It was AD. Mostly everyone except people who had been doing time with me from the beginning called me Lee Lee because Minister Gray, who had become a mother figure to me, introduced me as, "Your sister, my daughter, Lee, Lee," whenever I was about to minister through dance. So I was mainly known as Lee Lee on the compound.

The next time I saw AD was when I was at Wellness. I walked up underneath the pavilion, and she was posted up by the column. I didn't even say anything. I just sat down and kept quiet while I waited for the officer to come count us. Then I would start walking my laps. She noticed my presence right as we all began lining up by dorms for a head count. I probably would have walked in the opposite direction had someone not stopped me in need of some encouraging words. When I finished speaking to the young lady, AD was right there. With that look in her eyes. "Hey, Falicia. What's going on?"

"Hello, AD. Just going to get a little exercise in. How are you doing?"

"I'm good. Don't really want to be out here, but I guess it's not so bad since you here." I reared my head back. I had to see if she was just making a statement, or trying to flirt with me. She stood there with her hands tugged down in the sides of her pants looking toward the ground. Her locks hung over her face. She was so sexy.

God, what is going on with me? I asked as I just started walking.

"So, what's up with you and Jay?" she asked, right on my heels.

"Nothing. She do too much. She changed on a nigga."

"Man, who you telling." AD looked as if the thought of that truth still brought her some form of pain.

"I'm listening." She looked over at me from the distance she had just created between us.

"It was just a misunderstanding. A misunderstanding that Jayden just wasn't willing to see any other way." I listened intently as AD

271

recalled Jayden going to lockdown and her telling AD to keep an eye on her Hispanic girlfriend, Catalina. AD and Catalina did everything together, ate, watched TV, washed clothes; they pretty much spent the course of the day together. As to be expected, them folks started caring for each other! Though AD didn't admit it, I recognized the innocent gestures of the wrestling she mentioned; these were merely opportunities to sneak a feel on both ends. Likewise, the name-calling was a playful attempt to flirt. So I wasn't surprised that on any given day when Jayden was in an ill mood and sent her some hate mail from lockdown, Catalina turned to AD for comfort.

Just in the little time I had been getting to know her, there were things about AD that reminded me of Jay, when she was sweet and considerate. She continued to elaborate that because of the feelings she and Catalina had developed for each other, things could have gotten inappropriate, but because of their love for Jay it didn't. They decided to put some space between them for the sake of everyone's relationship. But Jayden is sharp and even from lockdown she realized something was different about their interaction, the sudden distance. Sending separate letters to lockdown.

After much badgering, Catalina was the first to confess and it was war after that! To Jayden, AD was flawed and always going after her girls. From this point on, they were enemies. Catalina went home shortly after and reached out to AD, being that Jay was so unforgiving. She pursued what she felt for AD and held her down financially for a minute. At some point, Jay reached out to her, and she started looking out for her as well, choosing not disclose to Jay that she was communicating with AD. Even though AD knew her dealings with Jay.

One day during a verbal altercation, it all came out and disloyalty was the lasting impression Jay had concerning them both.

"I just feel like a bitch shouldn't have come between us. As long as she was upholding her obligations, it shouldn't have mattered," AD concluded in her defense. I didn't say anything at first, because to me it was absolutely disrespectful to mess around with your friend's spouse.

"So, you don't see no wrong in what happened?" I stopped walking and looked at her.

"I mean, to some extent. I could have told my homie what time it was off top, and maybe even when she went home, but I didn't fuck the bitch, when I could have. If I wanted her, I could have had her. Jay didn't take that into consideration." I just nodded. Many things about that situation was all wrong, but I wasn't the one to judge. Here I was, attracted to my ex-girlfriend's, ex-best friend.

We talked about how Jayden and I broke up. Then how my experience with her led me to the Lord and how I had just been focused on healing and my purpose in this life. "So what do you do when you get lonely? Who holds you? Or—"

"Whenever I feel I need a little extra attention—" I cut her off. "I call on God. He has the power to quench any desire and what I seek in a companion, I have in my fiancé."

"Fiancé?" she asked, with her face twisted some. "I can see a nigga trying to wife you." This subject opened the door to a series of questions that were key things that people asked to know more about your situation without straight asking: So does your family stand by you? Do they support you financially? Do you prefer gold over silver? Do your rings represent anything significant? Did your fiancé give you those? Are you seriously involved with someone or married? Is he free? How often do you go to visitation? Who comes to see you? Do you have any children?

I had to give it to her, she was slick and I could see why women fell for her, but I loved God more and that conviction alone would be what I held on to. *Lord, please allow this woman to see you in me,* had become my prayer.

Tameka went home shortly after they arrived, and AD had already been making herself acquainted in the dorm and had her eye on a particular CO. Fridays at Wellness Walk had become our routine day to meet up and talk. Several people had begun raising an eyebrow because we had been spotted together on the regular. It's just the way it is in prison.

Anytime someone saw a stud with someone, it's an automatic assumption that something is going on. I just did my best to not allow the lines to get crossed, such as when she started pulling on me, or trying to tussle or wrestle with me. I reminded her that she had already told me how this played out between her and Catalina, so she was to keep her hands off of me!

"Whatever, Falicia!" We laughed about it. "But I do want to know what it feels like to have you in my arms." I just rolled my eyes, but her words played over and over in my mind during the times I tried not to think of her. It was other things too. Like how hard it was for me to tell her I was HIV positive.

"Do you recall Jay telling you something about me that would normally be the reason she would keep it pushing, but not so with me?" She thought about the question for a good minute, but couldn't come up with anything.

"So you don't know I have HIV? No one has just slid that fact in since we've been hanging out?" The look of disbelief that settled in her eyes told me she wasn't aware. My heart raced, not knowing what to expect, wondering how she would treat me from this point forward. Silence dominated the space between us on the bench.

"That's fucked up!" she finally spoke.

As I briefly explained how I got it, a part of me wished this would be the excuse I needed to be set free. To be able to sit down and write Shelton a letter without thinking about her. To go to church without looking around to see if she was present. To concentrate on reading my Bible without the distractions of a conversation we had. To go back to my life where no one had to wonder whether my interaction was in the will of God, or the need to be brought up for questioning. I wanted to stop feeling guilty for the attraction I felt because of the history. I wanted to be free! So as I concluded how Ike claimed to brush me off because he felt helpless and did not consider that he took away my choice to decide if I wanted to remain in that situation, I hoped AD would change how she felt regarding me, to some degree.

"Falicia, that's fucked up. I respect you keeping it real with a mofo. You so young and have already had a lot to endure, but from where I stand it's all good." She leaned over and tried to put me in a headlock.

"Girl, what I tell you about playing with me like that?" I pushed her arm away and finger raked my hair that was cut in an asymmetrical bob, the longer side falling inches beneath my chin.

"Who you calling a girl?" She jumped to her feet, ready to play.

"Go 'head on, you not slick." I swatted my hand at her, seeing through her.

"I'm just saying, a brother need a hug right now. We talking about some heavy shit!"

"Find another word," I demanded.

"What, Falicia?"

"I told you, you too smart to always use curse words. Find another word to use besides the one you used."

"Woman, get out of here!" She towered over me as if she was feeling aggressive. "I don't want to hear that sh—that smack you talkin'! I want a hug, or I'm going to take it!" I looked up at AD. She was smiling, but I knew she was serious. I slightly bent over, messing with my shoe, forcing her to step back a couple steps because I was still sitting on the bench. Right as she did, I jumped up and took off running toward the basketball court.

"Oh, so you think you slick!" she yelled as she ran after me. We ended up on the court like two kids in a world of our own. "Why you doing me like this?" she whined as she held on to my arms, facing me.

"I ain't doing you like nothing! You don't need to be touching me."

"Says who?" she snapped back. We both laughed as we walked off the court, toward the track. "For real, Falicia . . . You don't ever feel like you need someone to be strong for you."

"I'm good. God put people in my life to uplift me when I need it and carry me in prayer when I'm not strong."

"No, I'm talking about loving you, being the sjfjfirenenodfrlkfm when you mcmmfkf." I looked over at AD. Her lips were clearly moving, but whatever was coming out of her mouth wasn't audible. It sounded like gibberish. I kept blinking to make sure I was not trippin'. I wasn't. God had confused her language in my ears; it was time for me to go back to the dorm.

CHAPTER 44

I received a letter from Shelton acknowledging how many weeks had gone by without receiving any mail from me and enclosed in the letter was a vision he had of me. In this vision I was in this room with the door locked, sitting in a chair in the middle of the floor crying. He stood opposite the door, knocking.

"Baby, come open the door. Open the door!" he said several times, though I never moved. After some minutes passed, he began trying to look into the room. "Why won't you open the door?" Just then, my eyes reverted to something that stood against the wall out of view of the window. There inside the room with me stood a woman, who had the appearance of a man, locks just like his, but hers were shorter and thinner. Their complexion was almost the same, but she was slim and taller, where he was toned and short.

"Open the door," he repeated his plea, but just as before I sat there crying.

Shelton proceeded to tell me the meaning of the vision.

Falicia,

Just as Christ has said, I stand at the door and knock. Any man that opens the door, I will come in and dine with him. I am extending the invitation for you to re-open your heart for me. God has revealed to me that there is a woman in your life that has ignited a struggling in you, and oftentimes you are left feeling torn. I am here and willing to help you through this, but you have to allow me to help. I love you and still desire to be your husband, your brother in Christ, your everything, if you would just allow me.

Get up and open the door, Falicia.

I sat on my bunk speechless, blown away at the majesty of God. Here was the man that I had declared to love in the presence of God and even in my silence he prayed for me and God gave him clarity about the storm that was raging in our lives and particularly, the exact description of AD! On one end I felt blessed, and on the other end it seemed scary, as if I didn't have any privacy. One thing is for sure, God reveals Himself to whomever He wants to, however He chooses.

It took me a few hours to settle my thoughts and write Shelton a detailed account about the struggles I was facing concerning AD. It didn't feel good telling him how I felt, but I didn't want him to suffer any longer by my silence. After the letter was complete, I had a heart to heart with God. I tried, but I just couldn't get past his height. Judging from his pictures, I was lucky if he was five feet four inches tall.

Minister Gray had a natural ability to make everyone feel like they were her family, and during the course of time while working with her daily, Kayla and I addressed the issue that had developed between us as a result of how Jayden went about moving on without me. The two of us were like sisters. Miss Arlina easily became my auntie with the way she always made me feel she had my best interest at heart, and Minister Gray was hands down my spiritual mother, a woman God was using in a mighty way in my life.

Rapidly, God was doing a work in my innermost being, and it manifested in my actions! At times I didn't recognize my own response to various situations, and up until this point there wasn't anything that transpired with me that Minister Gray didn't know about. So fearing what she would say about my feelings for AD, set in motion a conflict within me. I needed to be forthcoming. And before I discovered the courage to address it, Counselor Warlike came to the Media Center to announce that they had hired someone for the position who would start the next day. I considered it a sign and decided to wait and approach the subject later. For now, Miss Arlina, Kayla, the other two orderlies, and I had to get used to our new supervisor, Mrs. Worthy. At first glimpse I felt she was beautiful enough to be a model. Somewhere around five feet ten inches tall, the deep chocolate skinned woman had a bright smile and healthy shoulder-length hair. Her dark brown eyes searched our eyes as she introduced herself. She was a woman of God and had experience in many fields, cosmetology, teaching, and fashion. The adjustment would be a smooth one, right? We all love the Lord, we'd get along just fine.

Well, one afternoon to my surprise as I was standing behind the counter checking out books, I looked up and AD was standing in front of me.

"What are you doing here?" It was a wonderful surprise, being that she hadn't been in the library since the day we officially met.

"I needed to see you." She slightly smiled as she slid a folded up letter across the counter.

"Falicia, when you finish, come to—" Miss Arlina called out to get my attention as she was about to walk into the Law Library. "Dang, what's up with you? You just lit up like a Christmas tree?" she said as her New York accent revealed itself in her sarcasm. A little embarrassed by all the extra attention, I looked away but looked back to see her still standing in the same spot, looking from AD to me.

"I'll be there when I finish," I replied, and set my attention back on AD. I tried not to show how uncomfortable I had suddenly become.

"What's this?" I tapped my pocket, signaling the letter she wrote.

"Just something I needed to get off my chest."

"AD, you do know that—"

"Excuse me?" Mrs. Worthy walked up behind me addressing AD. "Are you supposed to be in here?" She stood next to me, her arms crossed over her chest, looking like someone had just offended her. I had never seen her make that expression before.

"Well, ma'am, I don't know. I just got off my detail, and I stopped to fill out a Law Library form." I hadn't even noticed the form in front of AD. She must have suspected it might be something.

"You can't just come in here when you feel like it." Mrs. Worthy wasn't letting up, in fact it was beginning to seem as if she had a personal issue with her.

"Yes, ma'am. It won't happen again." AD slid the form in front of her and stepped back from the counter and headed to the exit door.

"I will not accept this! You can come in here on Wednesday night and sign up for this like you're supposed to! PI comes on Wednesday nights, not when you feel like it!" AD didn't even respond and neither did I. Her disposition was very offensive, and I could bet money that Mrs. Worthy conducted herself like that as a result of Auntie Arlina's comment. I stepped over to the next checkout box and finished checking those people out.

"Ms. Blakely, when you finish I need to see you." I wasn't surprised to hear my supervisor say that.

Apparently, my expression revealed what else I didn't say, because the next day, long before my work hour began, I walked into her office and Mrs. Warlike, who was in charge of all the Media Center dealings, was waiting for me in my supervisor's office. The second I walked through the door and made eye contact with her, I knew this meeting wasn't about Auntie Arlina leaving for the TC earlier that morning, after twenty-four years. This would be my first encounter of knowingly being mistreated for an underlying issue that most wouldn't even address.

"Good afternoon," I spoke politely as I stepped into the threshold of the overcrowded office. Mrs. Warlike sat behind Mrs. Worthy's desk, and she sat in one of the two chairs across from her desk.

"You may have a seat." Mrs. Worthy extended her arm toward the chair next to where she sat. Both, ignoring my greeting.

Lord, let me immediately die to myself, so that you may get the glory. I sat down, taking a second to look at them. Mrs. Warlike's healthy face sported the same miserable look she always wore. The jet-black pixie cut wig complemented her brown eyes, but was in contrast to the various colorful dashikis she wore every day. Some had even joked that her full figure made the attire resemble curtains that were seamed along the sides. And there was no room to question her off-colored sneakers. It was a given that she dressed for comfort, period.

"Mrs. Worthy has brought to my attention that you had an attitude with her yesterday when she asked someone to leave the library." She wasted no time getting to the point of the meeting.

I wasn't the one with the attitude, I thought. As if Mrs. Worthy had snapped my neck out of place, I instantly turned to look her in the eyes. What once was such a welcoming face now donned a mug that tried to conceal hostility.

"Are you serious?" I replied, genuinely surprised by the accusation. I did not understand how she could have assumed such a thing. I was trying to finish the task before me so I could go speak with her as she requested, but she called me before I was finished. Immediately, I stopped what I was doing and went to her office.

"You called for me?" I asked, standing in her doorway.

"Yes, if it is not someone's library day, you are not to permit them to sign up or utilize any service in the Media Center." Her chocolate face was firm. I knew she meant every word. I refrained from saying, "*Now* you want me to do your job *and* check schedules." Instead I replied, "Yes, ma'am."

"And furthermore, this is not social hour. I would appreciate it if your friends find another time to speak with you."

"Yes, ma'am," I respectfully replied once again, thinking about all the people who came to the library just so I would pray with them.

"You may leave now." Just as she had called for me, I was dismissed. In silence and with an aching heart, I finished the task of returning the books that had been checked in back on the shelves. Had Mrs. Worthy handled the matter differently, this wouldn't even be an issue. But I wasn't going to blame her. I knew she meant well. It was only her second time stepping foot in the place. Plus, here I was catching heat behind someone I barely knew. I could be mistaken, but I believed in my heart the only reason this was even being made an issue was because AD was gay. I couldn't wait to get back to the dorm so I could pray and release the tears I refused to shed at work. Even that night at choir rehearsal I found myself stretched out before God. Auntie must have picked up on something more than what met the eye because I had to answer to Minister Gray about "lighting up like a Christmas tree" as well.

"Let me make myself clear . . . I am the one asking the questions, not you! And if you have a problem answering them or respecting Mrs. Worthy, we can drop you." Drop you meant putting in a drop slip for me to be removed from the detail. I was taken aback, trying to understand how we had gotten to this point.

"With all due respect to the both of you, I am at a loss as to when I offended Mrs. Worthy. I love my detail, and even when you worked up here, Mrs. Warlike, I wasn't a problem," I stated in my defense.

"She told me how you get all quiet and act like you don't want to talk. I have seen you do that before, and she said you gave her a nasty look when she told you she wanted to speak with you." I was on the verge of just walking out. *Did I suddenly walk into a room with children? When did it become a crime to refrain yourself?* It's wise to keep your composure and opinion to yourself at work. It wasn't the appropriate time, but I burst out laughing. It was a defense mechanism. I laugh when I'm embarrassed, scared, frustrated, caught off guard, or angry. And right now, it was the latter. *Lord, have mercy,* I prayed. I was the only one laughing though!

"Mrs. Worthy, I apologize that I somehow made you feel I shot you a nasty look. I don't even have a reason to be upset about anyone you escort out of your area. And in reference to me shutting down or staying to myself, I don't believe that anything is wrong with that. I'm a woman and women can have multiple emotions throughout the course of their day. People come in and out of here all day with multiple personalities, and sometimes because of the things I may have on my mind, I can't deal with or overlook those personalities the same way I do on better days, but as long as I don't disrespect anyone, fail at being professional, or slack on my job assignments, I didn't think it would be held against me." Them broads looked at me as if I'd just asked them to eat dirt! Lips pinched together like they had been sucking on a lemon. Eyes burning a hole in me like it was necessary to watch my every move. When no one replied, I went a step further, being that I was in the presence of two women who proclaimed to be women of God.

"I'm not perfect, but being down right disrespectful isn't a part of who I am. Mrs. Worthy, I understand that you are new, but at any time you feel you need to address something or pull my coattail, you have free range to do so.

"God has seen fit for us to be working under your supervision at this appointed season. I don't ever want you to feel all this is necessary." I purposely did not look over at Mrs. Warlike as I addressed my supervisor. She took her time replying. I sat in silence waiting, believing I had gotten through to her.

"Well, I have observed you witnessing to many of the ladies that come in here, and you often speak of the Lord. I just want to be clear that you understand . . ." She sat up straight, put her shoulders back, and tilted her head in the air. You know that look when you find yourself looking up their nose, because they're looking down on you. "Sexual immortality is a sin. Homosexuals will not enter the kingdom of God."

If I hadn't already been on trial for my body language, my mouth would have fallen open, but I was particularly mindful of myself at the moment. "And the Bible also says, in loving kindness have I drawn you!" I wanted to scream back. None of this had anything to do with this so-called attitude I *didn't* have; it was all about AD being gay, and it appeared we had an interest in each other.

"You need to see to it that you keep your 'going through changes' in check *if* you want to remain on this detail," Mrs. Warlike concluded. I didn't so much as nod my head, I couldn't. For the first time I truly understood what it felt like to be disliked because of one's preference, and I wasn't even dating a woman. Just merely having a conversation. I couldn't be excused quick enough. How long would the people who professed to love God walk in hate? What will it take for us to understand that people only see the God we reveal? If they were that concerned about my soul, one of them could have sat me down and explained according to the word of God, how God has the power to fulfill any loneliness or lack I may feel. Even the power to sustain me and keep me from committing sexual sin. But instead, their method was to attack that which didn't meet their standards and that method caused me to have even more sympathy for AD. I longed to check on her and see how she was doing as a result of how Mrs. Worthy treated her, along with the other Christians who openly displayed their rejection of our friendship. I often prayed that God would allow her to see Him in me.

AD and I grew to be very close. She freely spoke with me about all her dealings with inmates and staff alike. I discovered that most staff despised her because they chose to believe she had a way with manipulating their coworkers into having dealings with her. That she used her eyes to mesmerize them. When in actuality, those women were just as attracted to her and their curiosity got the best of them. Just like it is with sin, period. You think about a thing long enough, you reason with yourself. Then you begin to justify why it's okay to do it. Once you're convinced, you find the guts to act on it. Just like that, you're in waist deep.

Time enabled me to see more than the reputation AD upheld. I saw the vulnerable her, and even though I found her to be very attractive, I was on a different path. I believed being with a woman wasn't in alignment for the journey that was set before me. We decided to be grown about it and just be friends, but in time our friendship was an issue for some. In prison, an attractive female and a stud equaled an intimate relationship, and I couldn't really be mad that we were being perceived that way because I was guilty of being just as narrow-minded in the past and passed the same form of judgment.

Minister Gray had been told that AD and I 'appeared' to be a couple because we hung out every Friday, and we 'seemed' to be into each other. However, no one considered she had the whole boo-thang in the dorm. Now granted, we did laugh most of the time we hung out, and we even had some very in- depth conversations at times, but there was nothing inappropriate about our interactions. However, being that my quest for life was to assist anyone into a relationship with God, the assumption made me self-conscious, and I questioned my ability to minister as effectively as I did prior to the accusations. But on the other hand, I felt slighted about disowning my new friend who didn't fit the profile of a good sister. So as an attempt to accommodate the issue at hand, I asked my best friend Tia to start coming out with us, so it wouldn't appear we were boo'd up.

Tia was a young mother of two teenage girls by the time she stole my heart. She had me by a couple of years, and we seemed to fool up with the same crowd of people. However, one day during the time I was devoted to Jayden, about twelve of us were sitting at several tables we had put together, that now appeared to be one long table, eating dinner. Pasta salad made of multiple bags of ramen noodles, a few vegetable cup soups, diced onions and pickles with homemade ranch dressing. Mayonnaise, chicken seasoning, creamer, black pepper and pickle juice. Tuna salad consisting of onions and pickles as well, along with boiled eggs, and crackers spread across the center of the tables. Jayden and Lil Rep suddenly started having words, and instead of just being the bigger person and letting it go, Jayden challenged her opponent.

"What's up? You want to hit?" She casually rose from her chair. I set my spork down and rolled my eyes in disbelief. These were our friends, the last people I expected her to get into an altercation with, but she was always doing the most. And as a result of that, I knew mostly everyone would ride for Lil Rep the way I rode for mine.

"It's whatever!" Lil Rep jumped up as well.

Just like in the free world, a commotion always drew a crowd. People started coming out of their cells, standing on the catwalk to observe what was happening. Some left from out of the TV room. Hell, someone might even get out the shower, so they didn't miss the action. I slid my feet out of my house shoes and removed my socks with my toes, to guarantee I didn't slip.

A girl named Tia, who was about two inches taller than me, grabbed Lil Rep. "It ain't worth it," she said. I didn't know her well, but we respected each other because of the same ring of people we affiliated with. She had been down about a year prior to me and had a life a sentence as well. I admired her outspokenness.

"Boo, this nigga petty!" she said, then retreated. No one asked me, but I agreed. Jayden was petty and in this situation, selfish. Making friends and associates choose which side they would fight for. I looked around the table and everyone, with the exception of one person, had rose to their feet. I looked at Jayden, and she didn't seem phased by the fact I was the only person riding for her. I could imagine how she had crossed them at some point because Lord knows she had crossed many boundaries with me. Just like me, they probably were choosing to walk in forgiveness. My heart began to pound as I stood and cleared the path between us. Swiftly placing the chairs out of reach, to make sure if anyone picked up one to swing, it would be me. Jayden and her opponent had a few more words, and I prayed that God wouldn't allow these broads to get the best of us. Tia stood the closest to where I now stood. I knew she and I would square up first. I stared her in the eyes, just waiting for Jayden to swing. I could see she didn't want to fight me, nor did I want to fight her, but what we understood as *loyalty,* was calling us to rise to the occasion. Just like many situations you may find yourself in. Doing things you wouldn't normally do, going against your own grain trying to prove a point to a lover. Stealing from work, making a drop off that could send you to jail, permitting someone to sell drugs out the house your children rest their heads in, engaging in sexual activities with other people along with the one you love as an attempt to please your lover. Do I need to say more?

One of the most important aspects to consider when pledging loyalty to another person, is that individual should hold her or himself to the same standard of loyalty to you. And in my opinion, not everyone deserves this degree of devotion. I know mothers who are locked up because they refused to cooperate with the police and turn on their children. One may argue that's stupidity, but in my opinion it's better to sit in prison for your children than a man, who will most likely be on to the next one as soon as you're out of the picture. At least with your seed you value the life of that child enough to take the fault or the blame so that the child might have another chance at life. But if that child doesn't maximize the moment and strive to reach his/her greatest potential, what was accomplished? If that mother is neglected by her child/ren, what principle was honored? Loyalty can call you to exhibit some of the highest form of devotion or sacrifices, just make sure you're putting yourself on the line for someone who would do the same for you and would be real with you, even when you're wrong. And standing there about to brawl with people Jayden introduced me to as family over nothing is a perfect example of being mindful of the type of people I surround myself with. Nine against two. But who cared, I was riding for my nigga. Who cared if this was unnecessary and I didn't have an issue with any of the other people that stood opposite me? Who cared that we might get hurt and we would go to lockdown and Jayden and I would no longer stay in the dorm together? Who cared, as long as I stood by her side, like the fool I was. Kimmie cared, the only person who didn't rise from the table. That's who cared!

"Y'all have to be some of the *dumbest* black women I have ever meet!" she yelled as she stood upright, forcing her chair to slam into the waxed concrete floor, making a loud clashing noise. "Just minutes ago we held hands and prayed together over our meal, and now you dumb motherfuckers about to kill each other!" Her baritone voice that was usually used to recite poetry or act out various characters for plays that she wrote demanded the attention of the entire dorm, even Jayden's selfish ass. "You think you tough? You think you being a friend by having someone's back because you consider yourselves loyal? That same ignorant ass shit you call loyalty is what brought you to prison, and that same loyalty is going to keep you in here! A real friend will lead their friend in the right direction, and this shit is irrelevant!" Kimmie turned to walk away, a chair sat in her path. She kicked it out of the way, causing another clashing sound as she stomped to her room. She was pissed, but her words had such an impact on the dorm, they began to clap. The unison must have gotten the officers' attention because she stood in the window looking at the dorm. All of us stood where we were. I knew she was right, but I didn't want to be the first one to walk away and leave Jayden in the middle of the floor alone. All of them looked at me, and it was as if Tia and I said "now." At the same time we turned to walk away. I reached out for Jayden's arm and made her walk away. The dorm began to applaud even louder as we all went our separate ways.

One thing I have discovered over the years is that most of the people whom I can't stand, or I have had some form of run-in with, ended up being someone that God has ordained for me to play a major role in their life, or for them to play a major role in mine. Tia always tells people the story about how we were about to fight each other and now we are besties. But it wasn't until she joined the choir that we realized we were kindred spirits and became best friends. Everything I endured she did too; it would be years later before we discovered the pattern.

Things didn't go as I had hoped with Tia hanging out with us. People still believed what they wanted, and it eventually resulted in Minister Gray asking me to put some space between us for the sake of the ministry. In the book of Romans chapter fourteen verse sixteen, the Apostle Paul was addressing all that were in Rome and stated don't let what you know to be good, be spoken of as bad. Now in this particular chapter he was addressing someone's faith being strong enough to eat anything, while others faith only permitted them to eat vegetables. The point he was making was don't destroy your brother by causing his mind to conflict with what you do because he lacked the ability to recognize the liberty God has given you. So I felt it was only fair I honor the request to pull back for the sake of those who couldn't wrap their mind around the fact some of us are mature enough to find someone attractive and not act on it. I noticed AD started coming to church more often to see me dance, and if I ran into her at the chow hall, it was always a great reunion. I never got any negative vibes from her.

One day someone came to the library to tell me AD had just gotten locked down about her locks. After some inquiry, I found out that unnecessary force was used on her, and she was told she would not be released back on the compound until she cut or combed her locks out. Being that I had been promoted as a clerk for the Law Library, I had familiarize myself with its content. I filled out a lockdown request for legal supplies in a fake penmanship and dropped it in the mail box. The next day the request was amongst all the other requests that Mrs. Worthy left on Kayla's and my desk as usual. I pulled some information on Georgia Department of Corrections (GDC) rules and highlighted where it stated they were not supposed to do certain things. I also included the appropriate amount of forms for her to file a 1983 constitutional suit. I attached a letter explaining how she was violated and what action she needed to take. Now, one of the first things you learn in Standard Operating Procedures (SOPs) is that as a law library clerk, we are not to give anyone legal advice. We are not paralegals nor lawyers. So I was taking a major risk by attaching the letter, but when I heard how she was handled, I knew she would have a solid case. It was time someone made these people be held accountable for their actions.

That Wednesday I took all of lockdown's requested material to lockdown. I went back to the dorm at lunch time as usual, then reported back at third track, but when I walked in the door Minister Gray was sitting in the office with Mrs. Worthy. Disappointment covered her face, and she could barely hold her head up when our eyes met. Her feelings were hurt. *What's wrong with Ma?* I wondered as I walked around the counter and went to go set my cup down in our office area.

"Ms. Blakely!" Mrs. Worthy used that "trying to keep from becoming hostile" tone with me. I immediately set my stuff down and was at her door in seconds.

"Lee Lee . . ." Minister Gray looked at me as if I had betrayed her. "This is your handwriting, right?" I looked down at the note I had written AD. *Are you serious?* I couldn't believe I was looking at it. *Why didn't she keep it?*

"Yes, ma'am." I swallowed down the emotions rising in my throat, and tears welled in my eyes. I didn't need anyone to tell me how much trouble I was in. I already knew. Trying to help somebody had just dropped me in a pit I wasn't ready for.

AD ended up getting shipped the next day. The unit manager had called to ask the lockdown officer what she was doing, and he was informed that she was reading Law Library material. The unit manager then instructed the officer to go get the material and let him know exactly what she was reading. When the officer went to the door and told her to give her the material, she just handed her everything, letter included, not thinking to keep it. Once the unit manager was enlightened about it, he called my supervisor and she called Minister Gray. The only reason I didn't lose my detail was because of the grace of God. Also, Minister Gray went to bat for me, pleading how I never got in trouble. The overall conclusion was AD had a way of manipulating people. Her reputation allowed grace to be extended toward me. But my feelings were hurt because I just couldn't believe she wouldn't think to keep that letter. Why incriminate someone who was trying to help you?

CHAPTER 45

It seemed the entire compound was relieved that AD was gone. At the end of October 2010, I went to work one morning, and got the shocking news.

"Congratulations, Falicia! You're starting cosmetology class next week!" Mrs. Worthy said. "You've got less than two days to train Kimmee, who will be taking your place. So get to it!"

Oh, my God! I suddenly made it into Cosmetology! I hadn't consulted anyone. Once my locks were out, I tried the press and curl thing, but I believe hair is supposed to have personality. I was in the choir, and we were always singing at a function. I wasn't satisfied with my nappy behind hair, and by the time all the curling wax was piled up in my head, I couldn't style that mess or nothing. So I ended up getting a relaxer. A stylist I respected and aspired to be like cut my hair in the dorm, and I rocked the baddest asymmetrical bob there was. I only went to Cosmetology every eight weeks for my relaxer. I imagined Mrs. Prease felt I was fit for the position once I removed my locks. I hadn't given it a second thought because I had put it in God's hands, and I continued my declaration of faith whenever I walked by. People had stopped acting so uptight with me. Mainly the church gladly propped me back on the pedestal they had set up for me. I personally wasn't feeling it. People had changed up with me because they believed I suddenly wasn't the picture perfect image they had come to believe I was. And the truth of the matter was, I wasn't. I am just a girl who has sinned more than the entire church put together. I love God and desire for everyone to get to a place where being in love with God is the most important thing in their lives, but just like everyone else, I am trying to find my way. I still stumble. I still make decisions based off my emotions, and I am destined to disappoint people. I believe in living a transparent life so

291

that no one has to assume when it comes to me, but I am growing to realize that no matter what I do or don't do, somebody will have a problem with me. No matter how hard I try to be the woman God created me to be, I will still come up short. So all I can do is look to the Lord from which cometh my help and take it one day at a time. And this is what I did for almost the next two years.

Cosmetology came at a time in my life when a transition was underway. Every morning we started our day with daily devotions, and then we prayed. Mrs. Prease didn't see it any other way. If you didn't want to participate, you sat at your station quietly until we were finish. One day Mrs. Prease felt compelled to take our morning devotion to another level. We all sat at a station as she played a few gospel songs we hadn't heard before.

"Let the words minister to you," she encouraged as the song filled the room. In time, almost everyone was crying. I bowed my head, just praying for the women in the room. Acknowledging that God had placed them in my life for a reason. Gradually, Mrs. Prease made her way around the room and was praying for us individually. When she reached me, she took the palm of her hand and rested it on my forehead. My initial reaction was discomfort because I don't believe in just allowing anyone to lay hands on you. I'm convinced spirits can cross. As she prayed, she commissioned me to go stand in the gap for my sisters. Once my tears stopped, I got up and began to go pray for them, individually as well.

After we finished, we spent some time in silence, just reflecting on God and what was said unto us in prayer. Then we eventually began our hair day. Which was a day set aside every other week to pamper ourselves. We did each other's hair. I mainly did everyone's pedicure and designed their toes. We did facials and manicures as well. It was what we considered a perk for working in Cosmetology. Being that we could not just style our hair on a normal day.

Around this time, the choir was planning for Minister Gray's birthday and choir anniversary. I was the secretary and the main praise dancer, so most of the choir looked to me to plan and organize the event and choreograph our dance. This particular year we were going to do an angel theme. I had given each choir member a blank angel to color and sign whatever greeting they wanted Minister Gray to have. I had spoken with the Recreational Department officer, and she was willing to allow us to have the angels hanging from the roof and to decorate the gym prior to her church service that Friday night. I had been collecting the angels, stapling them to the paper rings I had made to enable them to hang. Some of the members were dragging their feet and not showing up for dance rehearsal, setting back our progress, which was what normally transpired, but this year it was taking a toll on me. I found myself sitting in the corner of my cell next to my locker so overwhelmed and frustrated; I wanted to give up. All I could do was cry and ask God to strengthen me.

Now I had been at some very low places in life and suicide had never even been an option. And being aware of this, I began to petition God about what was really going on. After being in prayer about ten or fifteen minutes, I saw Mrs. Prease's face flash before my eyes. She was on her knees holding her head and bawling her eyes out. I began to pray for her, realizing that the burden I had been carrying was hers. That day she laid hands on me, I picked up on her burden. After talking to Minister Gray, I understood that God often allowed me to pick up on other people's burdens because He knew I would pray and if necessary, fast until the burden is lifted. Some people didn't know how to get rid of their burdens and just walked around with them, some found ways to cope with them and others remained oppressed. This really made me wary about people laying hands on me.

One of the most important virtues that I gained from my experience in Cosmetology is humility. My instructor perceived that I was spoiled, and set out to break me of my ways. As a result, we didn't always see eye to eye, and I learned to be okay with the fact. Not everyone will understand you and that's fine. What is important is that you have peace with God and yourself every day. Despite the fact I didn't agree with the way Mrs. Prease went about everything, I respected her work ethic when it came to her making sure we were qualified and ready for the State Board to obtain our Master Cosmetology license. Out of four classes totaling about twenty women, only one person did not pass the exam, and it was because she did not apply herself. Just like if you didn't pass certain exams to qualify for licensing, you would have to retest. Life had a way of bringing a test back around.

Metro Women's Prison was closing, and inmate.com was saying that all inmates classified under the highest level of security (close security) would be shipped out and housed together. I personally didn't want to leave the choir, so I signed up for vegan. None of the other female facilities provided the restricted diet. December came around, and I sent Jayden a birthday card like I had every year, only this time she replied. She was in a very dark place, and I tried to encourage her, but it was a little challenging; she's Muslim and believes that Christianity is a white man's religion. Something that was used in slavery days to manipulate and embed fear in slaves to obey their masters. We corresponded for a few months, and then one day while I was braiding Rocky, my old roommate's hair in E2 (the Honor Dorm), someone came in looking for me.

"I'm in the closet!" I replied.

Rocky had a chair sitting in the storage closet, and we were in there with the door open because it was a rule we couldn't do hair in the day area. I assumed because carpet was on the floor.

"Falicia, Jayden is here and she's looking for you."

"Jayden?" My stomach sunk. I thought all close security was going to Alto Prison. Instantly I had a bad feeling. "Thank you for telling me," I told the girl and continued braiding. I couldn't help but think about how I wasn't the woman I used to be, and based off her letters, Jayden seemed to still be the same, if not worse.

"Bunkie, this ain't good." Rocky was the first to speak, pulling me from my thoughts.

"I'm just in a different space, you know? I don't want to deal with this." I felt like crying, but crying wouldn't change my reality. Rocky knew Jayden and how she conducted herself at times.

Almost an hour had passed, and someone else came looking for me.

"Lee Lee, Jayden was at pavilion looking for you. She asked someone where you were, and when they told her in the dorm doing hair, she threw the cup she had in her hand against the wall and mumbled something." I looked down at Rocky as I finished her last braid.

"She do too much!" I could feel the tension building in my neck. "I don't have time for these scenes!" I was already frustrated.

"She on her way down here. She keep saying she didn't have no understanding as to why you wasn't outside."

"Because I have my own life, and I'm not going to drop everything for her!" My anxiety was increasing.

"Please, go outside. She on her way down here. I don't want her to come in here unauthorized and make an even bigger scene."

"Why is she making such a big deal about seeing me? We not together!" I retorted.

"Fe, maybe you should just go see her," Rocky chimed in, ignoring my question.

A few seconds later I was at the officer's desk with some excuse about why I needed to get out of the dorm. With the remains of blue grease and black gel on my hands, I stepped outside. By the time I was at the end of our yard, she was coming around the walkway at full speed, fists balled and shoulders broad. Face bawled up like she was rushing to a fight. I tried to smile, but the sight of her broke my heart. She wasn't the youthful, bright smiling, trash-talking young stud I had known five years ago. Her skin was pimply, as if she had broken out into a rash. Her eyes were dark and cold and her clothes were wrinkled. Jayden's locks were sprouted all over her head like the bottom of cleats. Even if you couldn't see with a spiritual eye, it was apparent Jayden was merely existing.

"Hey, Jayden. Why are you out here making a scene?" I asked, as we approached each other. She didn't say a single word, just continued to walk toward me like we were about to fight, as if I had disrespected her.

"Lord, set a hedge about me," I prayed, not knowing what was about to happen. The distance between us was closing, and she still was walking in full stride. I stood there watching as she approached me and then passed me. "Where are you going?" I was losing my ability to tolerate her madness already. She glanced back at me and kept walking as if she wanted me to follow her. "I don't understand why you all out here making scenes because I didn't come outside. Especially, when you just walked past me!" I snapped, suddenly sounding as if I was asking for a fight. She stopped in her tracks and turned to face me.

"Why didn't you come outside?" Her expression hadn't softened.

"Because I was doing something, and I don't go to pavilion like that."

"Fe, when they told you I was here, why didn't you come out to see me?" She closed in the space between us. Unexpectedly, the aggression began to subside and was replaced with sadness. "Everybody else came out to see me, but the one person I really needed to see was nowhere in sight." I stood there in silence. As I stared into her eyes, I couldn't help but think about how she had attempted suicide a year ago.

"One night I wrapped a net bag around the light fixture and then around my neck and jumped off the bunk. Immediately, I began to choke to death, and I thought I had succeeded until the light broke and I fell. I ended up hitting the desk stool and broke several bones.

"I even chipped my tooth on something. When I woke up and realized I was still alive I wanted to curse Allah, but I knew enough to understand it was a reason I still had breath in my body. I couldn't walk, stand up, or take a shower. It was hell having somebody do everything for me. But this particular day turned the tables for me. Lee—yeah, loud mouth Lee that keep coming back to prison, came in my room and asked if she could have a cup of coffee. I was propped up on my bed, extra pillows and shit. I figured it was easier for her to get it. So I told her to get it herself.

"Later on that day my lady went in my locker to fix me a cup of coffee and my entire Folger's jar was empty. Lee's bitch ass had stolen all my shit! Now, this is a broad I always looked out for her. There was never a time she went hungry and I knew about it. I confronted her about it, and instead of apologizing or even trying to explain, the bitch chumped me off! I knew the only reason she felt she could try me like that was because I was on fucking crutches, but I made that dumb ass broad a promise, 'Ho, on my mother you gon' see me!' I told that bitch, and I meant it from the depths of me.

"From that day forward, I started stretching and making myself walk. It was days I would be in so much pain, the lining of my cheek was eaten out from me biting down on it as I willed myself to walk and shit. It was extremely painful, but within months I was not only walking but running. I didn't make any sudden moves. I knew the time would present itself.

"One day all of us on my range were chilling. I was down the hall in Pop's room. Pop's is Stoven, you may not have met him, but he took me under his wing years ago.

"'Hey, Stoven! You straight?' a familiar voice yelled from the range door. Around this time, DOC had stopped selling cigarettes on the store and made them illegal to possess. It was normal for someone to come from another range looking to purchase cigarettes, and this time it was Lee. After she stole from me, she had gotten moved to another range.

'Yeah! I'm straight. Hold up a minute!' Stoven yelled back.

'Lil' Ugly.' He focused his attention on me. 'Go get me a pack.' I got up and ran to my room to get him a pack, making it my business to get a look at Lee at the door. When I came back, the bitch was in Pops room sitting on the toilet. Why did she do that? I took my foot and kicked that 'ho so hard she fell off the toilet and landed in between the toilet and the wall. Every punch I delivered and every time I kicked that 'ho, I told her why I was beating her ass! Stealing from me! Pops ended up putting me in a chokehold to get me to stop! I couldn't stop beating that 'ho. Tried me when I was down!"

"Jay, I can sympathize with how you feel, but acting out and being irrational isn't inexcusable. I lead a quiet life, and prefer it to stay that way." She stared at me a few seconds, and then just pulled me into her embrace.

"You look really good," she admitted with the first smile I had seen since we made eye contact.

"Thank you." I smiled back, wishing I could say the same. "You've been through a lot." She nodded yes. We talked a few more minutes as I walked her back up the walk toward the big side where she stayed.

"If they call gym call will you come out?" She looked like a desperate child hoping for a chance to discover something that manifested joy.

"If they call something tomorrow, I'll come out. I have choir rehearsal tonight." She seemed satisfied with my reply. We hugged and went our separate ways. We were a few yards apart when she yelled, "Fe, I love you!" I looked back, threw my hands in the air, and blew her a kiss. She smiled brightly, and my heart was grateful for that, but heavy at the same time because she looked so different, so detached from life.

Instead of going straight back to the dorm, I went by E5, where the Faith and Character dorm was now, to talk to my best friend Tia. She had already heard about how Jayden was carrying on and had begun to intercede for me. "Tia, I don't know why God trying to be funny, but this is one situation I don't want to deal with," I confessed as my bestie pulled me into her arms and hid my face as I shed a few tears. We sat on the bench of one of the picnic tables on her dorm yard.

Wednesday night came, and despite being exhausted from school, I went to gym call like I promised. I walked in the door and felt very out of place! Couples were ducked out behind bleachers, in the janitor's closet, behind other people, anything that shielded them in the least. They were fingering each other, making out. Hell, I even saw one girl laid out on the floor while her spouse gave some head in the hallway of the gym! I didn't know people openly disrespected themselves to this degree. My spirit was vexed.

"I am never doing this again!" I told Jayden as she tried to find us somewhere to sit that didn't have any action going on. We ended up on the floor by the restroom door that was secured and locked during gym functions.

"So what's up?" I asked Jayden, as soon as we were settled. I wanted to maximize the moment because this was definitely the first and the last. Jayden smiled and pulled me into her embrace. I didn't have to look around to know half the gym was watching me. Rumor had probably already surfaced: *Falicia's ex-girlfriend is back.* She held me for a few seconds and let me go. It made me very uncomfortable, but I didn't say anything. I sat there waiting for her to speak. Seconds later, she reached over and started grabbing at my sweater.

"What in the heck are you doing?" I swatted at her hands. I couldn't wrap my mind around why this broad was trying to expose my body in public!

"I just need to see it," she spoke frantically.

"See what? Have you lost your mind?" I felt myself getting angry, and I didn't like how this was beginning to be a common emotion when I was around her.

"My name . . . I want to see my name on your ribs. You don't understand I have been through hell since I left you. So many times I wanted to give up. I would just think about the love you have for a nigga, and all the ways you used to prove it to me."

"Jay, I'm sorry you have had such a hard time since you got shipped, but I'm not even going to sit here and waste time beating around the bush with you. You drug me, straight up. It took me a minute to get over what you took me through. I love you still, but not in the way I used to. I'm on a different path now, and what people think about the life I live matters to me. Why? Because I desire to live in such a way that someone may know God through me. I would appreciate if you never attempt to expose any of my body again, especially without my permission." There was a silence between us. "Furthermore, it's gone. Your name isn't there anymore."

"You got it covered up!" Her sad eyes searched my face for answers.

"No. When it healed, the ink came out. You can't even tell your first name was there at all, and only the first three letters of your last name is visible like it's scarred."

"What! Falicia, please let me see what you are talking about?" she asked repeatedly, to the point where I became embarrassed. And against my own will I stood up, turned my back to the gym, and lifted my sweater so she could see.

"Damn!" was her reply as she slid back into a sitting position on the floor. I purposely ignored all the eyes that were watching us. Very uncomfortably, I rejoined her back on the floor. It appeared she had checked out, and I remained sitting in silence, playing with my nails. I wanted her to process everything I had said. It was my goal that by the time we left the gym, the two of us would have an understanding and be on the same page. "I brought something for you." She suddenly broke the silence.

"Now you know you didn't need to bring me anything." I meant every word.

"You should have known I would . . ." She pulled out two bars of Caress pink soap and a bar of Tone soap and set them in my lap. "Especially when I found out they don't sell these here."

"Jay, I'm good. Thank you though." I tried to give them back.

"Falicia, you know me better than that." She pushed my hand away, refusing to take them back.

"I don't need any soap. You should keep them." Normally, I would have received them and believed God's favor had made it happen for me, but I was skeptical with Jay. This was how it all began, her sending me stuff. And I didn't want to give her the wrong impression.

"No, you just keep them until you need it. If you don't want them, give them away, sell them. Do whatever the fuck you want to do with them, but I gave them to you," she snapped. I eased away from her, slightly disapproving of how her tone had changed with me. My reaction must have spoken volumes because she began to apologize.

"My fault, I didn't mean to curse you. It's just you acting like a nigga ain't good enough for you."

"Excuse me?" I flipped. "It's not a matter of you being anything for me. I'm sitting here trying to help you understand that nothing is the way it used to be. You got your heart broken or whatever, and now you have discovered all this love for me. I'm good. All I can accept from you is your friendship and nothing more."

"This emptiness I live with ain't just about me getting my heart broke, Falicia. I got so low I wanted to die, and then one day I got a card from you saying you were praying for me! I had the choice of going to whichever prison, and I asked to come here because I knew if I could only see you, talk to you, I would find a reason to live. In your silence you gave me a reason to live. I'm sorry I'm not the same nigga you once knew. I'm sorry I started taking all those pills and now I'm throwed the fuck off. And I'm sorry I didn't recognize what I had when I had you. I was young and wild, Fe." As she spoke, she used her hands to further express the depth of her emotions. Six years ago I probably had prayed for her to come to that realization. But today, the thrill was gone. I had shed too many tears, and she had disrespected me in ways I felt I would belittle myself by just getting wrapped back up with her.

"I was young too, but I gave you my all and you hung me out to dry. The only thing I have to offer you is an invitation to establish a relationship with God, through Jesus Christ. That fool for love that you once knew died a long time ago."

CHAPTER 46

You would think things would have been chill because Jayden and I had an understanding, but it's vital to understand that some people have their own personal motive for being in your life. Therefore, it's best to seek God for guidance concerning everyone that is a part of your life. And that's exactly what I did. I woke up the following morning after praying fervently that if it was His will, for Jayden to be a part of my everyday life, then show me by revealing it to me. The second I opened my eyes, there was this knowing in my spirit and in my heart to separate myself. As I got dressed that morning, I prayed for strength and thought of the ways I could carry out God's will. I believe if you can see it, you can do it, but my downfall was I failed to listen. It had only been a few weeks since Jayden had been back, and all kinds of chaos was stirring. She often managed to get out the door first thing in the morning and walk me to school. She would take my books out my hand and carry them.

"I got it," I would protest, extending my hands to take them back.

"Naw, I got them. Why you act like I can't do nothing for you?" she questioned after a few days of going back and forth with me about the same thing.

"It's . . . I just—" I searched my brain to figure out how to say what I felt. We stopped walking, yards away from the crowd that was piled up in front of the door to the Programs building that I walked in everyday for class. "I just don't want you or anyone else to get the wrong impression."

"What's wrong with me holding your books, Falicia?" She stared deep into my eyes, her jaw twitched momentarily and frustration crept across her face and then disappeared. She was trying not to display her actual feelings. I casually looked around and took note of all the eyes

303

that were watching us. There had already been much talk about us being seen together a lot, and sadly some people sat back waiting to see if I would get involved with her again, instead of praying that I would remain strong.

"It's too familiar of the things you used to do for me. We are in a different place, and so certain boundaries need to be established and respected." I exhaled, feeling I had tactfully made my point.

"Different place, different time . . . all that doesn't change the fact I love you. We will forever be family. So if these motherfuckers"—She pointed toward those who were huddled a few feet away—"can't wrap their minds around that, then fuck them!" Her tone was beginning to rise, and I didn't want to make a scene so I just let it go. Which is something that an abuser will use as a method to get you to yield to them, because they know we want to avoid being embarrassed. I ruled out trying to be logical with her and just tried not to be so available.

The distance I tried to put between us didn't last long, because she ended up getting moved to E3, on the small side where I was. I wouldn't come out for yard call. Some days I wouldn't even go sign in for my vegan tray, even though we could only miss two meals each week because I wanted to set in motion a routine for Jayden that didn't involve me. I didn't want to feel as if I was going out to meet her every chance I got, like you would a girlfriend.

There was a girl named Ivory who they called my twin. She stayed in E5, in the FCBP (Faith and Character Based Program) with my bestie, who was a facilitator. She was gorgeous and black, with big eyes, long hair, and slim just like me. People used to think we were related.

Kayla also had taken a young girl named Catherina under her guidance. Catherina was very attractive, about five feet tall with long beautiful hair. They used to say she was a little Kayla, however, Catherina was way easier on the eyes than Kayla. Though Kayla was nice-looking too. I noticed the two of them had started spending time with Jayden, mainly during yard calls, and I was relieved because despite Jayden's shortcomings, she had the potential to be a good person, someone who can be very loving. Someone who I believed needed to be loved, but as a result of our past, I couldn't embrace her that way because she couldn't receive me in the manner I was coming. Any affection or concern I extended, fed a thirst in her for us to be in a relationship again.

"Fe, I can't believe how much Ivory looks like you," Jayden commented one day as she walked Ivory and me back to the dormitory from Cosmetology school. She not only resembled me, she was also attracted to people who didn't deserve a second of her time. She had been on and off with this young stud name Moolah, who just so happened to stay in the dorm with me. Moolah had taken a liking to hanging out with Missy, a Caucasian girl serving life. Missy was known for wrecking happy homes and dying her hair blonde with peroxide and heat.

"Yeah, that's my beautiful lil' sister." I gushed at Ivory, sincerely feeling blessed to have her in my life. Ivory was about five years younger than me. She had two sons who had just started grade school and were a year apart. They looked so much alike, people often asked if they were twins. One of the things that made me respect Ivory so much was her ability to express how she felt, and she was very in touch with herself. Despite the situations she put herself in.

Jayden and Ivory had been hanging pretty tight about three weeks. Going to pavilion together, as well chilling on yard call. They shared the same favorite color, pink. So I wasn't surprised to see Ivory with Jayden's big pink water bottle that she received from home. Ivory even had her Mp3 player, which was this little device that functioned like an iPod. Metro Women's Prison was the first to receive them, so it was new and exciting to us to see one.

One Saturday morning as my bestie and I sat in the small dining hall where they served special diets, she brought something to my attention.

"Girl, I believe Jay and Ivory are attracted to each other." She laid her spork down on her tray and watched it sink into the soy milk, where small remains of frosted flakes floated.

"Probably," I replied, nonchalantly. For some reason I wasn't surprised.

"But Ivory is our sister. Why would he pick her of all people?" I knew Tia already didn't care for Jayden, so she wouldn't see any good, nor be sympathetic toward her.

"Because she looks like me. And not taking sides, but why would she entertain him, knowing the history with us?" Tia just looked at me. "I personally don't care, if truth be told. All of this just really reveals who everyone is." I finished my breakfast as Tia continued to talk.

The sun didn't even have a chance to set before the drama began. Jayden came on my yard, unauthorized and stood in my six-inch wide, about five feet in length vertical window, pleading for me to come outside so we could talk.

"Jay, I really don't like being out in the sun. I'm already black as heck." I knew who she wanted to talk about. Somehow nothing is a secret in prison!

"Please, just a few minutes. Somethin' has come up, and I need to talk to you." I didn't say a word as I turned on my heels, pushed my cell door up, and made my way into the day area. There I set my ID down in the designated area the officer assigned for the IDs when we go outside. Before I made my exit out the sally port door good, she was approaching me trying to get a hug. I slid one arm around her and gave her a half embrace.

"Really?" She looked me up and down.

"Is there a problem?" I continued walking to the closest picnic table and sat down. I knew she didn't like the way I hugged her, but I wasn't in the mood to consider her feelings, and I wanted it to be clear I didn't want to be outside. Once she joined me at the table, I got straight to the point.

"What's up? What is so important that I had to come outside right now?"

"Well, a nigga barely see you. I respect you being tired when you leave school and all, but I came back to this prison for you, and it seems like you don't even want to be around a nigga."

"First off, I didn't ask you to come here. I didn't even know you were on your way."

Life after Life

"I'm just saying, like I was on the verge of giving up, and then I got that card from you in the mail. Corresponding with you gave me something to look forward to, to hope for. So I knew I just needed to get to you. Your love has always carried a nigga." I sat in silence trying to decide if I wanted to bring up Ivory or not.

"To God be the glory that you're able to hope again. I'm glad that I was able to contribute that aspect back into your life. However, I feel you hold certain expectations for me that I can't fulfill, and I'm just in a different space."

"So because you saved now, I'm not good enough to be graced by your presence?" I could see her jaw twitching a little. She was getting upset.

"It's not about you being good enough. It's solely the fact we have two different agendas, and from what I can see, you good. You haven't been alone. If you're not with Catherina, you're with Ivory. They both good people, so I don't really see the issue. Besides them, there's other people here you know. Kayla spends time with you." She sucked her teeth. "What, Jay? What's all that?" I knew she was about to unleash.

"Everybody you think are good people ain't always good people." She gripped the table with both hands and stretched her neck out toward me, staring me in the eyes as she spoke each word. Her eyes began dancing.

"All my friends are good people," I stated, as a matter of fact.

"Falicia, your friends ain't who you think they are," she warned.

"Why would you say that, Jayden? You only been here a good month. How do you know about my friends?"

"Because I do!" she yelled, upset that I was defending someone other than her. I just looked at her. She jumped to her feet. "I know because your twin pushing up on me!" She poked herself in her chest every time she said the word 'me.' "Trying to get with me." I didn't reply. I just looked at her. "As you know, I been chilling hard with her; she your family. I want to be close to who close to you, you know what I mean? You don't want to come out and see me, but she does. I let her

307

listen to my player. She even asked for my pink cup. You know materialistic stuff don't mean nothing to me." Something about her tone took me back to my days when she used to convince me she wasn't on the bullshit, and time always revealed she was. "Now, don't get it mistaken. It's all on the strength of my love for you. It does trip me out that y'all look alike, but I wouldn't go against the grain like that." I didn't believe a word she said.

"No, the truth is . . . you find yourself drawn to her because she looks so much like me. You can't have me, so you'll take her. But for real, if you want to be with her, go ahead." For the first time since we had been outside she was quiet. I watched her like a hawk as she sat back down and slowly looked me in the eyes.

"You think I would do you like that?" she asked quietly, after a long pause.

"Which one of y'all overstepped the boundary, is all I want to know."

"Falicia, I love you. The only reason we aren't together is because you don't want to be with me. I would never try and talk to your friend." I shook my head slightly. The fact she didn't give a direct answer spoke volumes.

"All right, Jay. Are we done? I'm going to go talk to my friend now and see if she wants to make any confessions, or get my permission to be in a relationship with you." I stood. "I would appreciate it if you respect our space and let us talk in privacy." I left her sitting on the yard and walked past E4 to get to E5. Now, I wasn't stupid enough to take her at her word. I hadn't spoken to Tia since breakfast, or Ivory since Thursday at school. Jay wanting to be heard first let me know it was more to the story. I waited for Ivory and Tia to come out for yard call. Tia stood by the window inside the building, next to the sally port door waiting to come out.

I could tell by the way Tia stood back on her legs with her hands folded across her chest, (and the fact she didn't smile when we waved at each other) something had transpired. The moment they stepped out the door, I could hear Jayden's big mouth yards away, being extra. I didn't see it then, but it was clear now. She didn't want the truth to come out. We all ignored her and just started walking up the black pavement that put you in the mind of a small suburban trail all leading to the front porch of each dorm. Each one uniquely decorated with beautiful stones and its own arrangement of flowers. No yard display was alike. As we made our way back and forth between their dorm and mine, I discovered Jayden left out a lot of details.

"Girl, so you not going to tell Fe y'all kissed?" Tia looked at Ivory and then at me, after we had been talking for a few minutes. There was no question my BF couldn't hold that in any longer. I had never known her to hide anything from me. And before I could reply, Jayden called out for me.

"Falicia, let me holla at you for a minute." She must have been studying our body language or something because she called out right as our chat was going to the next level.

"What? Are you serious?" Disappointment gripped my chest. I didn't expect that one, and I did little to keep my expression from displaying how I felt.

"Yes!" Tia was the only one talking. Ivory looked at the ground.

"Falicia!" I heard Jayden call out again.

"Not right now, Jay! I really don't want to talk to you right now!" I yelled, surprised to hear the rage in my own voice, and hating myself for making a scene.

"So, that's how we roll, Ivory?" I stopped walking and tried to make eye contact. Tia looked like she was ready to scrap. She was more offended than I was and appeared to be ready to fight my battle as always. Often she said that people tried me because I was humble, but she wasn't. "For real, if you want to be with her, then be my guest. I've had my share of pain behind that nigga, and if that's what you want, I won't stand in the way." I was trying to remain grown about it. I really wanted to slap them both, but not because they kissed—because Ivory and I were supposed to be closer out of the two.

"She kissed me," Ivory finally spoke up. "She was always saying how beautiful I am, and it felt kind of good to be noticed. When she kissed me, I asked her what about you. I just didn't feel right about it, so I gave her back her stuff and decided to just keep my space. I didn't mean for any of this to happen." As I stood there staring at her, I saw the younger me. I saw so many of my black sisters who had been battered emotionally, mentally, or even physically, and the least amount of attention can rob them of their ability to make wise judgments. Maybe I was wrong, but I wasn't upset with her. I just wanted her to consider what her actions could have caused. They didn't just kiss. Many factors played out to even put them in that position.

"Well, I've found out what I wanted to know. I'm going to head on in." I gave Tia a hug. Ivory looked at me with her big, beautiful, sad eyes. "Girl, come here." I grabbed her by the arm and pulled her into my embrace.

"I'm sorry," Ivory whispered in my ear. When we released each other, she swiped a tear away as she headed back to the dorm.

"You okay?" Tia asked, pulling me into her embrace.

"At the end of the day, Tia, the average female in here is looking for some form of comfort. Some type of relationship to feel validated, and if they can accept their nigga in the dorm hugged up with the next broad, they'll fall for the next broad. Regardless, if she's my ex or not, Jay ran to tell me Ivory tried him. I personally don't care. My ultimate focus is my relationship with God, but I do want Jay to stay away from me." After we finished talking, we hugged and parted ways. I started walking toward my dorm, and Jayden caught up with me.

"Baby, you all right?" She grabbed my arm in an attempt to make me stop walking.

"Baby?" I snatched away from her. "Falicia is more appropriate! I am not your baby and truth be told, I'm beginning to wonder if you're even my friend."

"Man, what that lil' bitch done told you? You out here acting pressured up."

"What you should be concerned about is why you chose to not tell me certain things." I looked her over once and just walked away.

"Yo, Fe. What you mean? You know we family." She was on my heels, but it didn't matter to me. I was done discussing it. "I should go slap that broad telling lies. So, you ain't going to talk to me?" I casually walked to the front door. I didn't want it to end like this. I'm not the type to show my hand. I would never give Jayden the satisfaction of even knowing I felt any kind of way about this.

"Jayden, do both of us a favor and find you someone who wants to be with you. All this love you suddenly have for me doesn't make sense to me anyways. Just do you, and I'm going to do me." The sally port door clicked, and I pulled it open.

"So, you just gon' walk away like that?"

"I'm going in my dorm because this discussion is over." I stepped in the sally port.

"I'll never stop fucking with you, Falicia." I let the door shut and grabbed the other door that led to the dorm. "I'll never stop . . ."

Her words rehearsed in my mind as I got my ID and walked to my room lost in my thoughts. Who would end up hurt or getting hurt just to get this woman to leave me alone?

CHAPTER 47

Her shirt was buttoned up wrong, her T-shirt hung from beneath her khaki shirt. Her eyes danced and her jaw twitched. There was little resemblance of the female I was once in love with.

"I plead the blood of Jesus," I declared under my breath, and she stood in the doorway staring at me. "Ms. Brown, may I take a few minutes to speak with her?" I looked at the officer, but she was distracted, staring at how deranged Jay looked. "Ms. Brown—" I was prepared to repeat my question.

"No, Ms. Blakely. I don't mind at all. Looks like you need to talk some sense into her anyways." We sat in the same chairs Memaw (the name I grew accustomed to calling Minister Gray) and I had sat in earlier. A garden tool (a scraper) had come up missing, and a rumor surfaced that Jayden stole it because she wanted to cut Minister Gray's neck with it. Plus, she had been trying to pick fights with my choir sisters. That's what Minister Gray had come to talk to me about. Now Jayden stood before me, appearing mentally and spiritually empty.

"What are you doing, Jay?" I was the first to speak.

"Why are you worrying about it?" She had the same disposition as she was sitting down.

"What I don't understand is, if you love me, why are you trying to hurt people who have been my backbone? People who have wiped my tears and encouraged me when I was down? Some of these same people were here for me when you broke my heart, was constantly lying to me and disrespecting me. They were here for me when you didn't give a damn if I was okay or not, especially Minister Gray!" I wasn't trying, but I started crying.

"How can you possibly say you love me, and all you're doing is wreaking havoc in my life? You don't see none of my sisters going out of their way to pick with you. Out of love for me, they're not even responding. They're letting you have that."

"Don't cry," Jayden finally spoke, trying to wipe away my tears. I leaned away.

"Thank you, but no thank you. Don't sit here and act like you care when your actions say you don't."

"Fe, I do love you!" she yelled. I just looked at her for a second.

"Maybe you do, maybe a little too much." She remained quiet but held my gaze. "I think you're jealous of the people that love me—that are in my life."

"I'm here now. I thank them for being here for you when I was being young and reckless. I even appreciate all that they have done, but I'm here for you now. You don't need them anymore. I got you now."

"It doesn't work like that, Jay. I'm not going to walk away from my friends just because you're here. I can't even trust you."

"Why can't you trust me?"

"Think about all the stuff you've done to me and the people I love. And tell me if you would trust someone like that." We sat in silence for a few seconds. Her expression began to soften.

"I'm sorry, Fe. I have done a lot of fucked up shit in my life. I don't mean to be this way; it's just when I'm mad or hurting, I react out of my pain. I need help . . . Will you help me, Fe?" I paused, thinking carefully of how to address her request.

"Truthfully, Jay, I don't know that I can. There are things about me that I can't change. I'm relying on my Creator to do so. You need God. He knows you better than you know yourself."

"Well, can you introduce Him to me?" I looked into her eyes; they were red and filled with pain but empty at the same time.

"Have you come to the place where you realize Islam isn't the way?"

"I have come to the place where if your God can give me the peace I see in your eyes, I want it," Jayden replied. I grabbed her hands and we bowed our heads as I led her in a prayer of repentance and then salvation. I held her for a few minutes as she cried. Then we stood up to hug.

"Jay, this is on you. You have to take the time to read the Bible and pray to God every day." I felt better as we parted. A part of me wondered if she was sincere, but I dismissed the thought because I'm not God, and I didn't want to judge her.

Jayden started popping up at church all the time. Tia didn't look too pleased to see her, but she was willing to give her the benefit of doubt. She asked me to come outside sometimes so I could answer her questions about the Bible. She gave me a silver band lined in diamonds, a friendship ring as a symbol of her devotion to regaining my trust and building our new friendship.

Things seemed to be heading in a better direction for about two weeks, until Minister Gray pulled me aside and asked if my involvement with her was more than I was letting on. I don't know if I mentioned that there were some rules that choir members were expected to live up to because we were viewed as leaders, ministers, model inmates, someone who reflected God, and for some, the only Christ some people would see because instead of picking up a Bible they observed how we lived to decide if it was any truth to God and His only Son. We were expected to respect all staff. Not to smoke cigarettes or even purchase them. Not to be active in a homosexual relationship and no Disciplinary Reports. If a violation occurred, one subjected themselves to be set down for a period of time. Set down meaning losing the privilege of singing with the choir for a time. If the choir was granted the privilege to sing at a graduation and we ate, you didn't attend, or if Minister Gray was feeding us for a special occasion, you weren't allowed to work. You could, however, come with your dorm.

I risked the loss of not being able to minister through dance as well. So, I was a little disappointed to be right back in the place I had been with AD, my interactions being questioned. I might have been wrong, but I felt it wouldn't do me any good to try to explain to Jay that people were reading more into our dealings than what it was, and for the sake of being in the choir I needed more space. So I made up excuses why I wasn't coming outside, and a few times I just didn't go to church so I wouldn't be seen with her. Now it saddened me that I had to go to such extremes, but I never forgot about the fact God had told me in the beginning to separate myself.

Maybe a week or two later, Memaw informed me that she was still catching smoke about Jayden and me. I found myself very frustrated because I knew I'd barely seen her. I started getting paranoid, like maybe one of my sisters in the choir was trying to get me kicked out. I wasn't sure who to trust, and in moments like this I needed Shelton's advice, so I sat down and filled him in on all he didn't know. As I hoped to receive a letter from him, knowing exactly what to say to me as he always had.

One morning in class after we did devotion and I had led prayer, I was still emotional and went to my station to clean my face. A young girl named Bre who styled my hair, whom I adored, was serving time for armed robbery and had been locked up since she was fifteen.

"Hey, Fe. You okay?" she asked. And for some reason I just opened up to her and told her my dilemma with Jayden and the choir.

"So you're telling me y'all not together?" Bre asked, jumping out of the styling chair she had settled in and closed in the space between us.

"That's exactly what I'm saying. We are just friends." I matched her tone.

"Girl, she tells everyone you're her baby. Like, she be asking people when they come in the dorm, 'Did you see my baby out there?'"

"Bre, I put it on God—me and this girl are just friends. We don't kiss; I barely hug her. Like, I don't lead her on, nothing like that." She shook her head in disbelief.

"Falicia, then why do you wear that ring?" We both looked down at my hands.

"This is a friendship ring. A symbol of her devotion to be open to my new life and the trust she's seeking to regain."

"Oh my God! This shit is unreal, Fe. Like, Jay asked me to pretend like I was you while she practiced proposing to you. He got down on one knee and everything, asking me which was the best way to ask you to marry him! With that ring!" If a fly was in the building, it would have flown in my mouth because I couldn't close it. I could not believe the nerve of Jayden! No damn wonder Minister kept hearing stuff about me. I was the only damn fool she was portraying a friendship with. Her whole dorm thought I was her woman! I was beside myself. I didn't go out that next day, but I did get up for breakfast that Saturday morning, and guess who was sitting in the dining hall waiting for me? Jayden. I got my tray and went to a table she wasn't sitting at. I knew she would get up and come where I was. I grabbed my fruit off my tray and gave the rest of my food to the ladies who sat at that table. As expected, she followed me to medical, to the pill call line. If you needed to take medicine, you went after each meal. Some medicines were distributed on SAMS (Self-Administered Medicines).

"Why are you avoiding me now?" She sounded as if she was the one exhausted.

"I just really want to be left alone, Jay." I didn't even turn to face her.

"Why? What has happened now?"

"Jay, please just leave me alone. For heaven's sake! Just let me be! . . . *Damn!*" I felt like I would cry any second.

"Falicia." She touched my arm. I just walked away and headed back to my dorm. When I bent the corner, I could see a small amount of people in the dining room eating. The closer I got to the larger dining hall, the clearer everyone came into view. It felt as if at the same moment we made eye contact, AD sat stuck staring at me. *God, I am not believing this!* But just as quickly as she spotted me, she must have spotted Jay because she immediately turned and slumped down in her seat. Clearly, she didn't want to be identified by Jayden, and I couldn't blame her.

"Falicia, why you just walking away like this?" Jayden called behind me. I twisted her ring off my finger and stopped in my tracks to allow her to catch up. "What's up?" she asked, once we were face to face.

"You! And you can have this back." I shoved the ring into the fist she was making. "All that talk and still telling lies. I don't have any use for your engagement ring."

317

"What?" She burst out laughing and remained in her tracks. "Who told you that?" she yelled after me and slowly started walking behind me. I was done talking. All day my thoughts had been on AD. I just could not believe she was back on the compound, and at the same time as Jayden. I was being tried and tested. Briefly, Jayden and I had discussed what really happened when AD was here. She had been informed wrong.

"Somebody told me y'all was down here together, living in the same dorm, happily in love and shit! Man, that shit fucked with my head, you feel me? Saying y'all making love and shit. I used to hang your pictures up and curse your ass out."

"Girl, something is wrong with you. AD and I are just friends. Yes, there was an attraction, but we were grown about it and just chose to be friends. Besides, when she left I sent her a card and she never replied, so that let me know where our friendship stood."

"I remember when he first got to Metro. We were outside on yard call and I saw the nigga. I said, 'Yo! AD, let me holla at you.' He said, 'Okay.' When that nigga walked up to me, I backhanded him, knocked his glasses off his face." Jayden started laughing as if he could see it in his mind.

"Jay, that isn't funny!" I shot her a mug so vicious she stopped laughing.

"So you taking up for him? He tried to fuck my wife, and as far as I knew, he had! So fuck him!"

"I'm not your wife, let's get that clear. You didn't respect me when we were together, nor appreciate what I was offering, so don't get your panties tied in a knot because the next man can recognize the woman I am."

"He ain't no saint, Fe. Why the fuck you taking up for him?"

"I'm not. You just tend to be a bully and that mess ain't funny."

Against my better judgment I went to pavilion that evening when they called it. I stood at the back door to see if Jayden was going. When I didn't see her, I waited until they called 'last call' and jetted out the door. I didn't see her anywhere in sight, so I allowed my mind to contemplate what I would say when AD and I were face to face. As I rounded the corner, I could see her coming down the sidewalk. My heart began to race. I don't know if I was excited to see her, or concerned about Jayden. Once I made it inside the gate that secured the gym and all the land that surrounded it, I bent down to fumble with my shoes to buy some time. I heard a set of steps approaching on the gravel, so I slowly stood up hoping it was AD. Something wet hit my arm, and I looked up just in time to see Jay spitting at AD as she passed in silence and without so much as a glance. I watched her spit land on the ground. *Where the heck did Jay come from?*

"Pussy ass nigga!" Jayden spoke loud enough for AD to hear.

"Jay, what is your problem! That is disgusting, you don't spit on people!" She shot me an evil look and started jogging a little like she was about to run up behind AD.

"Leave that girl alone!" I yelled as I ran and grabbed her.

"What the fuck!" AD turned just in time to see Jayden shake me off. She looked scared. "You turning on *me* for this kat!" she screamed like someone had died.

"It's not about that and you know it. You're wrong, period!" I watched as AD got out of the blind spot, on the side of the gym where we were, and Jay pushed off like she now wanted to fight me. Then I turned and went back to the dorm.

Jayden wrote me several letters over the course of the week. Most of her letters made me feel as if she was losing her mind. She begged me to never speak to AD again. Confessed how she wanted to end AD's life, and she wanted it to be clear it wasn't just about me, it was the disrespect AD dissed out. She apologized for hurting me and promised that when she went home she would hold me down for the rest of my life. I wasn't going to reply, but when she mentioned taking a life, I wrote her back and reminded her about her mother's health and the importance of going home. She had about a year left on the armed robbery sentence she was serving.

The following weekend was the Kairos reunion, and I went with one purpose in mind, to free myself. I had gone to the Kairos women's retreat, I believe in 2006. It was retreat number 26, and I sat at the table of Lydia with about eight women, two being volunteers from the free world. Kairos means God's timing. It was a weekend of being showered in God's love that began that Thursday evening. I can't tell you all the details because we made a vow to not reveal everything that happened over the weekend. So we wouldn't ruin it for those who have yet to experience it, but the most momentous moment for me was the prayer chain. It represented all of the people who were praying for us. That thing wrapped around the room several times! If you haven't been to a Kairos women's retreat, I encourage you to Google it for a date and time they will be in your city, and it's free with plenty of refreshments.

Once we experience the weekend, we meet up once a month to have a share and prayer session and enjoy some refreshments. I wasn't surprised to see Jayden, and she made a bee line to me once she saw I sat alone. I sat by myself on purpose. As if there wasn't someone at the front of the gym talking into the mic and standing at the pulpit, Jayden began her questionnaire.

"Do you love him?" I ignored her. "You never dated anyone after me. Is that because you are still in love with me?" I almost burst out laughing.

"I never dated anyone after you because I got saved! You proved to me that lifestyle is not for me, and I needed to take this time that I'm isolated from the world's everyday concerns to heal and fall in love with myself. God used you to push me to Him."

"I want to tell you something." She scooted closer to me on the bench. "I made a vow to Allah that if you ever dated someone else I would kill them." Cold chills raced down my back, and my stomach turned as I stared into her eyes. They weren't even dancing; they were empty. Two perfect round circles of emptiness. "And I put that on my momma!" Something in me was convinced she meant every word. I couldn't reply at first. I could only focus on how uncomfortable I suddenly felt. I looked around, and everything seemed normal, but I felt isolated. Seconds turned into minutes before my lips could even part.

"Jayden, do me favor." She looked at me.

"Anything."

"Stay away from me." I casually stood and walked out the door I had come in. I looked down at my hands as I walked as fast as I could to my dorm. They were shaking like my insides felt. *My God, what have I gotten myself into?* I prayed as I closed the distance from my dorm and the gym, never looking back. Unaware if she was behind me or not, I found refuge in the security of my room.

I didn't even say a word when I walked in the door, but Aimee felt something was wrong. I sat down on my bunk and was about to tell her what was happening when Jayden popped up at my window.

"Fe, if this is about me leaving, you don't have to push me out. I promise I'm not going to forget about you." I jumped to my feet and grabbed my soap dish and my shower robe.

"Just respect my request, is all I ask." I walked on the other side of the wall to get undressed.

"Bunkie, please talk to her!" Jayden pleaded with Aimee through the window.

"Just do as she asks, Jay." Aimee didn't know what was going on. "Just give her some time."

Dissatisfied with Aimee's reply, she began banging on the window and begging me to come talk to her. I could see she was crying, and the sight made me cry, but taking a life is not something you play with. I was officially scared for my and AD's life.

"Please!" is all I heard as I exited my room and got in the shower. By the time I came back she was gone. Aimee and I finally had time to discuss it. She prayed with me, and I did my best to give it to God. But when I just couldn't find any peace, I went and got my sister Rochelle.

Rochelle was Caucasian and a year younger than me. We got acquainted when I was in the FCBP, but we really didn't get close until I moved into the Honor Dorm. She had joined the choir and proved to be consistent in my life. No matter what. Rochelle was serving a life sentence for accidentally killing her best friend as he attempted to stop her from killing herself.

Now Rochelle prayed with me, and felt I needed to repent for being disobedient. I did and gradually began to have some peace about the matter. By now the sun was setting, and we were just talking about the Lord. Things He had done in my life, trying to encourage myself, and at about the same time I noticed, Rochelle asked, "Is that Jayden?"

This female was moving into E4 on A-Hall, directly across the hall I stayed on. Whenever it was dark outside you could see down the hall just as clear as if you were on it. I could not believe it. Rochelle and I went back into my room and prayed again. I wish I could say things got better after that, but all hell broke loose in my life. Jayden had gotten a mental health counselor she was cool with to make copies of letters that I had written her. For an entire week before my so-called friend Kimmie even told me, Jayden had been walking around showing people these letters, letters I had written her way back in 2004 when we were together. She had been portraying our correspondence as if they were recent, highlighting certain words like: *wifey, I'm in love with you.* And only God and the people she showed knew. Letters I had written her while she was at Metro and the letter I replied to about her hurting AD. She was telling anyone who would listen that she wasn't at my window for nothing. I had been telling her we would be together and that she was going to give Minister Gray a copy of my letters.

"I'm going to walk up to the pulpit and slam 'em down in Gray's face! See what she think about her daughter Lee Lee then!"

That didn't move me because I knew any letter I signed 'wifey' had to be old. Back then, I only thought it was cute to be called wifey (which means one who plays the role of a wife), but yet I wasn't rendered good enough to actually *be* one. That, however, was *before* I discovered my worth through my relationship with God. But what ate at my peace was finding out Kayla was the one showing everyone the letters! Now I was originally convinced that she and I had overcome our differences about

Jayden and even became sisters, but somehow Jayden managed to get in her head and turn her against me.

Then the next day, someone told me that Jayden was telling people I had told her to kill AD and stay in prison with me. This was the last straw. I got the letter out she had written me on the subject and highlighted where she stated it was something she wanted to do as a result of AD's constant actions and let the people who approached me with that read the truth. I was worried I might end up in lockdown, pending investigation behind her lies, so I carried the letter in the waistband of my pants, in the event I got called to security for questioning. I also told Memaw (Minister Gray) everything, in case something happened to me, and she would be able to explain everything.

I would be at church dancing mainly at Sunday school service; she dared not disrupt Memaw's service. She would jump up and down like she was moved by the dance, or scream I was Satan or Bishop Eddie Long. I'll never forget it. I was dancing to, "It Ain't Over." The song says:

> ♪ *It ain't over until God says it's over.*
> *It ain't over until God says it done,*
> *He says it's finish, He says Amen.*
> *It ain't over until God says it's over,*
> *Keep fighting until your victory is won.*
> *When people say you can't remember He can, He will.*
> *When you don't know what you're going to do,*
> *Please remember, He has the master plan* ♪

So I was dancing, declaring war on the enemy. I was fighting my battle in the spiritual realm, every move tearing down strongholds. Clapping, stomping, and kicking, all incorporated in my dance. I was fighting back and letting the enemy (Satan, not Jayden) know that I'm still standing, despite all the rumors, lies, and even broken friendships. I will rejoice because God is with me. I might get knocked down, but I wouldn't stay down.

Jayden jumped up and started waving her arms, jumping up and down screaming, "That's right. It ain't over. It ain't over!" Kayla pulled at Jayden's shirt and Jayden turned and screamed at her. "Don't touch me!" Jayden yelled. "Tell her to sit down!" Kayla was mortified. Jayden moved but remained standing and began to scream, "Satan!"

I witnessed the entire scene as I danced. The second my dance was over and people were coming up to me hugging me and crying. In that moment, I had a knowingness in my spirit. Jayden was putting the spotlight on me, and God was going to show out. I looked around the service that day, some faces looked at me with judgment in their eyes and others were sympathetic. One set of eyes broke my heart, and it was AD's. Her eyes were sad and uneasy. I mouthed, 'I'm praying for you.' I didn't know if she understood or not, but I knew God was listening.

Minister Gray covered me in prayer so much so that sometimes I saw her face when I was praying. Jayden began to get enraged and would show up everywhere threatening to do me harm when she caught up with me. Every morning before I left the dorm I would stand in the middle of my room and draw a circle around me with my finger by faith. "In Jesus name I declare a hedge about me. No weapon formed against me shall prosper. No evil will be able to penetrate this circle." In the midst of all of this, God was revealing some life-changing things to me. Memaw, Tia, and Rochelle were the only people who stood by me no matter what, and they never questioned if I was telling the absolute truth or not. They just knew I wouldn't lie. And even though God was with me in mighty ways, the thought to give up would pop up sporadically. At first I rebuked it, but then there were nights when Jayden would be standing in my window at eleven and twelve o'clock at night, after we were locked down and scared the heck out of me. As if she was taunting me, and I would lay awake most of the night praying that she got shipped.

The next day arrived, and I found out she didn't get transferred. I lost my appetite. The drama had been escalating for over a month. I was ready to stop being the topic of everyone's discussion, and I wanted Jayden to just move on. One night I stepped out on the hall because I needed to iron a uniform. Jayden stood at the end of her hall and was waving her arms to get my attention. Rochelle came out to talk to me and made it easier to ignore Jayden.

Maybe about ten minutes had passed, and I noticed Jayden had sat down on the floor by the window staring down my hall. I glanced at her but looked away. But something about the way she sat and how one arm rested in her lap and the other did this jerking motion disturbed me.

"Rochelle, I think this girl sitting in the window cutting herself." My mind immediately began to race with thoughts of her saying she would kill herself if I didn't talk to her. She had made such a habit of trying to torment me in the pill call line, but I just dismissed it. Very obnoxiously, she broadcast her lies about having had sex with Minister Gray, *and* with me, making me shake as if I was having a seizure. She even yelled that it was my fault she had AIDS. But here's the thing: we never had any type of oral sex—sex period—outside of using her hand. So, I'm not responsible for anything. Plus, I stood there trying to figure out if she was really infected with AIDS, or was she just saying that hoping to discourage others from wanting to be with me. When she said that, I just walked in Medical and told the officer to please give me a minute. God favored me and allowed that man to permit me to sit in there. Jayden had found my button when she said she was sick because of me and had sex with my spiritual mother. People stood around and laughed at the filth she spat, while very few of us prayed she would shut the heck up.

When I walked out of Medical after taking the medicine prescribed to me, Jayden yelled, "I'm going to kill my fucking self! You selfish bitch! You gon' come out the dorm, and I'm going to be dangling on that tree in y'all yard!" I kept walking as if she wasn't talking to me. The new people that stood out there every day didn't know the history with us, and they didn't have a clue she was indirectly addressing me every day!

"Rochelle, go tell the officer to call E4 officer and tell her to do rounds on A-Hall," I instructed my sister as I slowly approached the end of our hallway door. Fear gripped my heart as my suspicion became factual. Splattered blood was on the window. I could see big red spots on her T-shirt, and she must have heard the officer coming because she started wiping the window furiously, looking back and yelling for someone. Torn between trying to get someone's attention and maintaining mine, she jumped to her feet, and I could read her lips as she said, "Why don't you want to talk to me?" I couldn't answer if I tried. I was too taken aback by all the blood I saw running down her leg, all over shirt and on her hand. Tears poured from my eyes, and the sight shook me to my core.

"God please, tell me it's not my fault," I prayed, frozen in my tracks. Pookie, a heavyset sweet girl we both loved, appeared suddenly and handed Jayden a fresh T-shirt right as the officer stepped on the hall. Jayden was moving quickly, but she had already peeped out what was going on. She motioned for Jayden to come with her. At first she was hesitant, but she finally gave in and followed the officer. Immediately, Pookie came with a bleach bottle and began cleaning up Jaylen's blood. I went in my room and sat on my bed in stone silence. I was beside myself. The previous months came crashing down on me at once, and it was more than I could bear. I walked out my room in an attempt to get some water, and Pookie stood in my day room, waiting to get gloves and bleach from my officer.

"Fe, what's wrong with Jay?" She pulled me into her embrace. It was too much. I could only shake my head. Without saying a word, I started back toward my room. "Well, one thing for sure—she loves you, Fe! Pray for her. Pray for her." I needed to finish my homework for class the next morning because Mrs. Prease decided she wanted to push our test up a day ahead. I figured it would be the perfect escape.

Back in my room I struggled to concentrate. It was close to one in the morning, and I was still sitting on my bunk struggling to finish, dozing on and off.

"Fe, Fe, please! Talk to me!" Jayden suddenly appeared at my window, and it scared me so bad I accidentally threw my Cosmetology book on the floor! "Fe, pleaseeeeee!"

I began rubbing my hands trying to get them to stop shaking. Slowly, I sat up and looked at her. My heart stopped! The figure in the window didn't look like Jayden. Her eyes were wild, and her face looked different, as if her skin had broken out. Maybe it was the fact I hadn't looked at her in over a month. I noticed her arm was bandaged up.

"Fe, if I write a letter, will you read it?" Jayden asked. I couldn't move my mouth. I could only cry. I just wanted out. I can't tell you if I shook my head yes or threw my hands up or fell to my knees. What I do recall is kneeling by my bedside pleading with God to take my life.

"Lord God, I'm sorry for disappointing you and bringing shame to your name. I'm really sorry that I didn't listen and because of me, Jayden may never truly believe that you exist. Please forgive me for my sins. Please forgive the fact I'm still causing pain, and I'm the reason people are still hurting. I do love you, God, and I wish I would have done more with the life you gave me. I wish I didn't feel the way I do, but I don't want to live anymore. I am asking you to end my life. Just let me go in my sleep. I don't have the courage to take my own life, so I am begging you to just put an end to all of this. Please, allow my son to know I loved him with everything that is within me. May my friends and loved ones find comfort in the joy I brought into their lives. God please, take the breath from my body. I'm sorry, Lord, that I even allowed it to come to this." I got off my knees and sat on my bed. Aimee was still asleep. I stood up and kissed her on the cheek. She didn't stir in the least. "Lord, strengthen her," I prayed as I lay down. Tears soaked my pillow as I closed my eyes and pushed away visions of my family.

"Lord, I'm ready. Please take my life."

(To be continued)

327

Author's Bio

Falicia Blakely is a native of Jacksonville, Florida, but relocated to Atlanta, Georgia, where she experienced a rough upbringing as a child. This resulted in her committing various crimes as a teen and her inevitable imprisonment.

Since 2005, she has been an active member of The Children's Center, an organization which allows her to visit and interact regularly with her only child while she is imprisoned. As a victim of Domestic Violence and Human Trafficking, Falicia has dedicated her life to raising awareness about these social ills by writing books, skits (plays), and performing interpretive dances. Also, she has joined thousands in the fight against HIV/AIDS transmission after receiving a HIV-positive status in 2003.

In 2012, she devoted her life to becoming a mentor and now facilitates faith-based, self-help groups that focus on breaking the cycle of being victimized and wholeheartedly making peace with the past. She has obtained her GED and some technical college education and is now a licensed Master Cosmetologist/Barber, where she strives to uplift the self-esteem of other female inmates. Her mission is to live each day on purpose and speak out about her past in hopes of preventing someone else from making the same grave mistakes as she has. Today, Falicia trusts in Yahweh, her Savior, for His plans with her life.

Currently, Falicia is incarcerated in a North Georgia maximum security women's facility, serving a life sentence without the possibility of parole.

7 Figure Publications Titles

Traces of My Blood

Life of a Star

A Treacherous Hustle

The Falicia Blakely Letters: From a Pimp

Diary of a Black Rose 1

Diary of a Black Rose 2

Beautifully Ruthless

Murder Breeds Mayhem

7 Figure Publications Young Adult Titles

The Daily Life of Hailey Grace

Facebook: @7figurepublications

Instagram: @7figurepublication

Sign up for our mailing list by visiting us at:

http://7figurepublications.com

Write to us at:

7 Figure Publications

PO Box 9334

Augusta, GA 30916

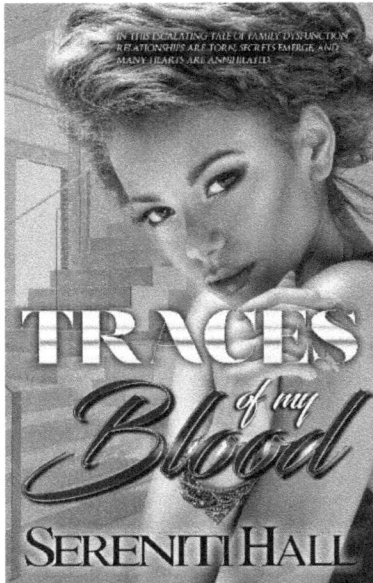

IN THIS DEVASTATING TALE OF FAMILY DYSFUNCTION, RELATIONSHIPS ARE TORN, SECRETS EMERGE, AND MANY HEARTS ARE ANNIHILATED.

TRACES
of my
Blood

SERENITI HALL

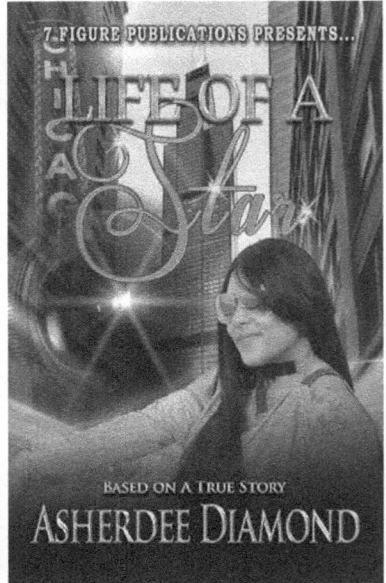

7 FIGURE PUBLICATIONS PRESENTS...

LIFE OF A
Star

BASED ON A TRUE STORY

ASHERDEE DIAMOND

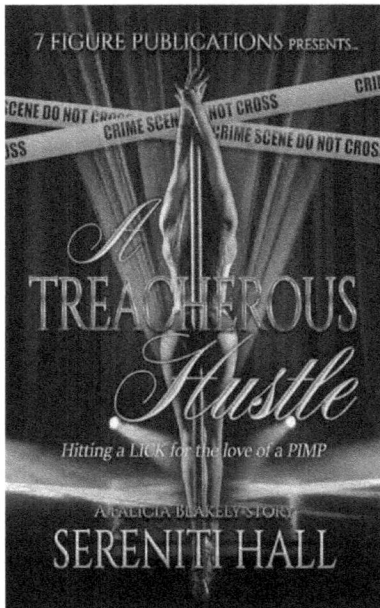

7 FIGURE PUBLICATIONS PRESENTS...

A
TREACHEROUS
Hustle

Hitting a LICK for the love of a PIMP

A FALICIA BLAKELY STORY
SERENITI HALL

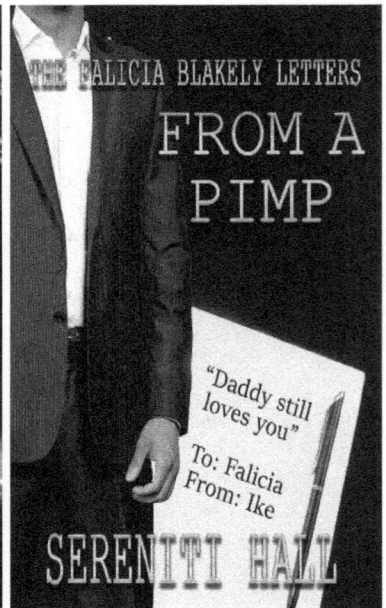

THE FALICIA BLAKELY LETTERS

FROM A
PIMP

"Daddy still loves you"

To: Falicia
From: Ike

SERENITI HALL

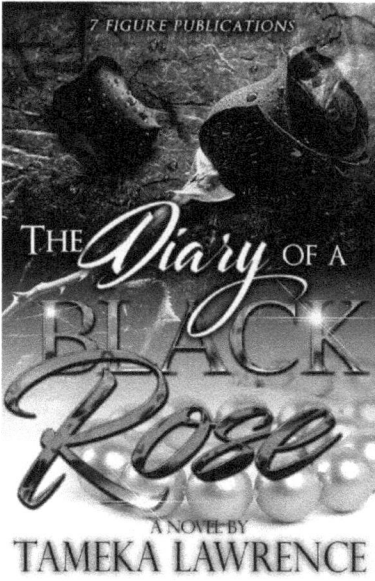

7 FIGURE PUBLICATIONS

THE *Diary* OF A

BLACK

Rose

A NOVEL BY
TAMEKA LAWRENCE

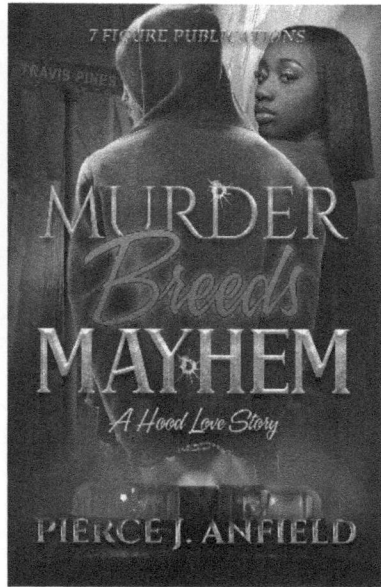

7 FIGURE PUBLICATIONS

TRAVIS PINES

MURDER
Breeds
MAYHEM

A Hood Love Story

PIERCE J. ANFIELD

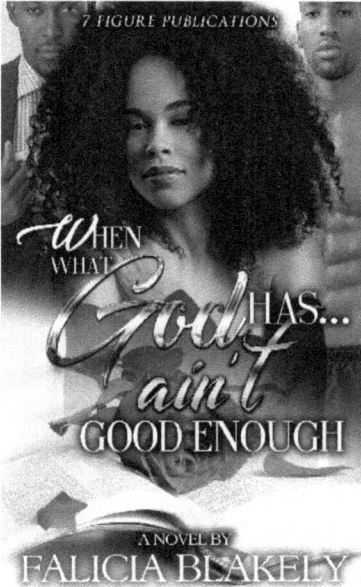

7 FIGURE PUBLICATIONS

When
WHAT
God HAS...
ain't
GOOD ENOUGH

A NOVEL BY
FALICIA BLAKELY

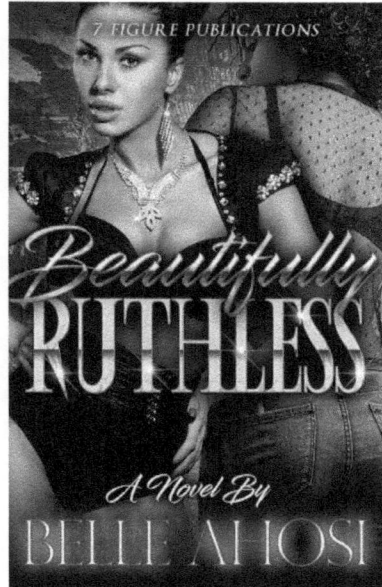

7 FIGURE PUBLICATIONS

Beautifully
RUTHLESS

A Novel By
BELLE AHOSI

www.ingramcontent.com/pod-product-compliance
Lightning Source LLC
Chambersburg PA
CBHW021958090426
42811CB00001B/78